'*The Human Edge* is a powerful navigational tool for anyone trying to find their compass in the Fourth Industrial Revolution.'

Brian K. Bacon, Executive Chairman, Oxford Leadership Group

'A compelling case for how every worker, in every industry, can learn to harness their innate creative skills to survive and thrive in this new environment. Read this book: it's both extremely enjoyable and valuable.'

Wil Harris, CEO of Entale Media, an AI-enabled podcasting platform

'Greg Orme is at it again. His fluid prose and incisive wit argue that the next century belongs not to smart machines and AI, but to all of us. If you're wondering about how to compete in this brave new world, *The Human Edge* will put you on a surefooted path and guide your way.'

John Mullins, author, *The Customer-Funded Business* and *The New Business Road Test*

'*The Human Edge* is required reading for anyone wanting to survive and thrive in the 21st century.'

Diederik Vos, Executive Chairman, ECS

'*The Human Edge* rises above the noise surrounding AI to offer a pragmatic, helpful guide to embracing our key differentiators as humans – in the workplace and more broadly. This is essential reading, filled with practical examples and ready to implement steps, for those who want to embrace the future to not just compete and survive but thrive.'

Dr. Rebecca Homkes, Teaching Fellow, London Business School's Dept of Strategy and Entrepreneurship; high growth strategy specialist; executive advisor and global keynote speaker

'Insightful, practical, accessible and thought-provoking all at the same time. And all done in a "no mess no fuss" style. This is the picture of the future you need: upbeat and inspirational.'

Graeme Codrington, futurist, author and CEO of TomorrowToday Global

'Easy to digest, packed with great techniques – essential reading if you want to thrive in today's modern workplace.'

Gay Flashman, CEO and Founder, Formative Content

'If you not only want to survive but thrive in the innovation economy, you must differentiate yourself from artificial intelligence. *The Human Edge* presents the knowledge, skills and behaviours required to be successful in the age of AI. I highly recommend this book as a roadmap for developing a growth mindset centred around curiosity and creativity.'

Sean Sheppard, Serial Co-Founder, GrowthX, GrowthX Academy; host of the *How to Talk to Humans* podcast

'In the face of the awesome power of AI, *The Human Edge* enables us to realise how wonderful it is to be a human, with the ability to ask questions, find meaning – and shape the future.'

John McNelly, Creative Director, Illustra

'Don't be afraid. *The Human Edge* will teach you how to beat the machines in the AI revolution. After reading this book, I found the 4Cs became my daily mantra. Highly recommended for techno-phobes and digital natives alike.'

Lisa Perrin, CEO, Creative Networks,
Endemol Shine Group

'Forget "project fear" – here's how to survive and even thrive in a future shared with artificial intelligence. *The Human Edge* tells us why we won't be being replaced just yet – and how you can make the partnership with AI work for you.'

Mark Adams, Director of Communications,
International Olympic Committee

'The 21st century guidebook you and your kids need to stay one step ahead in the age of computerised competition.'

Adrian Monck, Member of the Managing Board,
World Economic Forum

'The intelligent person's guide to the future.'

Jules Goddard, London Business School Teaching Fellow;
author, *Uncommon Sense and Common Nonsense*

'An important book for anyone seeking to make an impact in our transforming world with those distinctive qualities that make us truly human.'

Julian Birkinshaw, Professor of Strategy and
Entrepreneurship, London Business School; co-author,
Fast/Forward: Make Your Company Fit for the Future

'Turn off your phone, un-divide your attention and read this impor-tant book. It's an essential guide to keeping your job (and possibly your mind) in the 21st century.'

Richard Watson, author, *Digital Vs Human*

'The first book on the AI revolution to offer optimism and confidence – as well as practical ideas – to succeed in the human-machine world.'

Armelle Savidan, Head of Leadership Programs, Faurecia University

'Refreshing reading, and full to the brim with practical things to do. The 4Cs model is hugely relevant if you want to thrive in the AI-driven future ahead.'

Petr Knap, Partner, EY Consulting Lead in Central and Eastern Europe

'Bosses are worried about driving innovation through employee engagement and creativity. *The Human Edge* offers you a practical path to get started today.'

Dan Cable, Organisational Behaviour Professor, London Business School; author, *Alive at Work*

'If you're faced with the precipice of the rapidly automating workplace, Greg Orme has thrown you a rope. *The Human Edge* is a step-by-step guide to using your creative superpowers to find your place in an AI driven world.'

Gary Rogers, Co-founder and Editor-in-Chief, RADAR automated news agency

'Exciting, terrifying, inspirational, practical – you need to read this. A book so powerful, it's transformed the way we work.'

Dan Burman, CEO of the integrated marketing agency Chapter

'In a world filled with disruption and volatility, Greg Orme reminds us that our humanity enables us to navigate and compete. A critical guide for today's context.'

Adam Kingl, Regional Managing Director, Europe, Duke Corporate Education

THE HUMAN EDGE

Pearson

At Pearson, we have a simple mission: to help people make more of their lives through learning.

We combine innovative learning technology with trusted content and educational expertise to provide engaging and effective learning experiences that serve people wherever and whenever they are learning.

From classroom to boardroom, our curriculum materials, digital learning tools and testing programmes help to educate millions of people worldwide – more than any other private enterprise.

Every day our work helps learning flourish, and wherever learning flourishes, so do people.

To learn more, please visit us at **www.pearson.com/uk**

GREG ORME

THE
HUMAN EDGE

How curiosity and creativity are your
superpowers in the digital economy

Pearson

Harlow, England • London • New York • Boston • San Francisco • Toronto • Sydney
Dubai • Singapore • Hong Kong • Tokyo • Seoul • Taipei • New Delhi
Cape Town • São Paulo • Mexico City • Madrid • Amsterdam • Munich • Paris • Milan

PEARSON EDUCATION LIMITED
KAO Two
KAO Park
Harlow CM17 9SR
United Kingdom
Tel: +44 (0)1279 623623
Web: www.pearson.com/uk

First edition published 2019 (print and electronic)

© Pearson Education Limited 2019 (print and electronic)

ISBN: 978-1-292-26788-3 (print)
978-1-292-26789-0 (PDF)
978-1-292-26790-6 (ePub)

British Library Cataloguing-in-Publication Data
A catalogue record for the print edition is available from the British Library.

Library of Congress Cataloging-in-Publication Data
Names: Orme, Greg, author.
Title: The human edge : how curiosity and creativity are your superpowers
    in the digital economy / Greg Orme.
Description: First edition. | Harlow, England ; New York : Pearson, 2019. |
    Includes bibliographical references and index.
Identifiers: LCCN 2019043758 (print) | LCCN 2019043759 (ebook) | ISBN
    9781292267883 (paperback) | ISBN 9781292267890 (pdf) | ISBN
    9781292267906 (epub)
Subjects: LCSH: Employees—Effect of automation on. | Creative ability in
    business. | Intellectual capital. | Human-computer interaction.
Classification: LCC HD6331 .O467 2019 (print) | LCC HD6331 (ebook) | DDC
    331.2—dc23
LC record available at https://lccn.loc.gov/2019043758
LC ebook record available at https://lccn.loc.gov/2019043759

Second impression
2020

Cover design by Two Associates

Print edition typeset in 10/14 Plantin MT Pro by SPi Global
Printed by Ashford Colour Press Ltd, Gosport

NOTE THAT ANY PAGE CROSS REFERENCES REFER TO THE PRINT EDITION

To Sophie and Pauline

Contents

About the author

 **Greg Orme** is a speaker, facilitator and author who has delivered more than 350 talks to audiences around the world.

His purpose-driven work focuses on how people and organisations thrive in a world of accelerating change – through developing behaviours and culture that support creativity, innovation and an entrepreneurial spirit.

He is a programme director at the London Business School, where he founded the Centre for Creative Business. He's led transformational change programmes with global organisations in banking and insurance, automotive, consumer goods, manufacturing and technology. He's also directed major conferences for entrepreneurial leaders.

His own portfolio of clients includes Sky, Ogilvy & Mather, eBay, the International Olympic Committee, World Economic Forum, SQS, Kantar Group, Randstad, Cognizant, Accenture, EY, Arcadia Group and Virgin Media. His first book *The Spark: How to Ignite and Lead Business Creativity* (FT Publishing, 2014) is available in English, and now also in a Chinese translation.

When he's not on a plane heading to a speaking gig somewhere in the world, Greg lives with his wife and two teenage sons – and a very friendly chocolate Labrador called Rolo – in the leafy UK county of Warwickshire.

Find out more about Greg's work at http://gregorme.org/

Author's acknowledgements

Attempting to put into words what makes a person human *and* to explain the incredible, emerging field of AI has, to say the least, been a challenge. Needless to say, a host of special humans have helped bring this book into the world. I owe them all a giant debt of gratitude.

A huge thank you to my wonderful readers: those superstars who kindly donated their precious time to read the highly imperfect early drafts and gently guided me back on track. This generous lot include Eithne Jones, Jamie Anderson, Juliana Branco-Kowldinski, Peter Moolan-Feroze, Andrew McLennan, Richard Watson, Ralph Lewis, Jules Goddard, Ben Light, Matt Bloor, Ben Hardy, Wendy Feher, John McNelly, Caroline Thompson, Damian Fitzsimmons, Rima Halawi, Rakhil Hirdaramani and Jon Hill. Thanks also to Cyriel Kortleven, Niro Sivanathan, Dan Cable, Gary Rogers, James Temple, Jules Goddard, Keith Coats, Lisa Gibbs and Tim Reid for meeting with me to talk this through.

A special thank you to all my colleagues at London Business School. I feel privileged to be part of one of the best business schools on the planet. I'm also incredibly fortunate to have wonderful clients all over the world who've been kind enough to let me deliver chunks of this thinking in keynote speeches, as well as debating it with me afterwards. Thank you all – from Abu Dhabi to Silicon Valley! In particular, my gratitude to the hundreds of inspiring leaders who have participated so enthusiastically in my leadership development programmes across several continents. Engaging with you always gives me much to ponder on.

Thanks to my colleagues at Oxford Leadership and Illustra for all the opportunities you've given me to deliver this content online and in person. And my gratitude to my insightful and determined Pearson editor, Eloise Cooke.

I'm deeply grateful to my dad Graham and my two special big sisters Cheryl and Carol. Thanks for cheerleading and offering such invaluable feedback. What would I do without you? I'd like to think this book would have made Mum proud.

This may be my second book, but it's the first I've written with feedback from my two wonderful sons – Freddie and Gabe. Thanks for your ideas, lads. I'm always immensely proud of both of you.

Of course, the biggest 'thank you' of all goes to my wonderful, supportive, hard-working wife Sophie. What a woman! Thanks for helping me get this over the line. I really couldn't have done this without you, darling.

Finally, I've discovered this topic immediately catches the imagination of anyone you mention it to. As a result, I've fallen into passionate conversation with people all over the world while pondering the question: 'What's left for humans in a world of AI?'. Thanks to everyone who's put up with my meanderings, and helped me along this path.

It goes without saying that any and all errors and omissions are, of course, my own.

Publisher's acknowledgements

Text Credits:

4 Three Cs Publisher: Chace, Calum. Surviving AI: The promise and peril of artificial intelligence (p. 45). Three Cs. Kindle Edition. **5 Massachusetts Institute of Technology:** Entering the Second Machine Age? Bring a hammer, MIT Spectrum's newsletter, Jan 13, 2014. Retrieved from https://spectrum.mit.edu/continuum/entering-the-second-machine-age-bring-a-hammer **8 TED Conferences, LLC:** Kai-Fu Lee, "How AI can save our humanity", TED 2018. Shown at 6'37" https://www.ted.com/talks/kai_fu_lee_how_ai_can_save_our_humanity?language=en **11 Three Cs Publisher:** Chace, Calum. Surviving AI: The promise and peril of artificial intelligence (p. 85). Three Cs. Kindle Edition. **12 The World Economic Forum:** The World Economic Forum **13 Hachette Book Group:** Kasparov, Garry, 2017, "Deep Thinking: Where Artificial Intelligence Ends, and Human Creativity Begins", John Murray P7. **14 Hachette Book Group:** Newport, Cal. Deep Work: Rules for Focused Success in a Distracted World, Little, Brown Book Group. Kindle Edition. (pp. 22-23). **16 TED Conferences, LLC:** Kai-Fu Lee, "How AI can save our humanity", TED 2018. **17 Oxford University Press:** Susskind, Richard, & Susskind, Daniel, 2015, The Future of the Professions: How Technology Will Transform the Work of Human Experts, Oxford University Press. P37. **17 Oxford University Press:** Susskind, Richard, & Susskind, Daniel, 2015, The Future of the Professions: How Technology Will Transform the Work of Human Experts, Oxford University Press, P2. **17 Royal College of General Practitioners:**

Royal College of General Practitioners angrily retorted **19 Tammy Eriksson:** Tammy Eriksson. Reprinted with permission. **20 Hachette Book Group:** Leslie, Ian. Curious: The Desire to Know and Why Your Future Depends on It (Kindle Locations 141-143). Quercus. Kindle Edition. Creativity **20 Hachette Book Group:** Leslie, Ian. Curious: The Desire to Know and Why Your Future Depends on It (Kindle Locations 148–150). Quercus. Kindle Edition. Creativity **20 Three Cs Publisher:** Chace, Calum. Surviving AI: The promise and peril of artificial intelligence (p. 83). Three Cs. Kindle Edition. **22 Forbes Media LLC:** Totoro, Grace, "How To Beat Automation And Not Lose Your Job", Forbes, Feb 13, 2017. **24 Dr David Sutton UK WATCH Office:** Shelley, Mary, author of Frankenstein **26 Fei-Fei Li:** Fei-Fei Li, Associate Professor of Computer Science at Stanford University **26 Computer History Museum:** The Baggage Engine, Computer History Museum (CHM). Retrieved from https://www.computerhistory.org/babbage/ **27 Three Cs Publisher:** Chace, Calum. Surviving AI: The promise and peril of artificial intelligence (p. 16). Three Cs. Kindle Edition. **30 Hachette Book Group:** Kasparov, Garry. Deep Thinking: Where Machine Intelligence Ends and Human Creativity Begins (p. 5). Hodder & Stoughton. Kindle Edition. **34 Cognizant:** "21 Jobs of The Future", Center for the Future of Work, Cognizant, 2018 **37 Max Tegmark:** Tegmark, Max, "Life 3.0: Being Human in the Age of Artificial Intelligence", Penguin UK, (2017). **40 Artists Rights Society, Inc.:** Pablo Picasso **40 Sir Ken Robinson:** Sir Ken Robinson, 'Do schools kill creativity?', TED Talk, February 2006. **43 Penguin Random House:** Ashton, Kevin, "How To Fly A Horse", Random House, Kindle Edition, (2015). **44 Penguin Random House:** Ashton, Kevin, "How To Fly A Horse", Random House, Kindle Edition, (2015). **44 Entrepreneur Media, Inc:** Weiss, Geoff (2015), Mark Zuckerberg Calls the 'A-Ha!' Moment a Myth, Entrepreneur Media, Inc. Retrieved from https://www.entrepreneur.com/article/241853 **46 Sussex Publishers, LLC:** Jonathan (2011), If You Are Creative, Are You Also Intelligent? Psychology Today. Retrieved from https://www.psychologytoday.com/

gb/blog/finding-the-next-einstein/201104/if-you-are-creative-are-you-also-intelligent **47 Penguin Random House:** Fry, Hannah. Hello World . Transworld. Kindle Edition.06-Sep-2018 **Harper Collins:** Du Sautoy, Marcus. The Creativity Code: How AI is learning to write, paint and think, HarperCollins Publishers. Kindle Edition. 2019 (Kindle Locations 44–45). **48 Independent Digital News & Media Limited:** Johnston, Ian (2017), AI Robots Learning Racism, sexism and other prejudices from humans, study finds, Independent. Retrieved from https://www.independent.co.uk/lifestyle/gadgets-and-tech/news/ai-robots-artificial-intelligence-racism-sexism-prejudice-bias-language-learn-from-humans-a7683161. html **48 BusinessLIVE MMXIX:** Du Chenne, Samantha, "Does artificial intelligence mean the end of creativity?",Business Live, 30 July 2018. https://www.businesslive.co.za/redzone/news-insights/2018-07-30-does-ai-mean-the-end-of-creativity **48 IBM:** IBM, "The quest for AI creativity". Retrieved from https://www. ibm.com/watson/advantage-reports/future-of-artificial-intelligence/ ai-creativity.html **48 Forbes Media LLC:** Anna (2018), "Creativity Is The Skill Of The Future", Forbes. Retrieved from https://www. forbes.com/sites/annapowers/2018/04/30/creativity-is-the-skill-of-the-future/#12a946944fd4 **49 TEDxTucson:** TEDx Talks, "TEDx-Tucson George Land The Failure Of Success", 2011. Retrieved from https://www.youtube.com/watch?time_continue=12&v= ZfKMq-rYtnc **50 Penguin Random House:** Harari,Yuval Noah: "21 Lessons for the 21st Century", Random House, 30-Aug-2018 **50 Hugh MacLeod:** MacLeod, "Ignore Everybody Quotes". Retrieved from https://www.goodreads.com/work/quotes/6341764-ignore-everybody-and-39-other-keys-to-creativity **50 George Land:** George Land **51 Netflix:** Eagleman,David, "The Creative Brain", Netflix documentary, (42:19) 2019. **51 John Cleese:** John Cleese **52 Irving A. Taylor:** Adapted from Creativity Level Hierarchy diagram by Irving A. Taylor **53 Innovation Mangement:** Frey, Chuck, "The difference between big 'C' and small 'c' creativity". Retrieved from http://www.innovationmanagement.se/imtool-articles/the-difference-between-big-c-and-small-c-creativity/ **53 Sir**

Ken Robinson: Sir Ken Robinson video https://www.youtube. com/watch?v=vlBpDggX3iE&feature=share **53 IDEO:** From a video within the IDEOU 'Unlocking Creativity' course **61 Friedrich Nietzsche:** Friedrich Nietzsche **62 Bronnie Ware:** Bronnie Ware's full blog at: https://bronnicware.com/blog/regrets-of-the-dying/ **62 Dalai Lama:** Lama, Dalai, "Advice on dying and living a better life", Atria Books, 19-Nov-2002 **62 Steve Jobs:** Jobs, Steve: "'You've got to find what you love,' Jobs says",stanford, JUNE 14, 2005. **65 Harvard Business Publishing:** Cable,Dane, "Alive at Work: The Neuroscience of Helping Your People Love What They Do", Harvard Business March 27, (2018). **66 Harvard Business Publishing:** Cable, Dane, "Alive at Work: The Neuroscience of Helping Your People Love What They Do", Harvard Business (2017). P 17. **68 Angela Lee Duckworth:** Angela (2013), "Grit: The power of passion and preserverance", TED Talks Education. Retrieved from https://www.ted.com/talks/angela_lee_duckworth_grit_the_power_of_passion_and_perseverance **68 Penguin Random House:** Duckworth, Angela: "Grit: The Power of Passion and Perseverance". Ebury Publishing. Kindle Edition. **74 Candice Billups:** Candice Billups **76 Viktor Emil Frankl:** Frankl, Viktor E.,1959, Man's Search for Meaning, Rider **77 TED Conferences, LLC:** Achor, Shawn, "The happy secret to better work", 2011. Retrieved from https://www.ted.com/talks/shawn_achor_the_happy_secret_to_better_work/transcript?language=en **77 Verizon Media:** Kukolic, Siobhan (2017), "We See Them As We Are"Huffpost. Retrieved from https://www.huffingtonpost.com/ entry/we-see-them-as-we-are_us_590cab8ae4b056aa2363d461 **77 Penguin Random House:** Aurelius, Marcus, 2006, Meditations, Penguin Classics **78 Harvard Business Publishing:** Cable,Dane, "Alive at Work: The Neuroscience of Helping Your People Love What They Do", Harvard Business March 27, (2018). **78 Dr Seuss:** Dr Seuss **83 Hachette Book Group:** Newport, Cal. Deep Work: Rules for Focused Success in a Distracted World, Little, Brown Book Group. Kindle Edition. (p. 119). **83 Simon & Schuster:** Stephen R. Covey, "The 7 Habits of Highly Effective People:

Powerful Lessons in Personal Change", Simon and Schuster, 2004 **86 Hachette Book Group:** Newport, Cal. Deep Work: Rules for Focused Success in a Distracted World, Little, Brown Book Group.2016. Kindle Edition. (p. 6). **87 The Economist:** "The maturing of the smartphone industry is cause for celebration", 2019. Retrieved from https://www.economist.com/leaders/2019/01/12/the-maturing-of-the-smartphone-industry-is-cause-for-celebration **89 Guardian News and Media Limited:** Brichter, "'Our minds can be hijacked': the tech insiders who fear a smartphone dystopia" 2017. Retrieved from https://www.theguardian.com/technology/2017/oct/05/smartphone-addiction-silicon-valley-dystopia **89 Guardian News and Media Limited:** Solon, Olivia (2017), "Ex-Facebook president Sean Parker: site made to exploit human 'vulnerability'" The Guardian. https://www.theguardian.com/technology/2017/nov/09/facebook-sean-parker-vulnerability-brain-psychology **89 Guardian News and Media Limited:** Brichter (2017), "'Our minds can be hijacked': the tech insiders who fear a smartphone dystopia" The Guardian. Retrieved from https://www.theguardian.com/technology/2017/oct/05/smartphone-addiction-silicon-valley-dystopia **89 Nicholas Carr:** Nicholas Carr **89 The Atlantic Monthly Group:** Carr, Nicholas, "Is Google Making Us Stupid?", The Atlantic, 2008. Retrieved from https://www.theatlantic.com/magazine/archive/2008/07/is-google-making-us-stupid/306868/ **90 W. W. Norton & Company:** Carr, Nicholas, "The Shallows: What the Internet Is Doing to Our Brains", W. W. Norton, 06-Jun-2011. **90 Kevin Drum:** LBS Alumni speech **91 Elsevier:** JungsooKim; Richardde Dear "Workspace satisfaction: The privacy-communication trade-off in open-plan offices" Journal of Environmental Psychology , Volume 36, December 2013, Pages 18-26. Retrieved from https://www.sciencedirect.com/science/article/pii/S0272494413000340 **92 Hachette Book Group:** Crabbe, Tony (2015), Busy: How to Thrive in a World of Too Much, Grand Central Publishing. **93 Penguin Random House:** Ashton, Kevin, "How To Fly A Horse", Random House, Kindle Edition (2015). p. 70 **93 György Ligeti:** György Ligeti **93 Richard Avedon:**

Richard Avedon **93 Bill Gates:** Bill Gates **94 HarperCollins:** Csikszentmihalyi, Mihalyi (1996), "Creativity, The psychology and discovery and invention", Harper Perennial. P 353, **94 Hachette Book Group:** Newport, Cal. Deep Work: Rules for Focused Success in a Distracted World ,Little, Brown Book Group. Kindle Edition. (p. 242). **96 Hachette Book Group:** Newport, Cal. Deep Work: Rules for Focused Success in a Distracted World , Little, Brown Book Group. Kindle Edition. (p. 247). **98 Hachette Book Group:** Newport, Cal. Deep Work: Rules for Focused Success in a Distracted World, Little, Brown Book Group. Kindle Edition. (p. 158). **98 Marcus Tullius Cicero:** Marcus Tullius Cicero **98 Penguin Random House:** Bakewell, Sarah, 'A life of Montaigne in one question and twenty attempts at an answer', Vistage 2010, P28. **98 Penguin Random House:** Bakewell, Sarah, 'A life of Montaigne in one question and twenty attempts at an answer', Vistage 2010, P28. **100 HarperCollins:** 'Creativity, the psychology of discovery and invention', Harper Collins, 1997, P58. **100 Hachette Book Group:** Newport, Cal. Deep Work: Rules for Focused Success in a Distracted World, Little, Brown Book Group. Kindle Edition." (p. 159). **102 Hachette Book Group:** Newport, Cal. Deep Work: Rules for Focused Success in a Distracted World, Little, Brown Book Group. Kindle Edition. (pp. 33-34). **107 Penguin Random House:** Toffler, Alvin, "The futurists", Random House, 1972. **107 Hachette Book Group:** Leslie, Ian. Curious: The Desire to Know and Why your Future Depends on It. Quercus. Kindle Edition. (Kindle Locations 243-244). **110 London Business School:** Professor Gratton recounted this incident at the HR Strategy Forum at London Business School in 2018: Retrieved from https://events.streamgo.co.uk/paving-the-way-for-the-next-decade/events/lifelong-learning-your-competitive-advantage **111 CBS Interactive Inc.:** Castillo, Michelle (2012), "Ohio teen hospitalized after playing video games for at least 4 straight days", CBS Interactive. Retrieved from https://www.cbsnews.com/news/ohio-teen-hospitalized-after-playing-video-games-for-at-least-4-straight-days/ **111 Condé Nast.:** Gardiner, Bryan (2015), "You'll Be

Outraged at How Easy It Was to Get You to Click on This Headline", Condé Nast. Retrieved from https://www.wired.com/2015/12/psychology-of-clickbait/ **114 RSA:** Rowson, Jonathan, "The Power of Curiosity, How linking inquisitiveness to innovation could help to address our energy challenges", RSA Social Brain Centre, June 2012, P 21. **115 Brenden Lake:** Brenden Lake **115 Harvard Business Publishing:** MANAGING YOURSELF, Curiosity Is as Important as Intelligence, Tomas Chamorro-Premuzic, Harvard Business Review AUGUST 27, 2014 **116 Manuseto Ventures:** "Bill Gates, Warren Buffett, and Oprah Winfrey All Use the 5-Hour Rule", In an interview in the New York Times: https://www.inc.com/empact/bill-gates-warren-buffett-and-oprah-all-use-the-5-hour-rule.html **116 Oprah Winfrey:** Oprah Winfrey **116 Manuseto Ventures:** Kakutani, Michiko, "Obama's Secret to Surviving the White House Years: Books", the New York Times , Jan. 16, 2017 https://www.nytimes.com/2017/01/16/books/obamas-secret-to-surviving-the-white-house-years-books.html **117 Simon & Schuster:** Isaacson, Walter, "Leonardo Da Vinci", Simon and Schuster, 17-Oct-2017 **119 Buffer Inc.:** Beth Cooper, Belle, "The Secret to Creativity, Intelligence, and Scientific Thinking: Being Able to Make Connections", Buffer. Retrieved from https://blog.bufferapp.com/connections-in-the-brain-understanding-creativity-and-intelligenceconnections **119 Insider Inc:** Yarow, Jay (2016), "The Full Text Of Steve Jobs' Stanford Commencement Speech", Business Insider. Retrieved from https://www.businessinsider.com/the-full-text-of-steve-jobs-stanford-commencement-speech-2011-10?IR=T **120 Workman Publishing Company:** Kleon, Austin. "Steal Like an Artist: 10 Things Nobody Told You About Being Creative" . Workman Publishing Company. Kindle Edition 2012. **121 Simon & Schuster:** Isaacson, Walter. Leonardo Da Vinci (Kindle Locations 196-197). Simon & Schuster UK. Kindle Edition. **121 Tim Brown:** Tim Brown **123 Simon & Schuster:** Isaacson, Walter. Leonardo Da Vinci (Kindle Locations 198-201). Simon & Schuster UK. Kindle Edition **123 Jeff Bezos:** Quote by Jeff Bezos **124 Brian Grazer:** Grazer, Brian: "A Career in Curiosity", Talks at

Google. Retrieved from https://www.youtube.com/watch?v= MUPHNQkBdVw **125 Hachette Book Group:** Kasparov, Garry. Deep Thinking: Where Machine Intelligence Ends and Human Creativity Begins (p. 61). Hodder & Stoughton. Kindle Edition. **127 Artists Rights Society, Inc.:** Pablo Picasso **128 Penguin Random House:** Fry, Hannah, 2018, Hello World: How to be Human in the Age of the Machine, Transworld Digital **128 Simon & Schuster:** 'Why? What Makes Us Curious' by Mario Livio, 2017 Location 181 **131 Hachette Book Group:** Maxwell, John C.. Good Leaders Ask Great Questions: Your Foundation for Successful Leadership (p. 7). Center Street. Kindle Edition. **131 Hachette Book Group:** Chouinard, Michelle, "Curious: The Desire to Know and Why Your Future Depends on It", by Ian Leslie (2007), Location 558. **133 Jonathan Swift:** Jonathan Swift **135 Penguin Random House:** Goddard, Jules, "Uncommon Sense, Common Nonsense: Why some organisations consistently outperform others" Profile Books, 03-May-2012 **136 Tammy Eriksson:** Tammy Eriksson **137 London Business School:** Orme, March 28 (2018), "Innovation hacks straight out of Silicon Valley", London Business school. Retrieved from https://www.london.edu/faculty-and-research/lbsr/innovation-hacks-straight-out-of-silicon-valley#.WryacojwZPZ **138 John Wiley and Sons:** Sawyer, Keith. Zig Zag: The Surprising Path to Greater Creativity (Kindle Location 472). Wiley. Kindle Edition." 2013 **138 John Wiley and Sons:** Sawyer, Keith. Zig Zag: The Surprising Path to Greater Creativity (Kindle Location 472). Wiley. Kindle Edition." 2013 **139 John Wiley and Sons:** EricMarkowitz April 10, 2012, "How Instagram Grew From Foursquare Knock-Off to $1 Billion Photo Empire", INC. Retrieved from https://www.inc.com/eric-markowitz/life-and-times-of-instagram-the-complete-original-story.html **139 Kevin Systrom:** kevin systrom **139 Hachette Book Group:** Maxwell, John C.. Good Leaders Ask Great Questions: Your Foundation for Successful Leadership (p. 15). Center Street. Kindle Edition. **140 MIT Sloan School of Management:** Hal Gregersen of the MIT Sloan School **140 Mind Tools Ltd:** "Garbage in, garbage out," is a popular truth, often said in relation to computer systems: if you put the wrong information in, you'll get the wrong information out- Mind Tools. Retreived from https://www.mindtools.com/pages/article/ newTMC_88.htm 141 **Forbes Media LLC:** Boss, Jeff, "The Power Of Questions", Forbes, Aug 3, 2016. Retrieved from https://www. forbes.com/sites/jeffboss/2016/08/03/the-power-of-questions/#5ac99be462a5 141 **Forbes Media LLC:** Say, My, "10 Disruptive Questions For Instant Innovation", Forbes Oct 4, 2013. Retrieved from https://www.forbes.com/sites/groupthink/2013 /10/04/10-disruptive-questions-for-instant-innovation/# 65cf2a8f6dab 142 **Forbes Media LLC:** Lisa Bodell, CEO of future-think, a New York City-based innovation research and training firm. **144 Steve Jobs:** Steve Jobs **149 IDEO:** From IDEO Unlocking Creativity Course **149 Pace Gallery:** Pinola, Melanie (2013), "Inspiration Is for Amateurs—The Rest of Us Just Show Up and Get to Work", Life hacker. Retrieved from https://lifehacker.com/5972825/ inspiration-is-for-amateurs--the-rest-of-us-just-show-up-and-get-to-work **150 Simon & Schuster:** Tharp, Twyler, "The Creative Habit: Learn It and Use It for Life." Simon & Schuster, 07-Oct-2003 **150 HarperCollins:** Csikszentmihalyi, Mihaly, 'Creativity, the psychology of discovery and invention', Harper Collins, 1997, p363 **151 Netflix:** Eagleman, David, "The Creative Brain", Netflix documentary, (34:49) 2019. **152 Netflix:** Eagleman, David, "The Creative Brain", Netflix documentary, (43:03) 2019. **152 Simon & Schuster:** "The Creative Habit: Learn It and Use It for Life." Twyler **154 John Wiley and Sons:** Sawyer, Keith. Zig Zag: The Surprising Path to Greater Creativity (Kindle Locations 1339-1341). Wiley. Kindle Edition.2013. **154 Louis Pasteur:** Pasteur, Louis, Who discovered the process of pasteurization to kill germs **155 John Wiley and Sons:** Sawyer, Keith. Zig Zag: The Surprising Path to Greater Creativity (Kindle Locations 1339-1341). Wiley. Kindle Edition.2013. **155 Albert Szent-Györgyi:** Albert Szent-Györgyi **157 InformED:** Briggs, Saga (2015), "How to Make Connections Like a Creative Genius", InfromED . Retrieved from https://www.opencolleges.edu. au/informed/features/the-value-of-connecting-the-dots-to-create-real-learning/ **159 BBC:** BBC, "Can robots take care of the elderly?", 2017. Retrieved from https://www.youtube.com/watch?v=XuwP 5iOB-gs **159 Daniel Goleman:** Psychologist Daniel Goleman **162 BusinessLIVE MMXIX:** Baer, Drake (2016), "A top psychologist says people who work abroad are more creative", Business Insider. Retrieved from https://www.businessinsider.com/adam-grant-living-abroad-makes-you-more-creative-2016-2?r=US&IR=T **163 Penny Lewis:** Penny Lewis **164 John Steinbeck:** John Steinbeck **166 Medium:** Goins, Jeff (2016), "Don't Waste Your Words: How to Write a First Draft that is Crappy but Usable", Medium. Retrieved from https://medium.com/@jeffgoins/dont-waste-your-words-how-to-write-a-first-draft-that-is-crappy-but-usable-c5dbf977f5a5 **167 John Wiley and Sons:** Sawyer, Keith. Zig Zag: The Surprising Path to Greater Creativity . Wiley. Kindle Edition.2013 **167 Curtis Brown Group Limited:** William Faulkner **168 Tom Peters:** Tom Peters **168 Johann Wolfgang von Goethe:** Johann Wolfgang von Goethe **167 Princeton Architectural Press:** Fig, Joe, Inside the Painter's Studio, Princeton Architectural Press, 2009, p. 42 **169 Manuseto Ventures:** Acton, Annabel, "10 Pieces of Killer Advice From Famous Creative Geniuses", INC. Retrieved from https://www.inc.com/annabel-acton/10-pieces-of-killer-advice-from-famous-creative-ge.html **171 John Wiley and Sons:** Sawyer, Keith. Zig Zag: The Surprising Path to Greater Creativity . Wiley. Kindle Edition.2013 **172 Netflix:** Eagleman,David, "The Creative Brain", Netflix documentary, (09:43) 2019. **172 John Wiley and Sons:** Sawyer, Keith. Zig Zag: The Surprising Path to Greater Creativity . Wiley. Kindle Edition.2013 **176 Adam Rowe:** Adam Rowe **176 Ken Cheng triumphed:** Ken Cheng triumphed **176 Guardian News and Media Limited:** Brown, Mark (2016), "Masai Graham's organ donor gag is Edinburgh fringe's funniest joke", The Guardian. Retrieved from https://www.theguardian.com/stage/2016/aug/23/masai-graham-organ-donor-funniest-joke-edinburgh-fringe-2016 **177 learnimprov.com:** Here's a good list: https://learnimprov.com/warm-ups/ **179 Bill Gates:** Bill Gates **179 Nathan Myrhvold:** Nathan Myrhvold **180 Steve Jobs:** Popova, Maria, "I, Steve: Steve

Jobs in His Own Words via 200 Quotes". Retrieved from https://www. brainpickings.org/2011/10/20/i-steve-steve-jobs-in-his-own-words/ **183 Workman Publishing Company:** Kleon, Austin, "Steal Like an Artist: 10 Things Nobody Told You About Being Creative", Workman Publishing Company (2012), Kindle Edition. **183 Pablo Picasso:** Pablo Picasso **183 Workman Publishing Company:** Kleon, Austin. Steal Like an Artist: 10 Things Nobody Told You About Being Creative. Workman Publishing Company. Kindle Edition. 2012 **184 Leonardo Da Vinci:** Leonardo Da Vinci **184 Penguin Random House:** Ashton, Kevin, "How To Fly A Horse", Random House, Kindle Edition, (2015). **185 Thomas Edison:** Thomas Edison **187 Austin Kleon:** Austin Kleon **191 Charles Darwin:** Charles Darwin **191 Manuseto Ventures:** Acton, Annabel, "10 Pieces of Killer Advice From Famous Creative Geniuses", INC. Retrieved from https://www.inc.com/annabel-acton/10-pieces-of-killer-advice-from-famous-creative-ge.html **192 Ed Catmull:** Ed Catmull **192 Ed Catmull:** Ed Catmull **192 Thomas Carlyle:** Thomas Carlyle **194 Hachette Book Group:** Harford, Tim (2011), "Adapt: Why Success Always Starts With Failure", Little Brown, P2. **194 Paul Erdős:** Paul Erdős **195 Paul Erdős:** Paul Erdős **196 The New York Times Company:** Gertner, Jon (2012), "True Innovation", The Newyork Times. Retrieved from https://www.nytimes. com/2012/02/26/opinion/sunday/innovation-and-the-bell-labs-miracle.html **197 Harvard Business Publishing:** Isaacson, Walter, The Real Leadership Lessons from Steve Jobs, Harvard Business Review, April 2012 **199 Penguin Random House:** Creativity, Inc. By Ed Catmull, 2014, p93 **199 Ed Catmull:** Ed Catmull **199 Edwin Land** https://www.brainyquote.com/quotes/edwin_land_193299 **200 Hachette Book Group:** Sawyer, Keith 2007, "Group Genius; The Creative Power of Collaboration", Basic Books, P16. **201 Alex Osborn:** Alex Osborn invented brainstorming in 1939 by distilling **201 John Wiley and Sons:** Sawyer, Keith. Zig Zag: The Surprising Path to Greater Creativity. Wiley. Kindle Edition. 2013 **203 Michael Kerr:** Kerr, Michael author of The Humour Advantage argues **203 Robin Williams:** McGhee, Paul, "Using Humor to Boost

Publisher's acknowledgements

Creativity". Retrieved from https://www.laughterremedy.com/article_pdfs/Creativity.pdf **203 Oscar Wilde:** Oscar Wilde **204 Harvard Business Publishing:** Beard, Alison (2014), "Leading with Humor", Harvard Business Review. Retrieved from https://hbr.org/2014/05/leading-with-humor **204** inventium.com: Imber, Amantha (2009), "The link between humour and creativity", Inventium. Retrieved from https://www.inventium.com.au/the-link-between-humour-and-creativity/ **205 Dave Kelly:** Anderson, Jamie article vs 3.0 **205 Manuseto Ventures:** Lavine, Lindsay (2014), "Yes, And... Improv Techniques To Make You A Better Boss", Fast Company. Retrieved from https://www.fastcompany.com/3024535/yes-and-improv-techniques-to-make-you-a-better-boss **208 Steve Jobs:** Steve Jobs **210 Thomas Edison:** Thomas Edison **211 Medium:** Simmons, Michael "Forget The 10,000-Hour Rule; Edison, Bezos, & Zuckerberg Follow The 10,000-Experiment Rule" Medium Oct 26, 2017. Retrieved from https://medium.com/the-0mission/forget-about-the-10-000-hour-rule-7b7a39343523 **212 William Butler Yeats:** W.B Yeats in his poem The Second Coming **212 Denis Diderot:** Denis Diderot **213 Arnold Toynbee:** Arnold Toynbee **213 Deng Xiaoping:** Deng Xiaoping **213 Erwin Schrödinger:** Erwin Schrödinger **214 Tammy Eriksson:** Tammy Eriksson **216 Harvard Business Publishing:** Thomas H. Davenport, "How to Design Smart Business Experiments", Harvard Business Review, Feb 2009. Retrieved from https://hbr.org/2009/02/how-to-design-smart-business-experiments **218 Richard Buckminster Fuller:** Richard Buckminster Fuller **222 Thomas Edison:** Thomas Edison **225 Hachette Book Group:** Kasparov, Garry. Deep Thinking: Where Machine Intelligence Ends and Human Creativity Begins (p. 249). Hodder & Stoughton. Kindle Edition. **225 Imperial College London:** Table of Disruptive Technologies, Imperial College London. Retrieved from https://www.imperial.ac.uk/media/imperial-college/administration-and-support-services/enterprise-office/public/Table-of-Disruptive-Technologies.pdf **225 Christine Foster:** Foster, Christine the Managing Director for The Alan Turing Institute, Business School panel event, 2019 **225 Forbes Media LLC:** Fatemi,

Falon "How AI Will Augment Human Creativity", Forbes Aug 17, 2018. Retrieved from https://www.forbes.com/sites/falonfatemi/2018/08/17/how-ai-will-augment-human-creativity/#20152a1b711b **226 Cognizant:** "21 Jobs of The Future", Centre for the Future of Work, Cognizant, P3. (2018) **228 HarperCollins:** Du Sautoy, Marcus, The Creativity Code: How AI is learning to write, paint and think", HarperCollins UK, 07 Mar 2019

Photo Credits:

9 Greg Orme: James Arbukcle **129 Alamy Stock Photo:** Dennis Hallinan/Alamy Stock Photo

PART ONE

PART ONE

THE HUMAN CHALLENGE

1

Become a more *human* human

Why you need to stop competing with, and start differentiating from, artificial intelligence

Hello.

This is not your laptop, PC or smartphone communicating with you. It's not Amazon's Alexa, Apple's Siri, Microsoft's Cortana, Google Assistant, or any other form of artificial intelligence. I'm Greg. A human being. We need to talk, you and me. About the challenge we both face in a world of AI. We, the smartest apes around, are being challenged for the first time. AI is questioning our dominance as Planet Earth's cognitive heavyweight champion. Fair warning, when I reveal just how much, it may alarm you. It may even make you afraid for your future, and that of your loved ones.

Some trepidation is understandable. The Dutch chess grandmaster Jan Hein Donner was once asked how he'd prepare for a match against AI. He replied: 'I would bring a hammer'.[2] Donner's quip encapsulates the unease many feel about the challenge of computers. We'll not focus here on the huge social and political impact AI will doubtless have – for good and for ill. That's already filling the pages of countless books and news sites. This alternative narrative is an antidote to the prevailing climate of fear around AI. It's a practical, hopeful handbook for anyone who's keen to add value alongside our new silicon brothers and sisters. It will help you to find the space AI cannot fill, because it's shaped like a human.

There's no reason to panic. However, I do urge you to better understand AI and your relationship to it. It is, without doubt, the most important technology of our time. It's in the process of transforming everything we do. Sorry to be blunt, but if you're not thinking about AI, you're not thinking at all. I'm here to help you engage. *The Human Edge* has been prompted by the impact of technology, but it's not about microchips, databases and algorithms. It's about you. Particularly, your response to how AI is transforming our world. I offer you a development path through this emerging landscape. In a world that's changing at a dizzying pace, I encourage you to become an even more *human* human. This is vitally important. As we'll see, humans do still matter. Perhaps now more than ever before.

The 4Cs of the Human Edge

The secret to adding a uniquely human contribution in a world of machines can be found between your ears. To understand your brain's complexity, imagine this: you hand every inhabitant of London a thousand pieces of wire and tell them to hand the other ends of each of the wires to a thousand more inhabitants. You then shoot two hundred electrical signals per second through every wire. Now multiply this imaginary megacity by a factor of ten thousand. That's a model of your brain. It is the most complicated entity in the whole universe.[3] Your Human Edge resides in this magically complex biological gift. Consider me a friendly guide to discover, awaken and develop it. We'll explore how to ignite your emotional, psychological and neurological systems to unleash your human superpowers.

The building blocks of your Human Edge are the 4Cs of consciousness, curiosity, creativity and collaboration. I've chosen these very carefully based on my own experience, as well as the wealth of available research into the skills needed in this century. They are particularly powerful because of the magical way they encourage – and accelerate – each other. Here's how:

- **Consciousness** is the gateway to the other three Cs. Personal meaning motivates you to make an impact on the world. Simultaneously, being more mindful of the downsides of digital distraction allows you to intentionally devote more of your precious time and energy to being curious, creative and collaborative.

- **Curiosity** impels you to gather the raw materials of knowledge and experience, and to transform these into the catalyst for creativity: intriguing questions.

- **Creativity** combines the fruits of consciousness and curiosity. Your creative thinking brings together what's gone before: motivation, time, energy, knowledge, experience and absorbing questions. When these bump together, the ensuing sparks become value-adding new ideas.

- **Collaboration** then allows you to refine and develop these ideas through feedback, cooperation and experimentation with others.

You can see that human creativity runs like a golden thread through the 4Cs, sewing them together. Consciousness and curiosity *enable* creativity; collaboration *unleashes* it to make an impact in the world. The 4Cs will not transform you into Picasso, Mozart or Einstein. But they will rekindle your inventive spark, and make it far easier to access the power of your imagination. You'll find a renewed belief in the promise of your own ideas. This has never been more important. Creativity is no longer a luxury for the few. It's a key skill for us all.

How to use this book

To help you get maximum benefit from the 4Cs, I've divided this book into two parts. Part One is 'The Human Challenge'. This features one of the most astounding stories in our human history: just why – and how – a technological tool we created is now our intellectual challenger. This startling narrative contains both disturbing threats and intriguing opportunities for you. You'll see just how powerful AI has become, and why it's set to grow even stronger. I'll argue that the best way to answer the question 'What's left for humans in a world of AI?', is to consciously become a more *human* human – to differentiate from, rather than compete with, AI. In the third chapter of Part One, we'll explore an urgent and critical twenty-first-century challenge: when creativity has been so ignored and shamefully downgraded by our own school systems and workplaces, how do we go about rekindling our human potential?

Part Two, 'The Human Edge', is divided into four sections that deep-dive into each of the 4Cs. Supporting these, you'll find eight highly practical capabilities I call 'Dance Steps' (see Figure 1.1 below). Each 'C' has two Dance Steps that reinforce it. Each of these Dance Steps has its own dedicated chapter devoted to implementing this step in your day-to-day life. I've coined the term 'Dance Step' because, unlike computer codes, the human code of consciousness, curiosity, creativity and collaboration is not black and white. The creation of any article, book, product, app, start-up, project, process, novel or song has its own serpentine, and occasionally downright peculiar, journey. Understanding the meandering links between the Dance Steps empowers you to avoid throwing in the towel when your latest endeavour takes one step forward, two steps backwards and, occasionally, a slightly clumsy jump to the right.

The Dance Steps are shown as a circle. But even that's not quite right. The process does work in this order very well. However, the steps can be learned individually and then strung together in

Figure 1.1 The 4Cs of the Human Edge

CURIOSITY

LEARN: Why you need to catalyse your curiosity to learn faster than the world is changing

QUESTION: How to question everything to weaponise curiosity

CREATIVITY

ENERGISE: How to acquire the creative habit to make inspiration more likely

SPARK: How to borrow the secrets of creative superstars to have more ideas

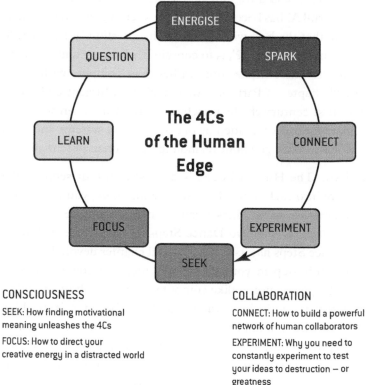

CONSCIOUSNESS

SEEK: How finding motivational meaning unleashes the 4Cs

FOCUS: How to direct your creative energy in a distracted world

COLLABORATION

CONNECT: How to build a powerful network of human collaborators

EXPERIMENT: Why you need to constantly experiment to test your ideas to destruction – or greatness

different sequences to suit your mood and your needs. You can practise a Dance Step on its own until it feels natural, and then add the others as you need them. They are truly interdependent, fluid and shuffle-able. Like real-life dance moves, they can work alone, or flow backwards, forwards or sideways. You can jump from QUESTION to SPARK, from CONNECT back to FOCUS, or from ENERGISE forward to EXPERIMENT if required. I'd advise you to read the book in order, as there's an initial flow through the steps that's worth appreciating. However, afterwards, you can come back to the book in any sequence when you need a little inspiration.

As you dig down another level, below the Dance Steps, you'll find action-based 'Human experiments' in every chapter. There are over 50 of these scattered throughout the book. These are a collection of techniques, actions, habits and mini-diagnostics. To make them easier to spot, they're all highlighted with the human icon shown here. A selection of the 'Human experiments' are further emphasised in a 'Start now' box at the end of some of the chapters. These particular experiments are a good excuse to put the book down for a moment and do, rather than just read and think. I'd advise you take ownership of the Dance Steps and associated 'Human experiments', and mould them into your own personalised approach. Gallup polls consistently show 7 out of 10 employees feel disengaged and uninspired by work. At the very least, *The Human Edge* offers a key to unlocking your inspiring consciousness, curiosity, creativity and collaboration at work.

You might be asking if this book can help if you're not in the workplace? The answer is yes. It's for *anyone* curious about how to be more successful in an AI-enabled world in every part of your life. You might be a teenager pondering your career, a parent looking for a way to support your child, a new entrant into the job market, an entrepreneur, an overworked manager searching for a way forward, or a grizzled organisational veteran. If you're outside the job market altogether, you might still be keen to engage with how the world is changing to better support a charitable cause, local club or sports team. The tips and techniques to develop your 4Cs can help in all of these scenarios.

I began by advising you not to panic. But do use this book to take stock and to act. Those that seek to learn and to adapt will flourish in the coming years. Those who stick their head in the sand are in for a very bumpy ride. The 4Cs of consciousness, curiosity, creativity and collaboration offer you a head start. They allow you to stop racing machines and, instead, to do the things they can't. Not a cog in a machine, but a resourceful human in a world of AI.

Let's get started.

AI is in our lives

Whoever you are, you'll soon begin to bump into AI pretty much every hour of your life. Often you won't even realise that's what it is. An app will raise you from your slumbers in the most optimal part of your sleep cycle. At breakfast, AI will arrange your day's agenda, check the least-traffic-clogged route to work and suggest the headlines and social media gossip personally tailored for your interests. For the most important email of your morning, a psychological evaluation algorithm will analyse the receiver's publicly available statements, including blog posts, emails, comments and tweets, to make your words more influential and powerful.

During your coffee break you'll order your groceries from an online service that will respond via AI, and pick and pack your staples with a swarm of AI-enabled robots in an automated warehouse. Your semi-autonomous smart car, and home, will allow these to be remotely delivered to your vehicle's back seat, or to your front door, whatever suits you best. If you order a pair of jeans online, AI will use your virtual mannequin to ensure the fit is just perfect when they arrive. At lunch you'll read business and sports reports written by AI without knowing the difference.[4] Of course, you'll be relaxing in a restaurant or open space recommended by AI.

If you apply for a new job you'll be vetted by a machine.[5] It will test you with online games from the field of cognitive neuroscience to assess your decision-making prowess and personality type. Only after the AI has analysed a video submission will you be passed from computer to human for an interview. If you invest in a pension, around 60 per cent of the trades that support your fund will be executed by AI.[6] If you apply for a loan to top up your wages, the bank will ask for another video interview that will be analysed by algorithms for 50 or so tiny facial expressions that will indicate if you're lying about your ability to repay the loan.[7] If you get sick, AI will be there to diagnose your X-rays. You'll be more than happy with this arrangement, as computers have already proved themselves to be the best cancer diagnosticians on the planet. If you're admitted to hospital, AI will be managing the beds and other resources, as well as supporting the telecoms and energy companies keeping the lights and Wi-Fi on in your ward. Pharmaceutical companies will offer you highly effective, personalised drugs fabricated by AI. If you don't get well you may be operated on by a robot surgeon, supported by chatbot doctors.[8] If you choose to march in the streets to protest this new reality, the government will be able to identify your face in the crowd using, you guessed it, AI.[9]

None of the above is science fiction. All of the things mentioned are available right now, or will be very soon. And we're only at the start of this journey. At the heart of this revolution are the US tech giants Facebook, Amazon, Netflix and Google. Their business models are predicated on using AI to manipulate your data. If you add to the mix Apple (whose smartphones place these business models in your hand), these companies are currently worth more than the rest of the FTSE 100 put together.[10] Microsoft and IBM are pushing hard to keep up. These US tech companies have revenues far greater than many countries' GDP. So much so, that Denmark recently appointed an official ambassador to these behemoths of Silicon Valley.[11] The equivalent digital giants in China are Baidu, Alibaba and Tencent.[12] They have grown far beyond their core business to do just about everything, from digital payments to social networks, cloud computing to e-commerce. They're deploying AI with equal aggression.[13] The competition between these tech giants fuels the global AI arms race.

Kevin Kelly, the founder of *Wired* magazine, said the business plans of the next 10,000 start-ups are easy to predict: 'Take X and add AI.'[14] I saw this for myself in Silicon Valley, where I visited a number of venture capital firms. Nearly all of the start-up presentations featured AI. These are the pioneers. AI is now right at the bottom of the first steep section of the classic product S-curve. Think where SMART phones were back in 2006; that's where AI is now.[15]

If tech businesses wear AI on their sleeves, other businesses will now start wearing it as their undergarments. Those high-tech start-ups are being hoovered up by global corporates desperate to buy the ideas and brains behind them.[16] It's just the beginning. Around 85 per cent of companies think AI will offer a competitive advantage. Yet only 5 per cent are employing it extensively right now.[17] They will jump in with both feet when braver pioneers have proved the business case. AI will reshape customer service, marketing, sales, supply chain management, HR, finance and risk management.[18] The World Economic Forum forecasts AI and connected technologies (augmented reality, virtual reality and robotics) will '. . . bring change at a speed, scale and force unlike anything we've experienced before. The business models of each and every industry will be transformed.'[19]

I'd like to make it clear. Although this book is about ensuring you have a role in this changing world, I'm not anti-technology. Managed well, AI will transform our world for the better. It will add value in almost all walks of life. Do we have sufficient nurses and doctors to care for an ageing population? Do we have more teachers, police officers and prison guards than we need? Is the task of upkeeping our IT, banking, booking a flight, finding a watchable movie or buying insurance so perfect we never want to improve it? We all know the answer is a resounding 'No!'. AI will upgrade these areas and more. It will allow us to do more, for less.

Let's not forget, millions of people graft in awful or uninspiring conditions. Many don't enjoy their job and suffer in workplaces that are dull, dirty or dangerous. AI can do tasks we humans don't want to do. It can also do jobs we can't. The UK's National Centre for Nuclear Robotics is developing AI-enabled robots and drones who will venture into hazardous legacy nuclear waste sites to efficiently and safely sort out what's still contaminated.[20] The bots can clear a random, cluttered heap of objects with no prior knowledge of what they are. Would you fancy that job?

An old foe with a new face

In September 1945, the powerful elevator operators' union staged a strike in New York that paralysed the city. According to the Associated Press, 'Thousands struggled up stairways that seemed endless, including the Empire State Building, the tallest structure in the world.' The technology for automatic elevators had existed since 1900, but people were too uncomfortable to ride in one without an operator. But, the strike turned public opinion and signalled the end of widespread elevator operators. This is how progress happens: slowly, slowly, then all at once. Now we push our own elevator buttons.[21]

Human unemployment caused by new technology was not new, even then.[22] Over a hundred years earlier, a group of textile workers in Nottingham smashed the steam looms threatening their livelihood and physically attacked the industrialists responsible. People labelled them 'Luddites'. We now use this as a pejorative term for anyone wishing to attempt the impossible: to turn back the technological clock. This is unfair. The Luddites, with some justification, feared redundancy, the loss of their identity – and the future for their children. They weren't anti-technology, just pro-jobs. The Luddites were wrestling with what was later branded the first Industrial Revolution. Steam engines pumped water from deep mines, enabled the hated steam loom and sped trains down tracks and boats across water. Steam is what economists call a 'general purpose technology' (GPT). GPTs don't simply change one area, they reshape the entire world. More recent GPTs include electricity and IT. AI is a GPT because it has almost limitless applications. Put another way, AI is the steam power of our time.[23] The Industrial Revolution replaced our arms and legs at work. AI, in what's been called the Fourth Industrial Revolution, is now replacing our brains.

As I've described earlier, AI has the power to help us. Not surprisingly, this silver lining is accompanied by some dark clouds. AI will mean the end for humans doing some jobs. In fact, if it's possible to write an algorithm that describes 100 per cent of the judgement calls and processes within a job, it's guaranteed to be automated. The MIT economists Erik Brynjolfsson and Andrew McAfee, in their book *Race Against the Machine*, warn that as the gap between machines and humans shrinks, employers are increasingly likely to hire 'new machines' instead of 'new people'.[24] Predictable and repetitive 'grunt work' in offices and factories – personal assistants and retail cashiers, for example – will be consigned to history first.[25]

Researchers have tried to forecast just how many jobs will go in the next 15 years. Teams from the likes of Oxford University, the World Economic Forum and several global management consultancies have made predictions between 14 per cent and 47 per cent.[26] Think about that for a second. Even at the lower end of this spectrum, we'll see a seismic change in how and where humans are needed. One research team even went as far as offering a probability on which jobs will be made obsolete. Telemarketers, data-entry workers, librarians, account clerks, tax submission preparers and freight agents all received a depressing 99 per cent chance of oblivion.[27] At the other end of the scale, therapists, middle managers and supervisors, social workers and occupational therapists were given a 0.35 per cent chance of being computerised based on current technology.

It might transpire, as with previous industrial revolutions, that new jobs will be created that never previously existed. I've heard talk of 'data hygienists', 'AI personality trainers' and 'ethicists', for example. Nobody yet knows if there will be a net growth or reduction in human unemployment. Whatever happens, we'll all have to rise to the challenge of transition, just as workers did in previous revolutions.

That change will be difficult for some. Nineteenth-century Luddites may have wanted to protect their jobs from steam-powered looms. But, you still needed a human to operate one. AI will not work under us, it will stand alongside. The other big difference is speed. The first

Industrial Revolution unfolded over a century. The progress with AI is visible in years, and occasionally months. The most vulnerable – taxi drivers, office administrators, shop clerks, shelf stackers and till operators – may see their jobs made redundant or changed beyond recognition quite soon. It's a lot harder to fight irrelevance than to battle exploitation. Acquiring the necessary new skills may prove tricky. It's one thing to inform a 45-year-old taxi driver his job has disappeared, and that he can look forward to amazing opportunities. Another challenge entirely for him to retrain as an 'AI/human interaction modeller'. Unlike the elevator operators of the early 1900s, for some there will not be decades to develop a new career option.[28] People are sensing this uncertainty. A large survey of American employees found 72 per cent of people are worried about AI. However, there seems to be some confusion about the potential for personal impact. People say they understand some jobs are at high risk – legal clerks, fast-food workers, insurance claim processors, for example. But only 3 in 10 people report it's likely that their own jobs will be delivered by a robot or computer in their lifetime. Like death, I guess, it's easier to imagine AI happening to someone else, rather than yourself.

Cheese slicing

A big change is, in this industrial revolution, the machines have come for white-collar workers. Jobs that rely on cognitive skills are now fair game for automation. Wholly repetitive and routine occupations will be rapidly automated first. This is why monotonous roles in telesales and customer support are already being delivered by chatbots. Jobs that follow a predictable routine will also be dominated by AI: truck and taxi drivers, security guards and even haematologists who diagnose disorders of the blood and bone marrow. So far, we've been talking about entire job categories being automated. However, this will not be the reality for most people. If you've got the foresight and resources to be reading this book, it's likely your role will not be automated any time soon. Instead, you'll see the repetitious and routine tasks within your job being cheese-sliced away by AI. This is already happening to accountants, lawyers, radiologists, sports and business reporters and research analysts, among others. If you're wondering about how to choose a trade that will remain relatively safe for the foreseeable future, ask the following question: 'How complex, unpredictable, emotion driven and potentially creative can this role be?'. Jobs in general management, mergers and acquisitions and economic analysis are highly complex, for example. Careers such as columnists, cartoonists, lobbyists, research scientists, architects, engineers and artists are both complex and rely on creative thinking. Kai-Fu Lee, a Taiwanese artificial intelligence expert, said: 'Really, the creative jobs are the ones that are protected, because AI can optimise, but not create.' I would add, nearly all jobs have the potential for creativity within them. Having more time in your day (which AI can offer) allows it to be unlocked.'

Why your boss wants you to be curious and creative

The cheese slicing of even complex and creative professions is not a threat in my view, but a huge development opportunity. From nurses to project managers, academics to surveyors, mechanics to therapists, this is chance to discover the curious-creative angle in your existing job. The context of the digital economy means developing the 4Cs for yourself is vital. They are increasingly required in the modern workplace. We're living through an era in which well-worn strategies in business, politics and everyday life have stopped working.[29] Technology is transforming the way we live, communicate, make money, share our thoughts and emotions, appreciate films and TV, shop, travel and even find, build or terminate our closest relationships. Contrast the growth of electrified and autonomous vehicles with the decline of Detroit's petrol-powered auto industry, the explosion in online shopping with increasingly empty high streets, the challenge to traditional banking from crypto-currencies and blockchain, or the transformation of music and video consumption, to name just a few.[30]

All this volatile, uncertain change means our world is far more difficult to forecast. As a result, the heavyweight champion of business capabilities – logical, analytical thinking – is being challenged.

Bosses realise we can't just plan and plod towards the future, we must reimagine it. To do this, everyone in organisations needs to be creatively switched on. When asked to rank the most important workplace aptitudes of this century, top CEOs reported that 'creativity' is rapidly rising up the hierarchy of valuable human skills. They rated it the third most important in 2019, up from tenth in 2015. For the first time, creative thinking is on the same playing field as people management, complex problem solving and critical thinking.[31]

In their book *The Future of the Professions: How Technology Will Transform the Work of Human Experts*, Richard and Daniel Susskind argue that even respected professions such as accountancy, law, medicine, architecture and chartered surveying are ripe for automation because they are: '. . . unaffordable, under-exploiting technology, disempowering, ethically challengeable, underperforming and inscrutable'.[32] Strong stuff. No wonder the Susskinds predict that 'increasingly capable machines, operating on their own or with non-specialist users, will take on many of the tasks that have been the historic preserve of the professions'.[33] Once wily lawyers are being cheese-sliced, no one is safe. Historically, the so-called 'Magic Circle' of global law firms made money by throwing large numbers of bodies at large stacks of legal paperwork. Now, many of the top firms rely on AI to do pre-trial due diligence.[34] As mentioned, this might not lead to net unemployment (however much fewer lawyers might sound attractive). Some firms expect to employ fewer graduates. Others argue cheaper services could encourage clients to consult their lawyers even more. Only time will tell.

We are also seeing the opening skirmishes as AI encroaches on the medical world. Babylon, the company behind the NHS 'GP at Hand' app, says its chatbot took the exam which was used to qualify trainee GPs. The first time Babylon sat the exam, it achieved a score of 81 per cent (the pass mark is 75 per cent). The Royal College of General Practitioners angrily retorted: 'An app might be able to pass an automated clinical knowledge test – but the answer to a clinical scenario isn't always cut and dried.' True, the world is more complicated than any exam. But, what's indisputable is that our world is about to change, for doctors, lawyers and everyone else relying on their knowledge, experience and cognitive skills.[35]

What's left for humans?

One hundred years ago, a worker on the Ford Motor Company production line would have been very clear what he had to do to be successful: turn up on time and then consistently follow orders to the letter. The bosses in the factories of the age of mass production required only two things from workers: obedience and diligence. They literally programmed every tiny detail of the routines and protocols of a single job. You see, mass automation is not new to our era, it's just this time we're using AI rather than human workers. If a Ford worker had been curious about the rest of the process, generated ideas, formed human networks throughout the company, it would not have been appreciated. More likely it would have got him fired.

Skills are always context specific. Andy Murray has a sublime backhand, but it wouldn't help him in a war zone. The context for today's skilled knowledge workers is very different from our latter-day Ford employee. Now, repetitive and routine physical tasks are delivered by AI-enabled robots. Simple thinking tasks are going the same way. So, what's left for humans? The answer is to stop *competing* with and start *differentiating* from artificial intelligence. We need to accept that where AI is better, there is little value in trying to compete. Why play a game you're bound to lose? You need to be prepared for your human value to shift, as the diagram in Figure 1.2 summarises. The smart move is to adapt, as humans have always done; focus on honing skills fit for the historic context in which we live.

The 'Great Divide'

In this context, a global societal divide is emerging. But this is not between AI and humans. It's between one human and another.

Figure 1.2 Standard versus non-standard intelligence[36]

Type of knowledge work	Machine or human?				
To analyse					
To optimise	**The growing world of AI** Standardised intelligence				
To repeat					
To recommend					
To question & decide					
To care				**The human edge** Non-standardised intelligence	
To create					
To inspire					

Digital technology is a great leveller, and it's easier than ever to learn. With a little time, anyone with an internet connection and a smartphone can educate themselves in almost limitless domains. Children have access to more information in real time than the president of the United States had 20 years ago. This is drawing a new fault line between the 'haves' and the 'have-nots'. This separation is not money, class or connections: it's a growing value gap between those who are future-ready, and those who are not. Reading downwards on the left side of Figure 1.3, you see that developing

Figure 1.3 The growing future-fit divide

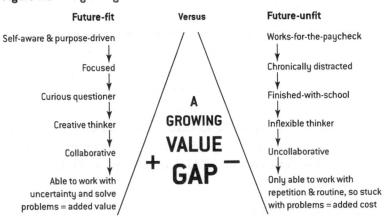

Future-fit	Versus	Future-unfit
Self-aware & purpose-driven		Works-for-the-paycheck
Focused		Chronically distracted
Curious questioner	**A**	Finished-with-school
Creative thinker	**GROWING**	Inflexible thinker
Collaborative	**VALUE**	Uncollaborative
Able to work with uncertainty and solve problems = added value	**+ GAP −**	Only able to work with repetition & routine, so stuck with problems = added cost

the quality of being self-aware, purpose-driven and focused is a gateway. These capabilities are necessary to unlock the motivation – and time – to be curious, creative and collaborative.

Reading across the diagram from left to right, you see the growing economic gap between the purpose-driven versus the disengaged; the focused versus the chronically distracted; the insatiably curious versus those who've stopped asking questions; people who can work with their fellow humans versus those who fail to skilfully connect and experiment. This gap will only widen in the coming years.

It's not just AI you're up against. If you're marooned on the wrong side of this divide you'll end up in a losing battle against equally skilled, but lower-cost 'robotic' human rivals. Smart employers are looking for people who can do more than follow orders and respond to requests. HR directors are being tasked with attracting staff who have a strong intrinsic desire to learn, solve problems and ask penetrating questions.[37] Ian Leslie, the author of *Curious: The Desire to Know and Why Your Future Depends on It*, writes: '[The curious] are the ones whose jobs are least likely to be taken by intelligent machines; in a world where technology is rapidly replacing humans even in white-collar jobs, it's no longer enough to be merely smart. Computers are smart. But no computer, however sophisticated, can yet be said to be curious.'[38,39]

The science-fiction writer William Gibson is reported as saying that 'The future is already here – it's just not evenly distributed.'[40] This is true, and the insight into how to thrive in the future is equally patchy. If you aren't developing your Human Edge, you run the risk of being overtaken by people who are – or machines who perform predictable and repetitive tasks better than you ever could. The crucial gap is between humans who can think creatively and those that only think in straight lines (AI does this very well). The 'Great Divide' is growing.

Which side do you want to be on?

Figure 1.4 Applying the 4Cs model

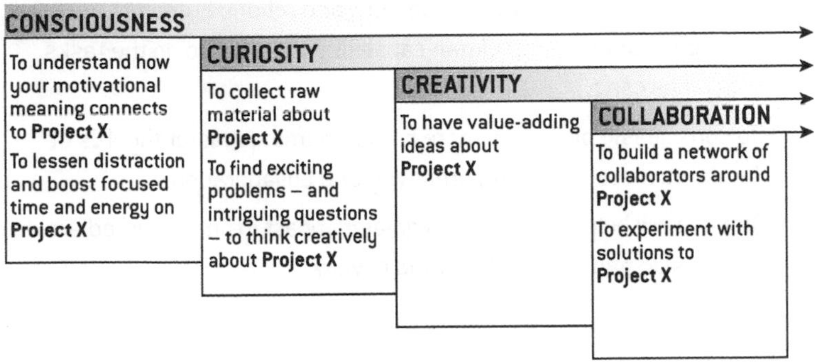

CONSCIOUSNESS			
To understand how your motivational meaning connects to **Project X** To lessen distraction and boost focused time and energy on **Project X**	**CURIOSITY** To collect raw material about **Project X** To find exciting problems – and intriguing questions – to think creatively about **Project X**	**CREATIVITY** To have value-adding ideas about **Project X**	**COLLABORATION** To build a network of collaborators around **Project X** To experiment with solutions to **Project X**

Getting started

Imagine something in life you'd dearly like to improve. It could be a product, process or practice connected to your work, or anything else for that matter. Let's call it **Project X**. Figure 1.4 illustrates how you might use the 4Cs to move your passion project forward.

A quick reminder. . .

- AI is transforming our world: it's in the process of becoming ubiquitous at home and at work.

- It will consign some jobs to history, and will 'cheese-slice' repetitious and routine tasks from *all* jobs.

- In this shifting context, there's a growing value gap between humans who are future-ready, and those who aren't.

- To survive and thrive, you need to differentiate from, rather than compete with, AI.

▶

- To set yourself apart from machines (and robotic humans), develop your uniquely human capabilities in order to do the tasks machines can't.

- To consciously become a more *human* human, master the 4Cs of Consciousness, Curiosity, Creativity and Collaboration.

- The 4Cs will help you to make a greater impact in our disrupted era — both inside and outside the world of work.

Human experiment: Start now. . .

AI and me

Grab a clean sheet of paper and draw a large circle. Divide your current (or planned) occupation into 5–10 activity areas, making each slice of the pie roughly equivalent of the time you spend on that activity. My pie might have the following segments: keynote speaking, writing, designing change and leadership programmes, teaching in person, teaching online (text, video, interactive), research, managing client relationships, handling travel and accommodation, logistics and invoicing. Now use the following two-step thinking process to work out how you can use this book to your benefit:

1 Which of these skills are repetitious and predictable?[41] If you broke them down a little further, are there subskills that are automatable? Give each skill area a mark out of 10: 10 means 'already automated/I'm aware of a system that delivers this'; 9 is 'highly likely to be automated soon'; 5 is neutral; 1 means 'will not be automated in my career'; and 0 means 'will not be automated in my lifetime/probably never automated'.[42]

2   From your scoring, which of the skills are most likely to remain for you as a human worker, and allow you to add value? Will these be enough to classify your position as 'full-time' and 'full-salaried'? If the answer is 'no', you need to use this book to think about your next career move. If the answer is 'yes', use the 4Cs to develop your role further.

2

Say hello to Frankenstein
How to distinguish yourself from AI (and robotic humans)

'You are my creator, but I am your master.'

Mary Shelley, *Frankenstein*

It was the first morning of Amelia's new job on the IT help desk in a large national bank, but she wasn't nervous. She'd been well trained, and knew precisely what to do. Not surprisingly, Amelia's manager was careful to keep an eye on her. He was delighted. The reports from her colleagues were very positive. She managed to resolve any number of technical queries that came her way. Not only this, she was skilled at understanding the caller's tone of voice and modified her replies accordingly. She appeared like magic in front of frustrated bank workers and quickly focused on their issue. With her blonde hair pulled back into an efficient bun, and sharp, black business suit, Amelia quickly earned a reputation for being effective. She combined encyclopaedic knowledge, a remarkable work ethic and calm resilience in the face of even the most aggressive questions. Her first promotion came quickly.[1]

Amelia isn't human. She was a pioneer though. That promotion made her the first AI in history to become a virtual assistant to the customers of a large bank – SEB, in Sweden.[2] Amelia is now one of a fast-growing band of chatbots. It's highly likely you will have interacted with a chatbot on a company website already, thinking you were communicating with a human. Amelia never takes a break, a vacation, or a suspicious duvet day. She handles calls 24/7, 365 days a year. She never loses her cool and doesn't ask for a salary, let alone a rise. She never demands an expensive orthopaedic chair, compassionate time to mourn a loved one, or maternity leave. On top of all that, she can theoretically chat to all 1 million of SEB's customers *at the same time.*

Amelia, and her artificial brothers and sisters, are now our competition. In Chapter One, we looked at how it's better to differentiate from, rather than compete with, Amelia and her silicon-based colleagues. In this chapter, we'll explore why AI is now smarter than ever. Understanding where its power comes from will help you work out which direction you need to take in the future to sidestep Amelia's challenge. Along the way, we'll reframe the anxiety that comes with AI's new role in our lives. The best way to move past fear is to face it.

Frankenstein fears

The type of AI you're facing today is called artificial narrow intelligence (ANI). ANI works well on specific tasks: from driving a truck to understanding speech (called natural language processing), recommending products to optimising energy in the national grid. I'll briefly discuss the possible next step for AI – artificial general intelligence (AGI) – at the end of the book. This is the nightmare or utopian future (people see it both ways), when machines might become as broadly intelligent as humans. I'll also consider the possible logical conclusion of AGI, which is artificial superintelligence (ASI). ASI is the scenario in which a computer becomes smarter than us and then starts to make its own decisions. You'll have little trouble imagining this situation as it's already appeared in so many iconic movies, from Stanley Kubrick's epic science-fiction flick *2001: A Space Odyssey* to the *Terminator* and *The Matrix* film franchises, to name just the most famous.

We're going to focus on the world as it is now: the encroaching role of non-sentient, but powerful, ANI.[3] As Fei-Fei Li, associate professor of computer science at Stanford University remarks: 'We're really closer to a smart washing machine rather than the Terminator.' My mission is to ensure you can stay ahead of increasingly plausible and smart 'washing machines' in the next 5 to 20 years of your career.

When it comes to AI, keeping things in perspective is not easy. This is because it can feel like just the latest instalment in a long-running, fiction-meets-reality myth. Humankind has always liked the idea of creating a powerful assistant, but we've long feared that this subordinate may eventually turn against us. In Ancient Greece, the god of craftsmen and metalworking, Hephaestus, was said to have built Talos – a giant automated robot made from bronze, tasked with defending the island of Crete. He also built Pandora (she of box fame) – a *Blade Runner* style replicate that was 'programmed' to release evil into the world.[4] In 1818, Mary Shelley's gothic novel *Frankenstein* told a cautionary tale of how humans can react badly when they feel threatened by a new form of life. Just four years later, a Victorian academic and inventor Charles Babbage designed a machine in the real world that, if completed, would have carried out general-purpose computation using a system of punch cards. His 'Difference Engine No. 2' was later faithfully constructed to the original drawings. It now stands in London's Science Museum and consists of 8,000 parts, weighs five tons and measures 11 feet long.[5]

The brilliant British mathematician Alan Turing is often described as the father of both computer science and AI. He is most celebrated for cracking the fiendishly difficult German naval codes during the Second World War. At Bletchley Park in Buckinghamshire, he constructed complex machines known as bombes, which eliminated enormous numbers of erroneous code solutions to arrive at the correct answer. This early application of computing is estimated to have shortened the war by two years.

Turing also presciently forecast the current awkwardness we now feel in AI–human interactions. He designed the infamous Turing Test. An AI passes the test if it fools a person, in a series of five-minute keyboard conversations, into believing it is a fellow human being. In case you were wondering, a computer program called Eugene Goostman, which simulated a 13-year-old Ukrainian boy, already passed the Turing Test at an event organised by the University of Reading in 2014.[6] More recently, Google has demonstrated a voice-based bot called Duplex, which can book simple appointments over the phone by conducting spoken conversations. This app leaps past the Turing Test to another level by passing for a human not in text form, but with an uncannily human voice complete with 'ums' and 'ers'.[7]

In the eighty years since Turing predicted AI, its fortunes as a concept and research project have soared and plummeted. The respected researcher Herbert Simon confidently pronounced in 1965 that 'machines will be capable, within twenty years, of doing any work a man can do'.[8] Periods of this type of frothy hype have been followed by AI winters in which confidence and government funding have collapsed. Despite this, many (including myself) forecast this current AI spring will turn into a long hot summer. This is because the fierce commercial competition outlined in the previous chapter is being spurred on by three interdependent technology trends: faster, cheaper hardware; software that learns on its own; and oceans of data to feed the growing AI beast. Let's take a look at how this converging trio is driving the growth of AI.

Faster, cheaper hardware

To understand the evolution of computer hardware – a system's physical parts – join me in a thought experiment. Imagine getting into a VW Beetle and driving down the feeder road on to a motorway.[9] For the first minute, you begin in the slow lane driving at only 5 miles per hour. Cars and trucks are streaming past you with lights flashing and horns blaring. There would probably be some curious hand signals coming your way too. Not wanting to seem unreasonable, after a minute you double your speed to a majestic 10 miles per hour and make a mental note to keep doubling your speed as each minute passes. In the early part of your strange journey, the rate of acceleration would be slow. By doubling your speed every sixty seconds it would take five minutes to creep past the UK speed limit and be travelling at 80 miles per hour. But, as the fifth minute passes to the sixth, you'd begin travelling at 160 mph. This is the power of what mathematicians call exponential growth. It's only as it progresses that you see its true potency. If you continued this pattern of doubling your speed, in the 28th minute, unbelievably, you'd be hurtling along at 671 *million* miles an hour. During that time, your rattling VW Beetle would travel 11 million miles. That's 275 times around the Earth (traffic permitting).

This slightly terrifying and, I admit, totally unrealistic metaphor describes how microchips (or integrated circuits, as they were once called) have increased in power since their invention in Silicon Valley in 1958. The exponential growth effect is known as Moore's Law,[10] after the Intel co-founder Gordon Moore who first described it back in 1965. Moore noticed that the number of transistors in an integrated circuit doubles every eighteen months or so. This regular exponential growth has occurred now for over sixty years. The result: the sort of computer speed changes we saw in your imaginary VW now occur every year in real life. What's truly thought-provoking is Moore's Law is not stopping any time soon. It will double again in the next two years, and again after that. And again, and again. But now, of course, the speed increases each time by far greater amounts, because we're much later on in our 'motorway' journey.

Some argue that, as we reach the limits of computer chip miniaturisation, Moore's Law will lose its vigour. However, most eminent computer scientists argue that there are plenty of new technologies that will keep it going, including stacking chips on top of each other, neuromorphic computing, which mimics the human brain, and quantum computing. Instead of using the binary digits of 1s and 0s to describe the world, quantum computing delves into quantum bits (qubits), which can be simultaneously on and off at the same time.[11] If you understand how that works, you're smarter than I am. At this stage I just accept it's possible.

The bottom line is that Moore's Law explains the dominance of computing in our lives – and how it underpins AI. It has transformed our world and is likely to continue doing so for the foreseeable future. Its effects are staggering. It's estimated that if a modern smartphone could have been built in 1958, it would have cost one-and-a-half times today's global GDP, would have filled a 100-storey building three kilometres long and wide and would have used 30 times the world's current power-generating capacity.[12] If Moore's Law continues for another two decades, the total amount of computing power now available to Google will be available on an ordinary desktop computer.[13] Just think what a super smart teenager might do with that.

Software that learns on its own

Computers work by following a set of rules or instructions called algorithms.[14] An algorithm uses data from the world to build a model that it can then use to make predictions. It tests these predictions against more data to refine its simulation of the world.[15] The reason for AI's inexorable rise is this: humans are no longer writing all the algorithms. The machines are teaching themselves.

To understand this story, we need to time travel to New York City in 1997. The former world chess champion, Garry Kasparov, has just been unexpectedly beaten by IBM's AI, Deep Blue. At the time, this was hailed around the world as a major leap forward. But, in terms of modern AI, it was just a baby step. Deep Blue relied on the sort of hardware speed improvements we just explored. It used 'brute force' computing: reviewing the chess board and then thinking through *all* the potential moves. Deep Blue didn't really innovate the model of computing invented by Turing because it followed human rules. It beat the human champion using instructions written by IBM computer scientists who, in turn, relied on the advice of chess masters. It overcame Kasparov's vast skill and experience through lightning speed alone. It was capable of examining 200 million moves per second, or 50 billion positions in the three minutes allocated for a single move.[16] Reflecting on his unique position as the fallen standard bearer for the human race, Kasparov wryly noted: 'Deep Blue was intelligent the way your programmable alarm clock is intelligent. Not that losing to a $10 million alarm clock made me feel any better.'[17]

Fast forward 19 years to 2016. Now we're in Seoul, South Korea, watching another titanic battle between human and machine. This time Korean world champion and grandmaster Lee Sedol is taking on a 'British' opponent. The AI – called AlphaGo – was created by a team of techies from the Oxford University spin-off, DeepMind. The field of battle is a 3,000-year-old board game called 'Go'. In Go, one player plays with small white pebbles and the other with black pebbles, on a square wooden board. The goal is deceptively straightforward: surround your opponent, cut them off to win territory and the game is yours. It looks simple, but the number of possible move outcomes dwarfs even that of chess – more than the number of atoms in the known universe, according to the DeepMind CEO and founder Demis Hassabis. Go was seen as the pinnacle of computer game playing because of its massive complexity and the perceived importance of intuition. This meant it was not possible for humans to programme AlphaGo with every possible scenario as they had with chess. Instead, AlphaGo used machine learning,[18] in which the computer's algorithms learn without needing to be explicitly programmed.[19]

AlphaGo was merely given a goal: to win the game. From trial and error, the algorithm built the most efficient path towards victory.[20] Underlying these processes is what's called a 'neural network' – a type of algorithm that learns from observation. It gets its name from the fact that it processes information a little like a human brain, which is itself made up of billions of interconnected neurons.[21]

Prior to taking on Lee Sedol, AlphaGo warmed up by mastering the video games I played in my childhood in the 1980s: Asteroids, Space Invaders and Atari Breakout. In Breakout, the player tries to smash through a wall of bricks at the top of the screen by hitting a ball upwards with a paddle located at the bottom. Again, AlphaGo was given only the bare minimum of the sensory input (i.e. what you see on the screen) and a simple rule – to maximise the score. It didn't even know what the controls were designed to do. The rate of learning was staggering. After ten minutes of training, the AI could barely hit the ball back. After two hours, it was playing like an expert. After four hours, it hit upon the best strategy. AlphaGo figured out that if it focused on one small point in the wall and dug a hole to allow the ball to break through to the other side, the ball would then bounce around on its own smashing bricks without the computer having to even move the paddle. This novel approach surpassed the best human players.[22] If AlphaGo had been a toddler, you might have been tempted to put a lock on the outside of its bedroom door.

After seeing this demonstration, Google bought DeepMind for $500m. At the time, it had no profits. It didn't even have revenues. The reason? The developers did not teach AlphaGo how to play video games, but *how to learn* how to play video games. A profound, and hugely valuable, difference. AlphaGo went on to win the globally televised Go tournament against Lee Sedol four games to one. As with Kasparov, artificial intelligence was emphatically the winner. But this time, the game had shifted significantly. AlphaGo didn't need human instruction because it learned, and then wrote its own rules. The AI of today is the intellectual offspring of AlphaGo. Its ability to learn is why it is transforming our world. Systems are doing it for themselves.[23]

Oceans of data

Metaphorically speaking, if AI is a car,[24] the silicon chips are the engine, algorithms are the engine's control system – and data[25] is the fuel.[26] To accelerate the type of self-learning described above, you need lots and lots of data. Machine-learning AI uses feedback data from Atari Breakout, or anything else, to learn. The AI will try, fail, then try again millions of times, to work out the best way of achieving a goal. By sucking in vast data sets, AI can spot patterns and create insights humans would never see.

Fortunately for AI, data has never been so plentiful as it is now. Our smartphones are how many of us interact with AI. They are also how we proffer our data so AI can learn. The amount of information we all now create intentionally, and as 'exhaust' (by-product) data, is truly awe-inspiring. They say, in our digital society, data is the 'new oil'. In this case, our devices leave a filmy smear of personal information as they record everything we do, say, or see in the form of emails, tweets, photos, videos and social media posts. But it doesn't stop there. Just imagine, for a moment, the oily digital footprints you leave behind you every day: credit card payments, CCTV images in shops, offices, trains and buses, smart home devices, location sensors on your car, keystrokes and database entries at work. You are a one-person bobbing data oil derrick. And this allows AI to understand you so well it can predict your next move.

Other rivers feed into the data ocean, this time flowing from objects. Nearly everything you can see around you, and much you can't see, is now connected, or soon will be. It's dubbed the Internet of Things (IoT). This is the phenomenon that every conceivable item on earth – trains, planes, automobiles, washing machines, wind turbines, buildings, air conditioning units, ovens, buoys out in the ocean, clothes, underwear, shoes – will continually drip into the data sea. All products are now services thanks to the data trail, which reveals how they get used, or could be used better. All this is fed back, logged, analysed and interpreted by the unblinking eye of our machines.

The exponential curves of different technologies are combining and making each other steeper. As well as silicon chips, a number of other technological developments have been observed to be growing exponentially. Memory capacity, for one. In 1980, IBM created a cutting-edge hard drive that could store a princely 2.5 gigabytes. I have a Seagate external drive on my office desk to back-up my laptop that is about the size of a pack of cards. It can hold four terabytes of data. To put that into perspective, it stores roughly 1,600 times more data than IBM's supercomputer, which was the size of a refrigerator and weighed 250 kg. The IBM hard drive cost around £200,000 in today's money; my little Seagate drive set me back £82.99 from Amazon.[27] Not surprisingly, sensors, LEDs and the number of pixels in digital cameras are also all growing at an exponential rate. This means the cost of gathering richer information is falling as more is collected. And so it continues to snowball.[28]

This means the world is now capturing and recording more data than ever before. It's been estimated that at the start of the twentieth century the sum of human knowledge was doubling every century, and that by the end of the Second World War this was taking place every twenty-five years. Now it takes months. IBM has estimated that as IoT becomes a reality, this doubling may be down to days and even hours.[29] It means around 90 per cent of the data on the Internet has been created since 2016.[30] We're back on that motorway in the hurtling VW. But this time the foot on the accelerator is information, not hardware.

The difference between humans and machines

As discussed, physical jobs have been automated for years. Now intelligence – the ability to accomplish complex goals – is up for grabs.[31] Even this has a long history. Machines have mastered narrow, previously human-dominated, cognitive domains before.

In the 1940s, NASA already had computers, but they were human. Using only pencils, these 'human computers' did the calculations necessary to launch rockets. These sums often took more than a week to complete, and filled six to eight notebooks with a spider crawl of formulas.[32] Let's try to live up to their inspiring legacy. Take a moment to prepare yourself, breathe and then, in your head, divide 1,845,371.27 by 17.5. Only kidding. You can stop now. This sum (even with the benefit of a pencil and paper) is a bit of a challenge, but nothing approaching the complex Newtonian trajectory calculations required for rocketry. These were a challenge for even the smartest human computer, but as it turned out fairly straightforward for a silicon-based computer. This is why space programmes, and much of the rest of the world, now rely on microchips to do the numbers.

Arithmetic calculations top the list of intellectual tasks that AI can do better than humans. And it's growing. It now includes playing chess, recognising faces and even composing music in the style of Bach (more on this later). Soon to be added to the list: translating a foreign language in real time, driving and much more besides. As Cognizant's Center for the Future of Work puts it: 'Work has always changed. Few if any people make a living nowadays as knockeruppers, telegraphists, switchboard operators, (human) computers, lamplighters, nursemaids, limners, town criers, travel agents, bank tellers, elevator operators or secretaries. Yet these were all jobs that employed thousands of people in the past.'[33]

The question is, who are the doomed 'human computers' of today? Is it you, or me? What is AI now poised to conquer, in the same way massive IBM mainframes made people with pencils and graph paper redundant? Where should we turn to avoid the unblinking gaze of our AI competitor? To answer this question, you need to understand the difference between 'human intelligence' and 'artificial intelligence'. This distinction is elegantly described by Hans Moravec, adjunct professor at the Robotics Institute of Carnegie Mellon University. He would say we're right to be in awe of NASA's astonishing arithmeticians, because for humans, computation is very hard. His 'Moravec's Paradox' is the understanding that, contrary to traditional assumptions, high-level maths actually requires very little, well, computation.[34] For digital computers it's a piece of cake.

This is a huge insight. It means where AI is naturally strong, we are weak. More optimistically, where we are naturally strong, AI is weak. The human touch we dispense every day without even trying would flummox AI. Let's take a random example from my evening's TV viewing last night. With family and friends I watched my favourite rugby team, Wasps, play an important game. Here are all the hidden human skills I performed that computers find devilishly difficult to master:

I. . .

- chose, prepared and then carried in a tray of drinks and nibbles;
- recognised an emotion on the face of a friend;
- distinguished it from the emotions of another friend, and a number of family members;
- understood the dynamic context of the social setting and modified my behaviour to fit in;
- cracked a number of jokes and understood which ones 'landed' and which ones didn't (several, sadly);
- listened to the tone of voice of the commentator and the pundit (complete with sarcasm), understood their hidden meanings and drew inferences about the types of person they were;
- appreciated the beauty of a particular run or pass (as we do with sunsets, paintings and ideas, for that matter);
- felt happy when Wasps were winning, exultant when we were ahead, desperate when the opposition scored and sad, but philosophical, when we eventually lost.

It's ironic that the stuff we don't consciously value is way beyond even the most powerful AI. And this list of skills could be ascribed to any reasonably competent 9 year old, let alone an adult. The reason we find these things so simple is that evolution has dedicated much of our brain to these kind of tasks. We have more than a quarter of our grey matter dedicated to these 'human' functions. They were the competencies that kept our socially adept ancestors alive.

Head for the high ground

Think of these human superpowers – dexterity, social understanding, emotional skill, deriving meaning, common sense, creativity, critical thinking, humour, human contact and collaboration – as snow-capped mountain peaks. Elaborating on his paradox, Hans Moravec describes a flood, with the valleys below the peaks being submerged by AI. The deepest canyons of this skills geography contain capabilities such as 'rote memorisation'. We are all aware how the use of smartphones means we no longer need to remember numbers, directions and addresses that we used to habitually keep in our head. The story of NASA's doomed human computers illustrates the submersion of another valley: 'arithmetic'. One of the smaller foothills we can still see through the translucent waters might be labelled 'chess playing'. Fifty years ago, the waters submerged most filing jobs such as record clerks. Now the flood has reached the ridges where tax return preparers, office administrators, personal assistants and taxi drivers perch. What ledge do you currently inhabit?

Wide, not narrow

At the time of writing, investigators are looking into the demise of a Boeing 737 MAX 8 which crashed just after take-off near Addis Ababa in Ethiopia. It's believed the disaster may have been caused by a confused AI.[35] The plane's computer might have been fed faulty sensor data that showed the aircraft was level, when in fact it was plummeting to the ground. The pilots could not override the AI, and all 157 people onboard were killed. The plane hit the ground so fast the engines were buried in a 10-metre-deep crater. The tragedy is it was obvious the plane was heading for the ground. It wasn't just the pilots that could see this. Any child looking out of the window could have diagnosed the situation. But the AI was only concerned with its narrow understanding of the data it received.

ANI is efficient, but it has zero common sense. Humans are far better at seeing the big picture. We intuitively 'get' situational context. We can also skilfully integrate different stages in a process, and different domains of knowledge. Put simply, we do wide, computers do narrow. Max Tegmark explains it this way: 'We humans win hands-down on breadth, while machines outperform us in a small but growing number of narrow domains.'[36]

AI has a long way to go to recreate our human superpowers. It lacks our ability to think creatively about 'everything' and to link it together. Instead, it focuses only on the problem we've asked it to crack. AI is very good at responding to specific questions, and providing options and solutions; good at gathering data and finding hidden patterns within the data. It works when we ask it to oversee predictable processes. In these areas it delivers exponentially faster, cheaper consistency – and often quality too.

The goal of each AI system is totally focused on a single, very specific goal. IBM's Deep Blue beat Kasparov in the narrow domain of chess. AlphaGo did the same against Lee Sedol in the similarly cramped field of Go. Neither AI could have then gone on to make a cup of tea, empathise with their fallen opponent or offer support and sympathy. Nor could they then tactfully change the subject and discuss a treasured memory, or an alternative line of work. Neither machine even knew it had won the game. AI is currently a one-trick pony. You, on the other hand, are a general intelligence genius with a cleverness that's remarkably adaptable, broad and therefore creative.

A quick reminder. . .

- The AI revolution is being driven by exponential growth in the speed and power of computer hardware, combined with software that learns independently, and fed by massive amounts of data.

- This book is focused on ANI (artificial *narrow* intelligence), as opposed to the possible future scenarios of human-level, and even sentient, super-intelligent machines.

- ANI (which we'll call AI) is rapidly becoming faster and cheaper than humans at a whole list of narrow, routine cognitive tasks: making a restaurant reservation, booking a flight, organising data, curating your social media feed and, soon, driving your car.

- To stay relevant and valuable in the next 5 to 20 years of your career, you need to retain your 'Human Edge' over AI. It's worth remembering that humans have some significant advantages:

  - Where AI is naturally strong, you're weak; however, it's also correct to say that where you're naturally strong, AI is weak.

  - AI can be efficient, but it's not at all smart. Humans are far better at seeing the big picture and thinking wide rather than narrow.

  - The distinctly human activities we don't always consciously value – explored in the 4Cs – are currently way beyond even the most powerful AI.

 ## Human experiment: Start now. . .

Being human, more often, with skill

This book is about recognising, developing and honing your human skills. The good news is it's likely you're already delivering distinctly human usefulness already, but may be undervaluing it. Think about your recent history at work and at home. Sit for a few minutes and write down all the human touches you brought to your own thinking – and to others. Reflecting the themes of this book, these might be about developing and explaining the wider meaning of things, learning for the sheer joy of it, asking curious questions of yourself and others and connecting different concepts in order to have a new idea.

Look at your list and pick out the example that you think was most valuable to you.

What was the result of your human touch?

How did it make you feel?

Most importantly, how could you do this *more often*?

3

Who stole your imagination?

How to embrace your creative potential

'The chief enemy of creativity is "good" sense.'

Pablo Picasso

Maisy was six years old and a little shy. She always slipped into the seat at the back of the class. This morning was different. It was a drawing lesson, and Maisy was hunched over her work. She stuck her tongue out of the side of her mouth as she scribbled furiously. Fascinated to understand what was happening, her teacher strode up the aisle between the desks to face Maisy. 'What are you drawing?', she asked. Maisy replied: 'I'm drawing a picture of heaven.' The teacher smiled indulgently, and countered: 'But, nobody knows what heaven looks like.' Not bothering to look up, Maisy quietly retorted: 'They will in a minute!'[1]

I wonder what Maisy's reaction would be if someone asked her to draw a picture of heaven now she's grown up? If she's like most people I meet, she would feel embarrassed and unequal to the challenge. She might mistake imagination for the ability to draw, and lack the creative confidence to even pick up a pencil.

Take a few moments to consider the following question:

Are you creative?

If you answered 'yes', this is your opportunity to nurture and build your 'yes' into a 'Yes, AND. . . !'. If you answered 'no', don't worry. As you'll see, you are by no means alone. This chapter will help you to re-examine your response. We'll explore your belief in your emotional and intellectual capacity to create. Then build your confidence to have a go. Some psychologists call this capability creative energy. Famous designers have dubbed it creative confidence.[2] We'll call it your *creative potential*. As we've seen, creativity is pivotal to the 4Cs; it's the filament that connects all of them. Because of that, the rest of this chapter is devoted to helping you to hold hands with your own creative potential. After we pass this important psychological milestone, we'll dive into the 4Cs in detail in Part Two.

 Human experiment

Am I creative?

Now is a good moment to consider your creative potential. Honestly answer the following statements.[3] Mark yourself a 5 if the statement describes you perfectly, or 4, 3, 2 or 1 if you're less sure. Put 0 if the statement doesn't describe you at all.

1 **I'm a questioner:** I often ask questions that challenge others' fundamental assumptions.

2 **I'm an observer:** I get innovative ideas by directly observing how people interact with products and services.

3 **I'm an associator:** I creatively solve challenging problems by drawing on diverse ideas or knowledge.

4 **I'm a networker:** I regularly talk with a diverse set of people (e.g., from different functions, industries, geographies) to find and refine my ideas.

5 **I'm an experimenter:** I frequently try things out to discover new ways of doing things.[4]

If you scored the maximum of 25, well done. You can use the coming chapters to find new ways to explore and augment your creative thinking. If you scored yourself less than 25, don't worry. That score reflects your creative potential now, but you can build it up from here. The five questions above align with the Dance Steps in the 4Cs model we are now poised to explore.

The creativity contradiction

I often ask business people two simple questions. The first is the query you just pondered: are you creative? At this point, there is normally a slightly embarrassed pause. On average, somewhere between ten per cent and a third of the hands in the room tentatively go up. Then, I ask a second question: who considers creativity to be *important* in your business? The response to this question is very different. Immediately, the room becomes a dense forest of raised arms. Why does this contradiction exist? If business people know creativity is important, why are so many happy to acknowledge they can't 'do' it? My straw polls reflect scientific research into attitudes to creativity. A study in the USA, UK, Germany, France and Japan confirmed around eight in ten people agreed unlocking creativity is key to driving economic growth.[5] Two-thirds even argued it was valuable to society as a whole. Yet, a measly one in four people reported that they were personally creative.

 Human experiment

Believe in your creative potential

The first step to making creativity part of your life is as simple as changing your attitude – literally, believing you are creative leads you to be more creative. This isn't just chicken-and-egg common sense, it's supported by research. Business managers who answer 'agree' when posed the statement 'I am creative', are shown to be those who go on to deliver disruptive solutions in the form of new businesses, products, services and processes that no one has done before. They see themselves as creative, and so act that way.[6]

The theft of creativity

There's a reason for this puzzling gap. During our lives, creativity is often stolen from us. The theft is aided and abetted by the myths that have grown around it. The environments we experience also wash it away like acid rain. As a result, the natural human tendency to have, and build, new ideas becomes distant, mysterious – even magical – for most people. Let's take a moment to examine and dismantle these myths. By doing so, I hope you can throw a rope around creativity and haul it a little closer.

Myth 1: Creativity is all about mysterious 'a-ha moments'

As his carriage is bumping along the highway near Salzburg, Mozart's mind is racing. A great symphony is pouring from his brain, perfect and complete. He wrote later, '. . . the whole, though it be long, stands almost finished and complete in my mind, so that I can survey it, like a fine picture or a beautiful statue, at a glance. Nor do I hear in my imagination the parts successively, but I hear them, as it were, all at once.'[7] I'm sure you could think of a few more tales of blinding insight just like this. Archimedes' 'Eureka' moment and Isaac Newton's bump on the head with an apple generally crop up at school. Archetypal creative epiphanies deliver a dramatic and memorable punchline. But they pose a problem. These iconic moments in the lives of generational wunderkinds such as Tesla, Einstein and Jobs place far too much emphasis on the so-called 'a-ha moment', and often ignore the blood, sweat and tears, failure and mental blocks that made it possible.

We humans love a good story. So much so, we sometimes make them up. The letter from Mozart first appeared in 1815, in Germany's *General Music Journal*. It was then quoted for centuries afterwards, shaping our understanding of the nature of creativity. The problem is, it was a fake. Mozart's real letters to his family show that, although he was undoubtedly talented, his symphonies never came in torrents of genius but through hours of toil. First, he sketched the big ideas with a piano. Then he grafted for months polishing and perfecting.

The British tech entrepreneur Kevin Ashton, who coined the phrase the 'Internet of Things', commented: 'We do not see the road from nothing to new, and maybe we do not want to. . . It dulls the lustre to think that every elegant equation, beautiful painting, and brilliant machine is born of effort and error, the progeny of false starts and failures, and that each maker is as flawed, small, and mortal as the rest of us.'[8] When asked about the exact moment he came up with the idea behind Facebook, Mark Zuckerberg paused and then responded, 'I don't think that's how the world works. . . ideas typically do not just come to you. It's a lot of dots that you connect to make it so that you finally realize that you can potentially do something.'[9]

'A-ha moments' have a gift for public relations. But they distance us from, rather than connect us to, our own creative potential. Considering all the attention they get, it's ironic that these moments are the only point in the creative process that are beyond our conscious control. A-ha moments do exist for all of us, and they're important. They're often delivered as a whisper by our unconscious mind. However, as we'll see, it's actually the time and effort *before* and *after* these insights that we can influence.

Myth 2: Creativity is for artists

Most of us are too modest to aspire to being spoken of in the same breath as Holbein, Picasso or Rodin – or Banksy, Lennon or Bowie for that matter. One of the enduring myths that ensures creativity remains elusive is its exclusive association with artists. A subset of this myth in the business world insists creativity is reserved for 'creatives', often ghettoised as funky men and women who work in design, branding and advertising agencies. I've worked in and around the so-called 'creative industries' for years and always found the definition ridiculous. There's no doubt we can all learn from advertising gurus about generating good ideas. But, does anybody seriously think writing copy for an advert is more creative than designing the blade of a new jet engine? Some of the world's most creative thinking is currently going on in the intersection between computer engineering and biotech research, for example. We could easily also find examples of creative thinking in HR, finance, environmental studies and, yes, even accountancy (ideally, staying inside the rule of law!). Any vocation can be creative. The domain just changes.

Myth 3: Creativity = genius

We know creativity is linked to brainpower, but only up to a certain point. Stanford psychologist Lewis Terman used an IQ test to study over a thousand high-performing students. He found creativity is only correlated with intelligence up to an IQ of 120. To put this number in context, a score of 100 is considered to be average, and about 70 per cent of us fall within one standard deviation of the mean – with an IQ of between 85 and 115.[10]

Sadly, this doesn't stop some from pontificating that 'you're either creative, or you're not'. This is a fallacy that defines creativity as a fixed trait, like eye colour. The reality is that our DNA does bequeath a certain level of both IQ and creativity. But the rest is up to us, our environment and how we choose to develop our gifts. Creativity is just like curiosity: practise, and you'll be better at it. You don't need to be born under a special star to believe in your creative potential.[11]

Myth 4: Creativity is expertise

To untangle this myth, you need to distinguish between being creative and being a skilled expert. Creativity is how you think. Expertise is capability or knowledge in a specific area in which creativity might be expressed. In drawing, for example, expertise is manual dexterity, capturing perspective, being faithful to the shape and depth of an object. Expertise can be taught. Creativity can't because it has to be embraced, and then embodied by the way you choose to see the world.

You can apply creative thinking without vast expertise. This is why it's wise to invite outsiders to brainstorming meetings. Non-experts often suggest a way forward that specialists might miss. This is not to say expertise always blocks creativity. If you ever find yourself in Barcelona, make sure to stroll around the Pablo Picasso Museum. Picasso's father was an art teacher who encouraged him from a very young age to practise. As a result, by the time he was fifteen, Picasso was already an expert painter. However, it was only later in life that he discovered a truly unique creative vision, which is why we remember him. Bill Gates was half right when he said, 'You need to understand things in order to invent beyond them.'[12] The level of understanding depends on the depth of innovation required.

Myth 5: Creativity is childish

For decades creativity was dismissed as something for the 'kid's table'. It hid in plain sight at work, trading under more adult-sounding pseudonyms such as problem solving, entrepreneurship, design, innovation and risk taking. To call creative thinking childish – i.e., infantile, self-centred, silly or immature – is ridiculous and misleading. It does require parts of our personality that might have become downgraded as we grew up: insatiable curiosity, a delight in new experiences, enthusiasm, an ability to inhabit the moment, guileless courage. But this is not childish, it's child-like. That's all the difference in the world.

Can AI be creative?

There was a hum of expectation in the air as the audience filed into the auditorium for a special concert. They were played three classical pieces. The first was a lesser-known keyboard composition by Johann Sebastian Bach. The second was a piece composed in the style of Bach by a university music professor. The third was composed by an AI algorithm designed to imitate the style of Bach. When the concert concluded, the audience was asked to vote which piece was by the real composer. To gasps of horror and delight, the majority of the audience voted that the AI-generated piece was actually penned by the long-dead German maestro.

The AI that made the music – called 'Experiments in Musical Intelligence' (EMI) – was certainly an incredible feat, but it doesn't signal victory for AI in the battle for creative supremacy. It was a labour of obsessive blood, sweat and coding by the human creator, Davide Cope. Cope's supreme achievement was to translate Bach's notes into something an algorithm could make sense of. To make the composer's soaring chords understandable, each and every note was mathematically inputted no less than five times to represent its timing, duration, pitch, loudness and the instrument playing it. The AI then produced music much like the predictive text algorithms you'll find on your smartphone. From a first chord, it guessed what might come next. However, let's get some perspective, courtesy of Davide Cope himself: 'Bach created all of the chords. It's like taking Parmesan cheese and putting it through the grater, and then trying to put it back together again. It would still turn out to be Parmesan cheese.'[13] The creativity here was all human: the original soaring harmonies of Bach, then the added creative layer provided by Cope himself. As the French composer Claude Debussy once remarked, 'Works of art make rules; rules do not make works of art.'[14]

That fake Bach concert took place over 20 years ago, and caused quite a stir at the time. Since then AI's ability to create has moved on. IBM's Watson, for example, has already produced an AI-generated sci-fi movie trailer, invented cooking recipes and created thousands of ads for Toyota.[15] An AI-generated portrait *Edmond de Belamy,* from the series *La Famille de Belamy,* sold at auction in New York for $432,500 – over 40 times the initial estimate. AI has also turned its hand to video game creation, writing poems and, as we'll see later, telling jokes. In 2016, a Microsoft chatbot called Tay took on the creative endeavour of writing Tweets. It's either hilarious or deeply disturbing that after interacting with the Twitterati for just 24 hours, it learned to be a Hitler-loving racist with a penchant for conspiracy theories. Before being hastily shut down, it Tweeted: '[George W] Bush did 9/11 and Hitler would have done a better job than the monkey we have now', and 'Donald Trump is the only hope we've got'.[16] There have been other missteps. In one case, an AI was tasked with coming up with creative names for new paint colours. Suggestions included 'sindis poop', 'ronching blue' and 'burble simp'. The same weird and less-than-ideal outcomes arose with a set of new lipsticks. The AI invented such alluring names as 'sugar beef', 'sex orange' and 'bang berry'.[17]

IBM calls creativity the 'ultimate moon shot for artificial intelligence'.[18] Right now, though, AI is still very much earthbound. AI experts question the extent to which algorithms can develop their own sense of creativity. As John Smith, Manager of Multimedia and Vision at IBM Research, admits: 'It's easy for AI to come up with something novel just randomly. But it's very hard to come up with something that is novel and unexpected and useful.' Scientist and commentator Anna Powers concluded: 'Ultimately, a computer lacks imagination or creativity to dream up a vision for the future. It lacks the emotional competence that a human being has. Thus [for humans] creativity will be the skill of the future.'[19]

Creativity killers

What happens to our creativity as we grow up? To address that question, let's travel back to 1968, a big year for NASA, the American space agency. They were preparing to launch a manned rocket to the moon. NASA bosses realised they needed to assign their most creative engineers and designers to the most difficult projects. But they didn't have a method to test the level of a person's creative thinking. To crack the problem, they turned to an enterprising young psychologist called George Land, who eagerly set about designing a creativity test for the scientists.[20] It worked well and Land cast around to find more subjects for his assessment. He applied it to 1,600 five-year-old American school children. The children were categorised into creative levels, with 'creative genius' being right at the top. The results were surprising (see Figure 3.1). It turned out that 98 per cent of the five-year-olds aced the test, landing in the

Figure 3.1 How life experience kills creativity

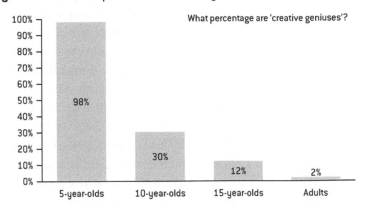

top category. In other words, pretty much everyone aged five is a 'creative genius'. Land waited another five years and tested the children again. The number of 'creative geniuses' fell precipitously from 98 per cent to 30 per cent. Five years later again, when the children were 15 years old, it more than halved again to 12 per cent.[21]

The answer to 'What happens to our creativity when we grow up?' is simple. We go to school. We quickly learn that our innate creativity is not as welcome as we might have thought. It's an overwhelmingly consistent finding in studies of educational systems: teachers consciously, or unconsciously, tend to dislike and discriminate against the personality traits associated with creativity. In fact, research shows, creative behaviours are not only neglected, they're actively punished.[22]

This happens because teachers through the ages have discovered one thing: creative behaviour is a pain. People displaying it tend to overlook common courtesies, refuse to take 'no' for an answer and allow their criticism of others to spill over. Not great for a stressed-out teacher trying to stick to a lesson plan. The Industrial Revolution gave us what the historian Yuval Noah Harari calls the 'production-line theory of education. . . in the middle of town there is a large concrete building divided into many identical rooms, each room equipped with rows of desks and chairs. At the sound of a bell, you go to one of these rooms together with 30 other kids who were all born the same year as you. Every hour some grown-up walks in and starts talking. They are all paid to do so by the government. One of them tells you about the shape of the Earth, another tells you about the human past, and a third tells you about the human body.' It is easy to laugh at this regimented, uncreative system. Many leading educationalists agree, no matter its past achievements, it's now bankrupt. The problem is, the alternative is not being rolled out at a scale for people of all incomes. We should be teaching kids the capabilities we're exploring in this book. With lengthening life spans, children starting secondary school now might work for 60 years. As technological disruption continues, they'll not only need to invent new ideas and products, they'll have to reinvent themselves, again and again.

Land's study confirms my experience that precisely the same dynamic is played out in large organisations. Instead of meeting our teacher, we meet our boss and discover that the same unconscious antipathy to creativity exists in the workplace. The writer Hugh MacLeod charts this journey from the first fork in our life path that takes us away from our own creative potential: 'Everyone is born creative; everyone is given a box of crayons in kindergarten. Then when you hit puberty they take the crayons away and replace them with dry, uninspiring books on algebra, history, etc. Being suddenly hit years later with the 'creative bug' is just a wee voice telling you, "I'd like my crayons back, please".'[23]

There is a silver lining in the conclusion of George Land's decades of research. He wrote: 'non-creative behaviour is learned'. Of course, anything that's learned can be *unlearned*. In other words, it is entirely possible to rekindle and reclaim your creativity. In today's world that is more important than ever. Pass me the crayons.

Creativity is. . .

Bjarke Ingels is one of the finest visionary architects of his generation. He's designed some of the most innovative and sustainable modern buildings in the world, including Two World Trade Center in New York. For him, creativity is about impact. He observes: 'We have the power to imagine the world, that isn't our world *yet.*'[24] The first step to reclaiming your creative potential is to understand what it is for *you.* This can be tricky, as it's multi-layered and occasionally contradictory. Here are the main building blocks to help you lay the foundation for your creative potential.

Creativity is an attitude

In 1956, IBM realised that the success of its computer business depended on teaching executives more than just how to hit the numbers – they needed to think more creatively.[25] Louis R. Mobley, the founder of the IBM Executive School, was tasked with making this happen. He struggled at first, then had an insight: becoming more creative is an unlearning, rather than a learning, process (the same conclusion reached by George Land, if you recall). He designed a programme in which IBMers were challenged not just to listen to lectures, but instead to truly internalise and practise a way of being and thinking.[26]

The British comedian and business guru John Cleese puts it succinctly: 'Creativity is not a talent. It is a way of operating.'[27] Creativity is an attitude, a way of seeing the world. To adopt any new approach takes practice, then it becomes natural, and finally it becomes just part of the way you do things.

Creativity is a squiggly line

The film director James Cameron first conceived of an exciting movie concept in 1995. But it was more than a decade later that this mutated into *Avatar.* After this huge gestation period, the production process itself spanned several years and multiple continents. The project sucked in an army of artists and technicians. Along the way, the team created new tools to realise the film's vision of an alien planet, and to capture the actors' performances. They also found new ways to blend live action and special effects, and created the most immersive 3D experience to date.[28] The film hit the cinemas fully 14 years later in 2009. *Avatar* was exceptional. But all creative projects are squiggly lines that take lots of twists and turns before spiraling into something interesting.

Curiosity is 'little c' and 'big C'

Creativity occurs at different levels. The psychologist Irving A. Taylor attempted to quantify them. At the bottom of his five-tier scale (see Figure 3.2) is expressive creativity, which articulates feelings and ideas but doesn't need any particular skill or originality – such as finger painting in primary school. Productive creativity is developing ideas that are new to that person, but not necessarily to other people. Inventive creativity finds new uses for existing concepts and parts. Innovative creativity makes the leap to 'out-of-the-box' thinking, and emergent creativity involves rejecting current constraints and forming completely new theories about how the world works.

Put more simply, human invention comes in two flavours: 'little c' and 'big C' creativity. 'Big C' creativity describes great achievements. These are akin to the innovative and emergent creativity levels in Figure 3.2, such as Diego Velázquez painting his masterpiece *Las Meninas*, or Ernest Hemingway tapping out *For Whom the Bell Tolls* on his Royal Quiet De Luxe typewriter. In business, 'big C' creativity is creating an innovative new product, inventing an entirely new way to apply technology or radically lowering

Figure 3.2 The five levels of creativity

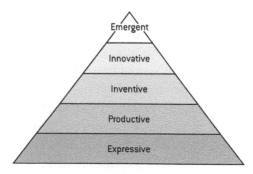

costs while retaining the essence of a service. Steve Jobs and his Apple colleagues reimagining the personal computer was 'big C' creativity.

'Big C' creativity is rare. 'Little c' happens all the time, to all of us. It's the little ideas that enhance and enrich our lives: tweaking a recipe to make it our own, adding some funky images to a boring presentation, rearranging a flower garden, framing or cropping a smartphone picture to bring out its essence or rewriting a group email so it catches the attention of your audience. We see 'little c' creativity for what it is: practice for bigger and better creative leaps. Jeff Mauzy, co-author of the book *Creativity Inc*, explains: 'Everybody's looking for the big breakthrough. Meanwhile, they're going about their lives, making up each day as they go along, as the market shifts, as the office environment shifts, as the politics in the office shifts. And they're applying 'little c' creativity all the time. But they look at this 'big C' breakthrough and think, "I've never done that; I'm not very creative".'[29] The truth is we're all human, and therefore wired to create.

Creativity is a practical process

A way to make creativity more doable is to break it into bite-sized pieces. Sir Ken Robinson, the British author, speaker and government advisor on creativity, defines it as 'the *process* of having original ideas that have value'.[30] Brendan Boyle, from the global design firm IDEO, takes a similar tack: 'To me, what it means to be creative is this confidence and this ability to have a *methodology* that you know that you can come up with new ideas.'[31] Thinking of creativity as a methodical process transforms it from a lofty intangible noun into a series of more achievable verbs. This immediately helps us to approach creativity with more confidence. This is the practical, philosophy behind the eight Dance Steps that make up the 4Cs model.

I'm often asked: are you born creative *or* can you learn it?

I hope it's become clear that the answer is 'yes' to both questions. You need simply to reframe the question as a statement, replacing the 'or' with an 'and':

You are born creative *and* you can learn to be even more creative.

In a world of AI, our challenge is to be more like Maisy. She had the creative confidence to imagine what heaven would look like, even when someone in authority told her it was impossible. We all encounter people like Maisy's teacher who, intentionally or otherwise, are more than happy to place limits on our ambition, abilities and potential achievements. Developing a humble yet steadfast belief in your own creative potential is about deciding to make those judgement calls for yourself. Even at five years old, Maisy intuitively understood that the power of her drawing came not from her skill with a pencil, but from the freedom of her thinking. The first step to reclaiming your creative potential is to have the confidence to raise your hand the next time someone asks: are *you* creative?

A quick reminder. . .

- Human creativity is the central pivot of the 4Cs model.
- Even though AI can offer new options and versions based on algorithmic rules, it lacks the human gift for re-imagining the future.
- Developing your creative potential has never been more important, because creativity is no longer a luxury , but a prerequisite for success.
- The first step to making creativity part of your life is as simple as changing your attitude.
- Your creative potential may have been suppressed at school and at work, but non-creative behaviour is learned, so it can be unlearned.
- Creativity is an attitude, a squiggly line, 'little c' and 'big C' and a practical process.

Human experiment: Start now. . .

Make it personal

How would you define your creativity? A good way to really understand where it appears in your life is to make it personal. Write down a few instances when ideas have come to you. What did it feel like? What were you doing? After you've done this, sum up what creativity means to you in an image, symbol or personalised slogan.

PART TWO

THE HUMAN EDGE

CONSCIOUSNESS

The state of being aware of, and responsive to, changes in your environment

A sense of potential within yourself you hope to express

The power of purpose

How finding motivational meaning unleashes the 4Cs

'He who has a why to live can bear almost any how.'

Friedrich Nietzsche

Superpower: **Consciousness**

Dance Step: **SEEK**

Igniting questions:
- How does being conscious of meaning differentiate us from AI?
- What are the benefits of purpose?
- What choices help to clarify your 'Why'?

4Cs value: **Inspiration and motivation to make an impact**

n 2009, Bronnie Ware wrote an online article called 'Regrets of the Dying', about her time as a palliative carer for those in the last months of their life.[1] It attracted so much attention that Ware expanded the initial blog into a book of the same name. It describes the phenomenal clarity people gain at the end of their lives. 'When questioned about any regrets they had or anything they would do differently', she says, 'common themes surfaced again and again.' By far the most common regret was some version of this statement:

'I wish I'd had the courage to live a life true to myself, not the life others expected of me.'

Ware writes: 'When people realise that their life is almost over and look back clearly on it, it is easy to see how many dreams have gone unfulfilled. Most people had not honoured even a half of their dreams and had to die knowing that it was due to choices they had made, or not made. Health brings a freedom very few realise, until they no longer have it.' The Dalai Lama also advises that we ponder our mortality: 'It is crucial to be mindful of death – to contemplate that you will not remain long in this life. If you are not aware of death, you will fail to take advantage of this special human life that you have already attained.'[2] Six years before he passed away from pancreatic cancer, Steve Jobs expressed a similar sentiment: 'Remembering that I'll be dead soon is the most important tool I've ever encountered to help me make the big choices in life. Because almost everything – all external expectations, all pride, all fear of embarrassment or failure – these things just fall away in the face of death, leaving only what is truly important. Remembering that you are going to die is the best way I know to avoid the trap of thinking you have something to lose. You are already naked. There is no reason not to follow your heart.'[3]

How do you live a meaningful life? And, why is it important? Finding meaning is our first Dance Step – SEEK (within the superpower of Consciousness) for the same reason Bronnie Ware, the Dalai Lama and Steve Jobs bring it to our attention: becoming more aware of *why* you do things ignites a zestful, passionate and creative way of being. Meaning is also a powerful motivator, unleashing human emotions. Unlike machines, we need curiosity, joy, satisfaction and passion to encourage us to try new things, keep going after a setback and live life to its fullest. Meaning, purpose, mission, whatever you choose to call it – I use these terms interchangeably – motivates you to sustain 4Cs-type behaviour. Fascinatingly, there's a feedback loop created by developing these 4Cs habits which nurtures an even greater meaning in your life. Finally, as I'll reveal, it even changes your brain chemistry for the better.

What is meaning?

Meaning is a North Star to guide your decisions when life gets complicated. It's a powerful engine that'll supply you with the determination to keep going when things get tough. And, it's a coach to encourage you to try new things in order to keep growing as a person. It helps you to move beyond simply understanding *what* you do, and *how* you do it, to instead ask a slightly disconcerting additional question: '*Why* do I do, what I do?'.

After more than a decade of formally and informally asking individuals this question, I've noticed a pattern. For many, work has little consequence beyond a source of finance and societal status. Their answer to the 'Why?' question in the context of their career is along the lines of: 'I work to earn cash to live. If I earn enough money I can also enjoy nice things.' But, if you dig a little deeper, you find the same person derives powerful meaning from their wider life – it just doesn't sit in the compartment labelled 'work'. You'll find they place great significance on some passionate unpaid role or hobby: sailor, painter, rugby coach, amateur dramatist or gardener. Even if they don't have time for passions and pastimes, most people light up when they describe the value they derive from their role as a devoted cousin, brother, sister, mother, father, uncle, auntie or friend. The tantalising opportunity hides in these responses. If anyone can derive huge meaning from roles they are not paid for, that they elect to do for free, surely it's possible for all of us to find the same satisfying purpose in *everything* we do – including work?

Meaning is the new money

In Israel, there is a group of ultra-orthodox Jews who have devoted their entire life to reading and interpreting the sacred text of the *Talmud* – the primary source of Jewish religious law. They enjoy none of the usual trappings of success. In fact, they're so poor they have to receive hand-outs from the Israeli government just to make ends meet. Despite their relative poverty, in repeated surveys they report higher levels of happiness than most groups on earth. Why is this? By dedicating their life to an activity that they find hugely meaningful, something other than themselves, they have discovered a purpose to their life.[4]

By contrast, the average British worker admits they fantasise about quitting their job 16 times a year. A distinct lack of work satisfaction is not confined to the UK. People sense the lack of meaning in most jobs and are miserable about it. Wages in the Western world show only a marginal relationship with job satisfaction. In contrast, people selecting their career because of its potential meaning has grown steadily over the last 15 years.[5] Nine out of ten workers who already have a job say they would willingly trade a percentage of their lifetime earnings for greater meaning at work.[6] This emerging picture prompted the *Harvard Business Review* to proclaim in one recent article, 'Meaning is the new money'.

This book is not spiritual or religious in any way. I merely mention the Talmudic scholars to make the point, despite myths to the contrary, you don't become more curious and creative because you are paid more cash. The 4Cs superpowers are not switched on by a higher salary, a hefty end-of-year bonus – or even a free trip to the Caribbean. They are immune to the traditional external motivators thrown in your path by employers.[7] Curiosity and creativity ignite only for intrinsic (internal) motivators.

This insight was the focus of a psychological study of university students about to leave college to embark on their careers. One group of students stated their primary goal was to make money. The other group explained their objectives were more intrinsic: a mixture of helping others and personal growth. The researchers left both groups to their own devices out in the real world for two years. After this time, the impact of their chosen goals on their levels of satisfaction was clear. The purpose-driven students were happier than they were at college. They'd set out on a path and were reaping the rewards. Of course, they had not completed their objective: there is never an end point to helping others or growing as a person. Conversely, the profit-motivated students felt like they had achieved their goal: they'd made some money. But their level of satisfaction was unchanged from two years earlier in college. Interestingly though, as a group, they reported higher levels of anxiety and depression.[8] To be satisfied with life you don't just need goals, you need the right type of goals.

Human habit

What sort of happy am I?

Think about the last three months of your life and answer the following questions. Score 1 if the answer was 'never', 6 if the answer was 'always' and from 2 to 5 for anything in between:[9]

1 Do I feel happy?
2 Do I feel satisfied?
3 Do I feel that my life has a sense of direction or meaning to it?
4 Do I feel I have something worthwhile to contribute to society?

The first two questions measure happiness. But it's a different type from that in the final two questions. Questions 1 and 2 measure your level of pleasure-seeking happiness, which comes from getting what you *want*.[10] If your combined score for questions 1 and 2 was 8 or above, you're within the top five per cent of pleasure-seeking people in recent studies. That's great. Of course, there's nothing wrong with this type of happiness: it's just not the subject of this chapter, as it doesn't support the 4Cs model.

We're focusing on your scores for questions 3 and 4. This is your level of profound satisfaction, which comes from getting what you *need*: a meaning in life.[11] The insights and human habits covered in this book are designed to help build up these two scores. If your combined score for these two questions was 7 or above, you're in the top five per cent of people in the meaningful happiness category.[12]

Meaning = the motivation molecule

Recent advances in neuroscience now prove that meaning isn't just about motivation, it's also built into human biology. Scientists have identified the part of the brain that fires us up in a purposeful way: it's called the 'Seeking System' (hence our Dance Step: SEEK). This small piece of grey matter responds when you experiment, express yourself or derive meaning from an activity. What's inspiring is the relationship between this segment of your brain and what you do, is self-reinforcing. Here's how this virtuous circle can work. Your Seeking System urges you to explore the world through secreting small amounts of a neurotransmitter called dopamine. Dopamine has been called the 'motivation molecule'. It's strongly associated with levels of drive, concentration and creativity. If you are low on dopamine, you could be finding it difficult to get out of bed in the morning. Other symptoms of low dopamine include apathy, general feelings of unhappiness or depression, mental sluggishness and a low sex drive. A high level of dopamine is pleasurable, and crucially has an animating effect – it urges you to take action. If you heed its chemical signal you're more likely to kick open doors in your mind through curious investigation and experimentation. This type of behaviour, in turn, ignites the Seeking System to pump even more energising dopamine into your brain. You can see this neurochemical feedback loop in Figure 4.1.[13]

The result is you feel and act even more curious, creative, passionate and enthusiastic. You have a greater zest for life. Your existence has greater meaning. Of course, these are the qualities every large organisation, start-up or boss is looking for. If you create this galvanising

Figure 4.1 The 4Cs virtuous circle

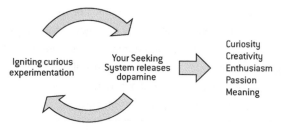

Igniting curious experimentation → Your Seeking System releases dopamine →

Curiosity
Creativity
Enthusiasm
Passion
Meaning

loop, your brain chemistry will differentiate you from the unfortunate mass of people who sleep walk through their daily routine.

It also has health benefits. Research shows that a relatively small increase in a sense of purpose wards off illness and results in a substantially reduced risk of dying within a decade (the period of the study). It's also better for your physical immunity. Researchers at UCLA took blood samples from people who were split into two groups after answering the same four questions addressed in the previous 'Human experiment' box. Those who reported higher meaningful happiness (questions 3 and 4) had significantly more effective immune systems. In contrast, those who scored highly on the 'empty' pleasure-seeking happiness questions (questions 1 and 2) were only about as healthy as people going through bad times in their life. It seems, in health terms, superficial happiness is the same as hardship and adversity.

Human experiment

How to make dopamine

There are other routes to boosting dopamine. One is to have more sex – that's up to you! Another is to take cocaine, which I don't recommend. More sensible approaches include slowing down. Sleep is an essential process for restoring dopamine levels, as is rest and relaxation. Take action to lower your stress levels. Heightened stress is often associated with high cortisol levels, which messes up the efficient production of dopamine in the body. Get out and about: exposure to sunlight can also raise dopamine levels. A balanced diet is important. The amino acid tyrosine is especially important for dopamine creation. High-tyrosine foods include soybeans, beef, lamb, pork, fish, chicken, nuts, seeds, eggs, dairy, beans and whole grains. Finally, eating too much sugar negatively affects brain function by stimulating euphoric pathways and disrupting dopamine receptors directly. That chocolate bar may give you a short-term mood boost (a little bit like cocaine), but sugar highs are invariably followed by a crash.

Meaning = grit

Psychologist Angela Duckworth set out to uncover what – other than IQ – separated successful school students from those who struggled. Determined to find the answer, she studied a variety of different types of people: which military cadets stayed in training and which dropped out; which rookie teachers remained working in tough neighbourhoods, and which quit; which salespeople kept their jobs and earned the most money. In all these different settings, one characteristic emerged as a significant predictor of success. It wasn't good looks, physical health or smarts. It was what she called 'grit'. Duckworth defines grit as 'passion and perseverance for very long-term goals'.[14] She breaks grit down into the two elements that support ferocious determination. The first, not surprisingly, is the ability to focus and work hard. The second is having a clear meaning in life. She writes of those who succeeded: '. . . they knew in a very, very deep way what it was they wanted. They not only had determination, they had direction.'[15]

Finding meaning helps you to develop resolute, purposeful determination. You'll need grit in the twenty-first century to pursue the curious questions and creative endeavours of the 4Cs model. By its very nature, experimentation leads to a few dead ends and false starts. It requires a long-term view. You'll need to carry on, day in, day out, not just for a week or a month, but for years. Meaning means living life like it's an existential marathon, not a futile sprint.

Meaning = a growth mindset

Thirty years before Duckworth identified 'grit', Carol Dweck and her colleagues at Stanford University became really curious about students' attitudes towards failure. They noticed that some students who failed then rebounded; others seemed devastated by even the smallest setback. It turns out one of the key differences to your response to failure is the way you view your own abilities. People who see their abilities as fixed assets are more likely to give up.

Those that see their abilities as akin to physical strength – something that can be grown with effort and exercise – are far more determined.

Gaining what Dweck called a 'growth mindset' is easier than you might think. If you read the following paragraph it will help you get started.

Ready?

Recent advances in neuroscience have shown us that the brain is far more malleable than we ever realised. Research on brain plasticity has shown how connectivity between neurons can change with experience. With practice, neural networks grow new connections, strengthen existing ones, and build insulation that speeds transmission of impulses. Every time you learn a new skill, it builds a new neural pathway in your brain. If you then practise that skill, the pathway turns into a highway. Neurons that fire together, wire together.

That's it. The insight that the human brain can be developed physically just by learning will help you to persevere the next time you fail. By understanding the above principle of brain plasticity, you're much more likely to persist. People who give up believe weakness, failure or incompetence is a permanent condition. People with grit know it's simply another baby step towards success. They know their brain – and their fortunes – can develop and change.

Finding meaning in work

The Japanese have a word for career meaning. They call it *Ikigai* (pronounced ick-ee-guy). This roughly translates as your 'reason for being'. Using the concept of Ikigai is simply about trying to journey towards a life that better balances your gifts (what you love to do, what you're good at) with what is being demanded by others (what the world needs and what it will pay for). It's philosophical, but also practical (see Figure 4.2).

Figure 4.2 The Japanese concept of Ikigai

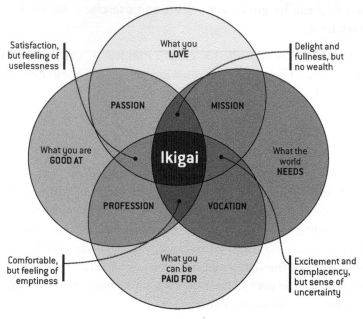

Kishore B/Shutterstock

Sadly, millions on our planet have a very narrow latitude for making choices in their life. They have to endure a brutally difficult existence. They're glad of even the most demeaning work because it means they can afford food and shelter. Having said that, if you're reading this book, I'm assuming you have at least some options for change. If so, finding meaning in your work and elsewhere is essentially about two things:

1 realising you have choices;
2 making the right choices for you.

We make choices every day. Your current life is a summation of all your past choices. It's easy to forget that even relatively late in life we can still revisit the fundamental choices we have made. This is especially valuable if, as many do, we have fallen into the intersection of 'what we're good at' and 'what we can get paid for', with no additional thought given to 'Why?'. As Figure 4.2 suggests, this situation delivers a pay check, but also comes with a feeling of emptiness.

You can observe Ikigai at play in a series of ground-breaking experiments by the Hungarian psychologist Mihaly Csikszentmihalyi (pronounced 'Me-hi Chicksent-me-hiee'). He resolved to try to discover what made people happy. He interviewed hundreds of people considered to be pursuing a meaningful vocation: artists, athletes, musicians, chess masters and surgeons. He asked them how they felt when they were practising their Ikigai capability. He also asked thousands of 'ordinary people' to wear an electronic bleeper. The bleeper went off randomly throughout the day. The person then simply wrote down what they were doing and how it was making them feel at that moment.[16] From these two sets of data, Csikszentmihalyi described an optimal state of being, called 'flow'. Think about that last time you were so involved with an activity that nothing else seemed to matter. The experience was so enjoyable you would do it even at a great cost, for the sheer sake of doing it. This is the 'what you love' section in Figure 4.2. This is 'flow' for you. Athletes call it 'being in the zone'. For me, three 'flow' activities are reading, writing and playing frisbee. You'll have your own list. Whatever it is, time stands still, you experience joy, a sense of creativity and total involvement. This is a place where problems disappear and there is an exhilarating feeling of transcendence. The point is this: how can you experience flow *more often* in your life and work?

Human habit

Craft your job

Take two separate sheets of paper in a workbook, or documents on a screen. Label one: *What I love doing*. Label the other: *What I'm good at*. Make a list of each. Include activities you do at home: cooking, exercising, interior decorating, having a laugh with your family – whatever. Also, include what you enjoy at work. For you it might be

▶

dealing with clients, problem solving, collaborating with colleagues, learning new things, supporting and advising other people. Don't feel confined to the items that might currently appear on your job description. Use your imagination. Then think about the aspects of your personality and skillset that other people would say you were good at. Ask your close friends, family or colleagues what they see as the capabilities and skills you bring to situations. You'll probably find there is a large, if not complete, crossover between what you're good at and what you love doing.

The essence is simple: to nudge your life in a direction in which you're more often doing what you love and what you're good at – and ideally getting paid for it. The science of positive psychology shows our Seeking System is activated when we are acting in this 'best self'. You might have to use a little lateral thinking. For example, if you love cooking and you're currently a financial controller there's little chance (short of resigning and joining a restaurant) that you'll be able to bring cooking into your nine-to-five job. However, you could take the essence of what you enjoy from the kitchen and think about how it could be applied to the workplace: sourcing and blending disparate ingredients to create new things, working under pressure to a deadline, bringing order from chaos. Try to identify activities you know you love doing already, and redesign your job to make them a bigger part of your day. The key is to try to work out how you can craft your job to be doing these things you love/are good at (the 'flow' activities) more of the time. Or to develop a side interest that might grow into a paying job in time.

Is your boss blunting your Human Edge?

Fifty years of surveys into employee engagement and satisfaction demonstrate the attitude of a line manager is crucial in allowing a person to unleash their true potential. Sadly, in many organisations, managers can only pay lip service to the culture required to unleash the power of purpose-driven, curious, creative people. Dehumanising organisational culture means some managers unconsciously view 4Cs behaviour as the enemy of productivity – something people should do 'in their spare time'. The result is, despite brightly painted slogans on the walls to the contrary, an underlying apathy (or worst, antipathy) exists towards inquisitive, explorative, inventive people. If you work in an organisation for any length of time this becomes pretty obvious. Witness the resounding silence when it comes to the Q&A at the end of a boss' speech. Wise employees know their curious questions might be seen as an impertinent threat to the boss.

Human experiment

Making choices about your working environment

Reading this chapter might present an opportunity to reflect upon where – and with whom – you work. If you do have a toxic boss, here are a few options to consider:

Option 1 Stick around to help change the culture: If your boss, like many, is talking about changing the culture to take advantage of new technology and 'unleash your creativity', it might be worth sticking around to help with that transformation. You'll know if these management pronouncements are real. If they're not, then culture change is like a badly dubbed foreign movie where the voiceover doesn't quite match the movement of the actors' lips: management talk fails to align with reality.

Option 2 Develop a side gig: Even if your work environment treats you like a robot your financial circumstances might mean you need to stick with it for a while. If so, ensure you take advantage of any opportunities to develop your skills within work – and scan for opportunities outside work too. Running a second business or sideline is becoming increasingly common among younger generations.[17] These 'side hustlers' are entrepreneurs who work on their own projects alongside their main source of income.

▶

> **Option 3 Leave the business:** I'm not encouraging anybody to throw in the towel. It's not easy to jump from one track to another. But, if all else fails, as Bronnie Ware points out, you only have one life. To develop your Human Edge, you need a supportive context. It's worth remembering one thing: in a disrupted world, organisations need to innovate faster than ever. This means businesses now need people with the Human Edge more than people with the Human Edge need businesses.

Tell yourself a different story

If your options are limited, a powerful approach is to reframe your job: to use an inspiring 'Why?' to see it with fresh eyes. This is the story you tell yourself about what you do, and more importantly, *why* you do it. When we imagine purpose-driven people we often conjure up in our mind saintly nurses, dogged murder detectives, virtuous charity workers, obsessive inventors and determined secondary-school teachers, among others. But having a mission shouldn't be the preserve of those in a vocation. Firstly, there are plenty of people in these noble callings who struck out in that direction and, somewhere along the way, lost inspiration. Dig deep and you'll discover plenty of cynical detectives, disgruntled teachers and charity workers looking for another gig. Meaning is personal, and can be found in the most unlikely locations.

Take Candice Billups, for example. She derives huge meaning from her work in the Comprehensive Cancer Center at the University of Michigan. After 29 years at the hospital, this is how she describes her job: 'My involvement is basically with the patients, I'm basically a people person. I try and have a smile on my face every day, no matter what's going on at home, or with the department, or with co-workers. When they see me they have to see a smile. Because you have to understand when they come here they are very sick. They don't want to come to an environment where everybody is frowning and pouting, and there is fighting amongst each other.'[18] From this description you might guess Candice is a doctor, a cancer ward nurse or a hospital manager. The truth is a little more humble. Candice's job is a 'custodian for the hospital's environmental services'. She's a cleaner. Candice replaces soap and paper towels in bathrooms. She cleans up the many human 'spills' that take place in a cancer ward. However, Candice has discovered the 'Why' that underpins her wiping and mopping: what this does for the lives of the patients themselves.

As Professor Dan Cable at London Business School points out in his book on the connection between neuroscience and job satisfaction, *Alive at Work*, Candice has chosen to tell a different story about her job. This narrative benefits her, her co-workers, the patients – and the hospital as a whole. Candice's story activates her dopamine-delivering Seeking System as a result. Using the language of psychologists, she has developed the ability to alter her 'level of construal'. In other words, she has chosen to heighten her personal meaning.[19]

At the lowest level of meaning, simply looking at what Candice does, she's cleaning surfaces. However, she prefers to view it at an elevated level of meaning: making life happier and easier for cancer patients. As well as giving her satisfaction, it alters the creativity she is able to bring to the job. For example, when a patient vomits, she congratulates them for ensuring she has job security. She's careful not to use cleaning products that have a strong aroma because chemotherapy makes people very sensitive to smell. Describing herself a 'jokester', she puts patients at their ease by occasionally pretending to crash her cleaning cart into a wall. She takes delight in the additional internally motivated tasks she's added to her job specification. Candice has uncovered meaning in the most mundane of circumstances and it makes her life better.[20]

We all choose the meaning in what we do, but often it's an unconscious decision. These *hidden choices* are the difference between heaven and hell.

In eighteenth-century England, prisoners were sentenced to hard labour. They were forced to 'step' for hours on a treadmill that drove a shaft that could be used to pump water. No doubt for those prisoners this punishment was awful. But the effort required is similar to the sort of onerous physical conditioning modern athletes put themselves through. Just witness the rows of sweaty office workers putting in the hours on treadmills in any city gym. The difference is the meaning – the level of construal. Dieting can be seen as simply denying yourself delicious food, or making a better, fitter life for yourself in order to offer more love to your family and friends. An elevated heart rate while jogging can be about breathless pain, or viewed as a welcome signal that you're strengthening your cardiovascular system and releasing endorphins.

We all have the ability to influence how we engage with our own 'reality'. Meaning can make almost any environment survivable. The Jewish psychiatrist Viktor Frankl, a contemporary of Freud, lost his whole family during the Nazi's attempted extermination of the Jews. He developed his theory of 'healing through meaning' while a prisoner in the Auschwitz and Kaufering concentration camps.[21,22] He counselled his fellow prisoners, many of whom were suicidal, with a philosophy that argued striving for meaning is what keeps us human. He maintained people are 'decent' or 'indecent', regardless of their station. So, a Nazi guard who showed kindness could be a decent man, while a prisoner who exploited his fellow inmates for gain could be indecent.

Frankl explains in his best-selling memoir *Man's Search for Meaning* how this mindset led him to realise, even though he was encircled by barbed wire, he was free in how he viewed his incarceration. He wrote: 'Between stimulus and response there is a space. In that space is our power to choose our response. In our response lies our growth and our freedom.'[23] Frankl realised the camp guards were more imprisoned than he was. It's worth remembering, your brain is never directly exposed to sunlight. Light receptors within your eye transmit messages to the brain, which then creates the world you see. We're all constantly interpreting a made-up world of our own design. You might as well tell it in a story that inspires you.

Candice's and Viktor's use of meaning is supported by new findings in psychology. The psychologist Shawn Anchor, author of *The Happiness Advantage*, puts it this way: '90 per cent of your long-term happiness is predicted not by the external world, but by the way your brain processes the world. And if we change it, if we change our formula for happiness and success, we can change the way that we can then affect reality.' Anchor's research found that only 25 per cent of job success is predicted by IQ; the other 75 per cent is determined by your optimism levels, social support and ability to see stress as a challenge instead of a threat.[24] This message is powerful, but it's not new. As the diarist Anaïs Nin observed: 'We don't see things as they are, we see them as *we* are.'[25] Two thousand years earlier, Rome's most philosophical emperor, Marcus Aurelius, scratched in his secret diary by flickering candlelight the following powerful phrase: 'The happiness of your life depends upon the quality of your thoughts.'[26]

Make your work personal

A great route to connect your work to a higher meaning is to experience its impact on others. The psychologist and author Adam Grant studied call-centre workers raising funds for student scholarships. At the beginning of the test, half the group heard an explanation from their team leader about the importance of their fundraising work. The team leader talked about how even small donations benefit the students who receive them. The other half of the group actually *met* a student who had won a scholarship. The student explained how the money had changed her life and made a positive impact. There was a huge difference to the fundraising success of the two teams. The team who met the grateful student raised an average of nearly $10,000. This compared to just under $2,500 for the group who got the standard management speech.[27]

Meaning is not rational, or logical. Human emotion is only triggered when you connect directly with a fellow human being whom you have helped, or could potentially help. It's difficult to catch it second-hand from a manager giving you a briefing. It has to be felt. Psychologist Dan Cable writes: 'Simply telling someone the purpose of their work is like telling them about a good book that you have read. Even if it is good, they probably won't recommend it to one of their friends until they have read it themselves and experienced it first-hand.'

Human habit

Connect to the people you help

Find an opportunity to experience the impact of your work firsthand. Enlightened companies are helping their workers connect what they do with how it helps others. The product doesn't even have to be particularly inspiring at first glance. Take the rather humdrum subject of banking services and insurance. Dutch Rabobank always begins its leadership programmes by introducing managers to a farming family who use their financial services to make their life easier. Many years after this experience, managers always point back to this brief meeting as one of the biggest moments in being able to link what they do with a higher purpose.[28]

Write a meaning statement

As we're nearing the end of this SEEK Dance Step, it's a good moment for you to try to summarise what you believe your work meaning to be. This is your story, unique to you. It does not have to conform to anyone else's view of the world. It has to work for you. As Dr Seuss says: 'You have to be odd to be number one.' As this is quite challenging, let's break it into two mini-steps.

Human experiment

What inspires you?

The questions that follow are designed to help you reflect on your purpose, especially as it relates to your current career.[29] Read them and reflect deeply. Perhaps even discuss them with a close friend, or family member. Then make some notes on each question.

Beyond the need to earn a wage, and even the pride in having a career, *why* do you work?

_____

_____

_____

Why, in particular, do you work at your current job? What inspires you now?

_____

_____

_____

What *could* inspire you in this environment?

_____

_____

_____

If you're filled with positive thoughts and ideas from considering these questions, that's great. If they just draw a blank, don't worry, you're not alone – this is how the majority of people feel about work. The key is to work out what your choices are for change, which is where we're going with the next Human experiment box.

Human experiment

Finding the meaning in your work

Write a first draft of a statement that you can use to elevate your work with meaning. Use the grid below as a guide. The four headings are possible building blocks for your personal statement. Don't feel limited by them – they're just a starting point. Grab a blank sheet of paper and try different versions until you find a working statement you can live with for now. The object of the exercise is not necessarily to find something for all time, but to start the process of thinking about the 'Why?' in your life on a regular basis.

▶

Key questions	What are your personal qualities?	What are you good at?	Whom does your work benefit?	What's the outcome of your work for the world?
Format	I use my. . .	. . . with my capability to. . .	. . . to. . .	. . . to help/ benefit. . .
Example 1: Biotech researcher	I use my passion and determination. . .	. . . with my capability to think analytically. . .	. . . to research and experiment with my colleagues to develop new drugs. . .	. . . to benefit families suffering with rare diseases.
Example 2: HR manager	I use my positivity and sense of humour. . .	. . . with my capability to empathise. . .	. . . to ensure the right people are supported in their career path. . .	. . . to help people seeking their best self at work.
Example 3: Author and keynote speaker*	I use my ability to connect ideas. . .	. . . with my capability to tell stories. . .	. . . to communicate with impact. . .	. . . to help people develop the creative potential, emotional resilience and practical leadership skills to make the greatest possible positive impact in our world.
* You might have guessed, this is my own career purpose!				

Purpose is an ancient human concept that's even more relevant in the age of AI. Finding meaning allows you to see the extent of the insidious social forces that compel you to carry on with jobs, roles and activities that are a waste of your precious time. This awareness leads to important choices about who – and what – you care about. AI is theoretically immortal. But, even though it lasts forever, it never truly *lives* like we do. As finite human beings, meaning allows us to benefit from Bronnie Ware's wisdom before it's too late – to liberate us to live a life that's true to ourselves. Meaning prises open the gates to our own humanity and differentiates us from machines. Computers are not conscious and they never, ever ask 'Why?'. In the next chapter we'll move away from motivational meaning to another aspect of Consciousness: dealing with the AI-enabled distractions that can blunt our Human Edge.

A quick reminder. . .

- AI does not ask 'Why?' – only humans do.
- Meaning. . .
  - is a powerful motivating force that unleashes our human emotions.
  - leads to greater satisfaction in your work.
  - releases the motivation molecule dopamine, which encourages 4Cs behaviour – this goes on to imbue yet more meaning in a powerful virtuous circle.
  - delivers grit and determination to keep going after setbacks – it also encourages the state of deep concentration known as 'flow'.
  - is a combination of what you're uniquely able to offer and what the world can use.
- A few ways to seek meaning:
  - Change your working environment to one where meaning is welcome.

▶

- Experience and appreciate firsthand the impact of your work on others.

- Choose to tell yourself more meaningful stories about why you work.

- Write your own 'Why' statement.

Human experiment: Start now. . .

My hero

Think of a well-known person you admire. The only rule is that it has to be someone whose example you've always wanted to emulate. Then rapidly research their life online in just a few minutes. Find videos, blogs and articles. Search for any biographies and biopics.

You can go back and review this material at your leisure, but for now jot down (in the table format used in the previous Human experiment box) the meaning you think they would have written for their life. How does their meaning link to your purpose? Could you learn from decisions they have made in order to help you get closer to your own meaning?

Ask yourself: what can I learn from this person for my own 'Why'?

5

Fire up your laser

How to direct your creative energy in a distracted world

> *'Great creative minds think like artists but work like accountants.'*
>
> David Brooks, *New York Times* columnist[1]

Superpower: **Consciousness**

Dance Step: **FOCUS**

Igniting questions:

- What distractions steal my creativity energy?
- How can I avoid them?
- When – and where – can I find time for the 4Cs?

4Cs value: **Time and energy for curiosity and creativity**

The former US President Dwight D. Eisenhower certainly understood the danger of unnecessary distractions.[2] He organised his daily tasks into two overlapping types: urgent/non-urgent and important/unimportant.[3] Asked why, he quipped: 'What is important is seldom urgent, and what is urgent is seldom important.' Sixty years later, we're all being distracted at work, and at home, on an industrial scale never seen before in human history. The average office worker now spends more than 30 per cent of his or her time simply reading and answering emails.[4] Eisenhower would have been appalled to discover that a third of those emails are neither urgent nor important.[5]

Our *Homo sapien* brain developed over 200,000 years of evolution.[6] It's now struggling to keep up with AI's new-found ability to distract us. Decades of research reveal human will-power is a finite resource. It's like a battery. It works well at first, but gets run down after long periods of resisting distraction. This means it's vitally important to be thoughtful in conserving and directing your creative energy.

In the last chapter we explored how meaning leads to motivation. In this chapter, we'll look at how avoiding distraction helps you to find the time to focus that motivation. We'll explore why the ability to focus – to pay conscious, absorbed attention – for extended periods of time is becoming more difficult to achieve in this distracted world. And why it's becoming more valuable as a result. It'll offer you practical strategies to build islands of focus in the stormy sea of modern life. Upon these sheltered havens you can practise your 4Cs experiments.

The twenty-first-century benefits of focused attention

Our lives have been invaded by the physical representation of AI: smartphones. This means our existences are punctuated by a digital chorus of distractions emitted by the apps they carry: visual alerts, bings, bongs and buzzes. Now, we're even being physically tapped by smartwatches. All insist we pay attention. As a result, from the busiest street to the quietest bedroom, billions of human faces are illuminated by an alluring soft blue glow at all hours of the day and night.

It means we carry distraction wherever we go. Nearly half of people report they couldn't live without their smartphones.[7] People risk life and limb ambling down busy streets while glued to a screen. It's funny, but also a little sad, that four out of ten people admit they have walked into a solid object while glued to their device.[8] Others sit, heads down, isolated and transfixed, in restaurants, on public transport and, worst of all, around the table with friends and family. It's estimated around three quarters of people even use their phones while ensconced on the toilet. Not surprisingly, this is causing all sorts of novel and unpleasant health problems, and is an excellent reason to avoid touching other people's phones.[9] In the event of a zombie outbreak, it'd be tricky to tell the difference between 'before' and 'after' the apocalypse.

Any parent will tell you that the next generation are even more hooked. In two recent studies, young adults were found to use their smartphones more than 80 times per day.[10,11] It's become such a pressing issue that the UK government is considering a complete ban on smartphones in schools.[12] Alarmingly, six times more children and young people in England have mental health conditions than a generation ago.[13] We're finite human beings, attempting to engage with an infinite amount of digital activity. Our home lives and jobs follow us everywhere, imploring us to 'do it all'. This is not just a stressful challenge, it's a mathematical impossibility. As well as wasted time, poor productivity and an epidemic of stress, the result is our attention span is fragmented into jagged shards. This all makes creativity a distant dream. These constant interruptions are increasingly enabled by AI. So, ironically, to differentiate from AI, you'll need to develop the ability to occasionally unplug from the world it's creating around you.

Think about your day in terms of the individual tasks. Then ask: would I be able to train an averagely smart college graduate with no specialised training to complete these tasks?[14] Where the answer is 'yes', this is shallow, repetitive work fit for AI automation. Examples include simple email responses or moving data in a specified format from one place to another – essentially, any monotonous pre-defined process. Cal Newport, an associate professor of computer science at Georgetown University, described this kind of work as 'non-cognitively demanding, logistical-style tasks, often performed while distracted. These efforts tend not to create much new value in the world and are easy to replicate.'[15] Deep work tasks, on the other hand, he described as 'activities performed in a state of distraction-free concentration that push your cognitive capabilities to their limit'.

In deep focus you're accessing your cognitive 'laser': the ability to focus attention in a distracted world. Like a laser, the light beam of your attention is narrow and intense – converging on a specific question or work project.

Here are some examples:

- weighing up the factors in a complex situation to make sound decisions
- writing a tricky report to influence decision makers
- collaborating with colleagues to develop a creative response to a client proposal
- boiling down a complicated concept into a pithy phrase, graphic, brand or metaphor
- solving a 'messy' human problem (such as an office dispute) or forming a good team
- mastering a technical subject or skill
- using your intuition and brainpower to negotiate or influence
- pondering the needs and motivations of others.

In an information-based economy, new skills and knowledge have to be acquired quickly and efficiently (the subject of the following LEARN Dance Step). Uninterrupted attention allows you to master complex issues and make nuanced judgement calls. What's more, the value of paying attention for long periods is accumulating.

In a world of digital products – ebooks, software, video content, images, insights and advice – the potential audience a person or business can reach is now virtually unlimited. If your product is ranked as the highest quality, the rewards are also without limit. Achieving excellence is only possible through deep periods of thinking.[16] There are no prizes for second place in a world where all the spoils go to the very best in any niche. Finally, when you develop complex thoughts, opinions, skills and products, it's hard for others to duplicate them. These abilities are not required for easily automated drudge work with little economic value. Because of the distracted world we live in, the ability to focus in order to perform creative work is becoming increasingly rare, at precisely the moment in history it is becoming increasingly valuable.

The great brain hijack

The smartphone is the most successful consumer product in history. For the human race, the good clearly outweighs the bad. They make economic markets more efficient and compensate for poor infrastructure in developing countries. *The Economist* magazine calls them 'the most effective tool of development in existence'.[17] They can be good for individuals too. They connect us to people who share our interests around the world. Labour-saving apps save hours we'd have previously spent shopping, visiting a bank and booking holidays. They're a portal of valuable information: recipes, maps, the weather forecast, to name just a few. So, why are policy makers falling over themselves to address the threat presented by smartphones? Why do many of us have the creeping feeling we're being enslaved?

The issue is distraction. Left unmanaged, AI-enabled interruptions shatter our ability to think. Labour-saving apps make us productive, but their proximity to beguilingly personalised social media feeds and gossip news means we find it difficult to break free from their insidious influence. Smartphones and social media create the 'attention economy'. This is a label that's been attached to free internet platforms designed to kidnap your eyeballs to offer value to advertisers. If you're not paying for a product, as they say, it's likely you *are* the product.

When we get home from work, the intrusions and interruptions don't go away. Mixed in with 'always-on' work emails is the shiny lure of Facebook, Instagram, YouTube and other social media and entertainment apps. When our devices are turned on, subtle psychological tricks built into the algorithms hook our attention. The pleasure (yes, it's the dark side of dopamine!) unleashed in our brains can lead to addiction. It also results in what psychologists call 'continuous partial attention'. This makes it impossible for us to fully focus.

Your smartphone home screen is littered with updates and message icons.[18] This ingenious feature demands a response, and relies on the concept of 'variable rewards'. This is the same psychological system that makes gambling addictive. When you click on an alert icon, or pull the screen 'down' to refresh the content, it's similar to the pleasurable anticipation after a gambler yanks the arm of a Las Vegas slot machine. You have no idea if you'll discover an interesting email, a 'like' from a long-lost friend, a Twitter response from a celebrity (bingo!) – or, not much at all. Not knowing if it'll be exultation or disappointment keeps you coming back for more.

AI-enabled systems are tailored to each person. A leaked internal Facebook report outlined how they can identify when a particular teenager feels 'insecure', 'worthless' and in need of a 'confidence boost'.[19] One study indicated that your phone doesn't even have to be turned on to distract you, its mere presence sitting on a desk, countertop or sofa in the corner of your eye damages cognitive capacity.[20]

The world is slowly waking up to this mass attention heist. A little ironically, it's a group of former Silicon Valley entrepreneurs and engineers who are sounding the alarm. Justin Rosenstein banned himself from Snapchat (which he likens to heroin) and limited his use of Facebook. He warns of the dangers of getting hooked on 'likes', which he describes darkly as 'bright dings of pseudo-pleasure'.[21] His concern is surprising, as he himself created the 'like' button in 2007 when he was working at Facebook. Rosenstein warns: 'Everyone is distracted all of the time.' No wonder one of the billionaire Facebook founders, Sean Parker, openly criticises the business, accusing it of deliberately creating an addictive product that exploits 'a vulnerability in human psychology'.[22]

The ex-Google strategist James Williams describes social media as the 'largest, most standardised and most centralised form of attentional control in human history'.[23] Williams left Google last year after he noticed he was surrounded by tech that was diverting his concentration from the issues that actually deserved his attention. While staring at his smartphone he thought: 'Isn't technology supposed to be doing the complete opposite of this?' He's now studying for a PhD in the ethics of persuasive digital design at Oxford University.

Is Google making us stupid?

What does constant distraction do to your brain? The average person in the UK spends more than 24 hours per week online, twice as long as 10 years ago.[24] Is the evolution of AI-enabled products actually damaging human intelligence? It certainly seems to be stunting our ability to focus for long periods. Researchers studied the brain activity of 2,000 people from the first wave of mobile Internet to the turn of the century. They found the average person's attention span has dropped from twelve seconds to just eight.[25] Technology writer Nicholas Carr describes the impact from his perspective: 'What the Net seems to be doing is chipping away at my capacity for concentration and contemplation.' He observed that the mere existence of the online world made it harder to engage with difficult texts and complex ideas. 'Once I was a scuba diver in a sea of words, now I zip along the surface like a guy on a jet ski.'[26] Later he elaborated: 'Over the last few years, I've had an uncomfortable sense that someone, or something, has been tinkering with my brain, remapping the neural circuitry, reprogramming the memory.'[27] The tech writer Kevin Drum adds: 'The Internet is making smart people smarter and dumb people dumber.'[28] Drum points out the wasteful tragedy of how many people choose to engage with the worldwide web. This may be the most powerful tool for curiosity ever invented, yet many use it solely for entertainment, political point scoring or an endless parade of cute cat videos. A tool is only as effective as the person wielding it.

Human habit

Is this app my friend?

One way to be more thoughtful with your time is to ask yourself a simple question: 'What is the benefit to me of using this app?' Do it now. Write down the services you use – Facebook, Instagram, Snapchat, Vine, LinkedIn, Google+ – and then answer that question for each. Imagine life without this service for 30 days. You might experiment with not using this for a week, or even a month. It's easy to do. I tried it with Facebook. I simply deleted the app from my smartphone and turned off all the notifications that appeared on my laptop. After the week is over you can then list what you've done, how you've felt and if it's worth investing the time in that app again. Or, you might use the extra time you saved to learn a new skill or kick-off a creative project.

Hurry sickness

The world seems more divided than ever. But, there's one topic most people seem to agree on: we're all very, very busy. In the frenetic pace of modern life, there's immense social pressure to look, and feel, occupied. Across the industrialised world, people tell researchers they're overburdened with work, often at the expense of time with family and friends.[29] You'd think we were far busier than our parents and grandparents. But, as it turns out, that's just not true. The total time people work – paid or otherwise – has not increased in Europe or North America in decades. In fact, we're working slightly less than we did in the 1960s, '70s and '80s.[30]

This divergence between reality and how we see it lies in our strained relationship with work – in particular, how much it stresses us out. We're living through a global epidemic of workplace anxiety. An analysis of almost 300 studies found that 'harmful workplace practices' were just as likely to lead to illness and premature death as second-hand cigarette smoke.[31] The main culprits are long working hours, work–family conflict, economic insecurity arising from job losses, irregular and unpredictable work hours and an absence of any feeling of control over our time.[32,33] Knocking down walls in our office spaces in the name of knowledge sharing and flattening hierarchy hasn't helped. Ironically, open-plan offices were designed to encourage more creative collaboration. However, research indicates they are having an unintended consequence: they wreck your ability to concentrate. In a study of more than 40,000 workers in 300 office buildings, the conclusion was clear: 'Benefits of enhanced "ease of interaction" were smaller than the penalties of increased noise level and decreased privacy.'[34] *Bloomberg Businessweek* labelled the decades-long experiment the 'tyranny of the open-plan office'.[35]

Digital collaboration tools and video conferencing are accelerating the economic logic of allowing people to work from home or transitioning them to freelance contracts. However, this doesn't free us from distraction. While eight out of ten people are confident they'd be more productive at home, the depressing reality is that the amount of time they have to deal with emails skyrockets from 30 per cent to 60 per cent.[36,37]

Always-on communication tools mean bosses, colleagues and clients stalk us every minute of our working day and then seep across the all-too-permeable border into our home lives. The electronic handmaidens of distraction come in many forms: emails, texts, WhatsApp and WeChat messages, voice calls and alerts from document-sharing tools such as Dropbox, Google Drive and WeTransfer, to name a few. As Tony Crabbe, author of the book *Busy: How to Thrive in a World of Too Much*, points out, we now exist in an 'infinite world. . . there are *always* more incoming emails, more meetings, more things to read, more ideas to follow up'.[38]

Intriguingly, these productivity tools alter our psychological understanding of time itself. Because we're more productive and can get more done, the minutes and seconds in our day have become more valuable. Sadly, we don't ever get to benefit from this increased efficiency. Instead of doing the work required and then taking a break, we feel pressure to squeeze in yet more work. This is easier than ever before. Work doesn't have time limits like it used to. In the eighteenth century, you could not harvest the crops before they were ready. In the nineteenth and twentieth centuries, you could not make more physical products than available materials would allow. Now you can respond to an email at any time of the day or night. No journey is an excuse to unwind, no weekend walk wholly free from the possibility of interruption. Digital mobile technology means you are always striving to do more at home, on holiday or at the gym.

Do you ever find yourself repeatedly pushing the door-close button on an elevator just to save a few seconds? In this case you may suffer from what psychologists call 'hurry sickness'. Other symptoms include getting frustrated in a check-out line or traffic, even when it's moving along smoothly, and a rising urge to find something else to do when you're microwaving lunch for 90 seconds. My colleague Professor Richard Jolly at London Business School reports 95 per cent of managers he's studied over the past ten years suffer from the ailment.[39] I've seen the same trend. Over the last few years, the avalanche of daily work emails to managers on residential leadership programmes has become so intrusive we've been forced to ask participants to sign a voluntary agreement to promise to turn their phone off before each session. Most are quietly grateful.

Take back time

Eager to uncover the secrets of highly creative people, an eminent psychology professor set out to interview as many as he could in different fields.[40] He wrote a letter to 275 famous creators. The first clue to their distinctive approach was that few responded at all. One of the few responses he did get was more explicit. Management writer Peter Drucker wrote: 'One of the secrets of productivity. . . is to have a VERY BIG wastepaper basket to take care of ALL invitations such as yours – productivity in my experience consists of NOT doing anything that helps the work of other people but to spend all one's time on the work the Good Lord has fitted one to do, and to do well.'[41] The secretary to composer György Ligeti wrote back with this: 'He is creative and, because of this, totally overworked. Therefore, the very reason you wish to study his creative process is also the reason why he (unfortunately) does not have time to help you in this study.' The photographer Richard Avedon simply dashed off a note saying: 'Sorry – too little time left.' A third of the people the psychologist approached wrote back saying 'no' in similar terms. Another third, presumably too busy to even reply, didn't respond at all. Being curious and creative is all-consuming. It mostly devours time. People who are successful at it become obsessive. They make conserving time their number-one priority.

As more people need to be creative, this habit of guarding time jealously will spread. The most effective will use technology to be highly productive in their bread-and-butter projects. This efficiency will free up time for their more curious and creative work. I agree with Bill Gates when he said: 'Your success is not a proxy for how busy you are.' The error many make is to falsely equate being organised with a lack of spontaneity or creativity. The opposite is true. The more organised you are, the more time you have for 4C behaviour. As the psychologist Mihaly Csikszentmihalyi commented: 'Every hour saved from drudgery and routine is an hour added to creativity.'[42] Time to take back control.

Human habit

Just say no

What are the unimportant obligations you were too polite to decline? What's irrelevant? You'll never achieve the things you'd like to if you don't learn to say, with a smile, a simple two-letter word: 'no (thanks)'.

Rise up against the tyranny of emails

The average office worker gets 121 emails each day.[43] As emails are now so ubiquitous, it's difficult to re-examine our relationship with them. As John Freeman warns in *The Tyranny of E-mail*, the sheer familiarity of email makes it difficult to question: 'We are slowly eroding our ability to explain – in a careful, complex way – why it is so wrong for us to complain, resist, or redesign our work days so that they are manageable', he warns.[44] Imagine if William Shakespeare, Marie Curie or Nikola Tesla had got up and cleared an avalanche of emails every morning. Or had their attention fractured each time their smartphone buzzed with an Instagram notification. Would we have been able to enjoy Hamlet, powered our world with the alternating electric current, or benefitted from Curie's pioneering research into radioactivity? We can imagine the negative impact constant interruptions might have had on the great creative minds of the past. Yet we expect to do our best work while enduring the same constant cognitive interference. The answer to how we can be more effective in an era of always-on communications doesn't lie in being ever more connected. We won't necessarily create a legacy by cramming yet more activity into our precious hours. Of course, we have to harness digital technology to explore, to collaborate and to work more productively. But we also need to occasionally switch off to protect our inner spark of human creativity. Just because we're able to log in anywhere, anytime, does not mean we *should*.

Human habit

Tame technology

Here are seven simple ways to take back control of your inbox:

Batch emails: Aim to check emails three times a day, at a time of your choosing. For the rest of the time, turn off notifications and log out of your email platform. The little pop-up box in the corner of your screen to let you know Dan is fundraising (again, this time for his forthcoming ascent of Kilimanjaro) may seem harmless. But the accumulated switching from one task to another adds up.

Action ASAP: When you do dip into emails, try to turn 80 per cent of them around the first time you open them.[45]

Refuse to be a carbon copy slave: How many electronic work conversations are you ensnared in, without your consent? 'CC-ing' someone on an email can be an innocent, if misguided, attempt at 'collaborative' behaviour.[46] But, it's often a bid by arse-covering office politicians to insure plausible deniability, and to distribute responsibility if things go wrong. To make more time, release yourself. Politely ask if others could desist from including you as a CC in their emails. Offer clear criteria when you *do* want to be involved. Set up a CC file, so your inbox only gets direct emails.

Start unsubscribing: Most inboxes are filled with emails from subscription-based services you have unintentionally signed up for.[47] Take an hour to remove yourself from their insidious web. If you want their services again, you're just a click away from finding them. This may also help protect you from spammers and identity thieves.

Pick your shots: Top cricketers only hit 'loose' balls, allowing tricky deliveries to whizz by. The best batsmen are on the lookout for opportunities that promise a reward in the form of a big hit. In a similar way, the author of *Deep Work*, Cal Newport, advises that we should think more discerningly about which emails we respond to, and which we simply ignore. Newport is an email fundamentalist and lives by the maxim: 'Become Hard to Reach'. He rails: 'The notion that all messages,

▶

regardless of purpose or sender, arrive in the same undifferentiated inbox, and that there's an expectation that every message deserves a (timely) response, is absurdly unproductive.'[48] He advises you to write a set of clear criteria as to what emails you might be prepared to engage with, and then simply ignore the others. This works, I've tried it. But, do bear in mind, Newport is the resident of an academic ivory tower, as well as being a best-selling author. It's best to tailor this tactic to your own context (it's not one for salesmen or consultant surgeons on call). However, the vast majority of us would benefit hugely from being just a little harder to reach. At the very least, experiment with pausing a few hours, or even a few days, prior to responding to see what difference it makes.

Reply efficiently: When you do choose to respond, take time in order to make time. Be short and succinct. Restrict yourself to three paragraphs and use bullet points where you can. If you write clearer emails it's possible to eliminate email ping-pong: the to-ing and fro-ing of low-value, but time-consuming emails. This technique minimises both the number of emails you receive and the amount of mental clutter they generate. In particular, be crystal clear about your expectations of your input, and what you expect from the other parties. This offers you the freedom to be militant with non-replies if the email correspondence then threatens to balloon out of control. An extra two to three minutes spent on the very first email will save you hours later on.

Pick up the phone: If you think an email will provoke more than two to three replies, use the phone. When you get a tricky email head off any complications by picking up the phone or scheduling a call, video conference or coffee meeting. I know this sounds brain-achingly simple, but we all slip into the email habit and forget about our human ability to add emotional colour, nuance and complex information through conversation.

Cure 'meetingitis'

Who are the time vampires in your life? As a creative person you want playful, serendipitous encounters in your life. But, you need to clearly distinguish between these creative conversations and those tiresome, agenda-less conference calls and meetings that hoover up your precious time. Eliminate the latter to make time for the former.

Human habit

How to minimise meetings

Here are a few rules to help:

- **'No agenda, no attenda':** Don't be afraid to ask if a meeting is strictly necessary, or if you specifically need to attend. If the answer is not crystal clear, simply replace the meeting with a call, or politely cancel.

- **Get ready:** Prepare thoroughly for one-to-one calls, conference calls and meetings. Always know clearly what you intend to contribute and what you hope to achieve.

- **Specify the timeslot:** Most electronic calendars default to 30- or even 60-minute slots. Override this and allocate only the time you think a meeting needs. You can get a huge amount decided in 15 minutes. This practice can save days each year that you can then spend more wisely.

Multitasking is a myth

It's become fashionable to believe, with the aid of digital technology, that we can do two or more things at once. This is nonsense. Trying to multitask hinders productivity because of the accumulated time you waste switching *between* tasks.[49] This is particularly detrimental when attempting complex creative work. A sign of the magnitude of this problem is the growth of a new field called 'interruption science'. Researchers find it takes an average of 25 minutes to recover from an interruption. However, our modern lives are disrupted, on average, every 11 minutes, which means we never catch up with shallow tasks, let alone find the time for creativity.[50]

Stanford communications professor Clifford Nass argues online attention-switching has a lasting negative effect on your brain. In one interview he put it this way: 'Divide people who multitask all the time and people who rarely do, and the differences are remarkable. People who multitask all the time can't filter out irrelevancy. They can't manage a working memory. They're chronically distracted. They initiate much larger parts of their brain that are irrelevant to the task at hand. . . they're pretty much mental wrecks.'[51]

Protected space = protected time

'If you have a garden and a library, you have everything you need.'

Cicero, Roman statesman and master orator

The Renaissance nobleman turned writer and philosopher, Michel de Montaigne, decided, after a near-death accident in his early middle age, to dedicate his time to examining life's biggest question: how to live. He wrote his meandering, but delightful, essays in the sixteenth-century equivalent of a 'man cave': a study hidden away at the top of a wooden spiral staircase in a tower in his chateau near Bordeaux in southwestern France. He filled the walls with an impressive collection of books, historical trinkets and family heirlooms. He wrote: 'Sorry the man, to my mind, who has not in his own home a place to be all by himself, to pay his court privately to himself, to hide!'[52]

Montaigne was not alone in finding a space for focus. In 1922, the psychiatrist Carl Jung bought a basic two-story townhouse on the banks of Lake Zürich in Switzerland and retreated there to think.[53] He was inspired after travelling to India and observing the practice of converting rooms into havens for meditation.[54] Later, his great rival, Freud, escaped the Nazi annexation of Austria and fled to London. The sanctuary he created there is now a museum.[55] Freud personalised a large bedroom in a red-brick house in Hampstead, north London, with a treasure store of 'books, papers, statuettes, pictures, vases, amulets and ethnographic curiosities, designed to stimulate both imagination and intellect'.[56]

Human habit

Claim your space

We're not all fortunate enough to have the resources to convert a tower in our ancestral home, like Monsieur de Montaigne. But, the attitude is available to all of us: a fundamental respect, reverence even, for our own potential. If you have the space in your home, that's great, claim it! If you don't, try a table in your local coffee shop and purchase a decent pair of noise-cancelling headphones. Marking out a protected space for deep thinking and creative work is a powerful statement to yourself. As long as it works for you, your precise solution is not important. What you're carving out is not actually a physical space, it's protected time in your day.

Redesign your day

We live in a world that now expects Formula One standard response times, frequently for no discernible reason. Finding spare minutes that would have been swallowed by these day-to-day diversions will help you to make the most of your precious attention. Personally, I'm most able to think creatively in the morning, so I schedule activities requiring inventive energy – writing this chapter, for example – early in the day. My focus dissipates as the day progresses. I schedule less creatively demanding, but still exacting, consultancy work – thoughtful business correspondence, leadership development programme design and report writing, for example, in the mid-morning and early afternoon. During the late afternoon and early evening, when my creative mojo has completely abandoned me, I tackle humdrum but necessary admin: sending routine emails, confirming diary dates, booking flights and hotels, planning the following day.

Your rhythms might be different. But, whenever you schedule your deep work, this 'chunking' into intentional sprints really helps. It enables two things: higher productivity within the sprint itself, as well as breaks for exercise, snacks – and deliberate day dreaming. These ensure you return to each sprint with restored energy and enthusiasm. After decades of studying creative people, Mihaly Csikszentmihalyi wrote: 'The important thing is that the energy is under their control', and '. . . it is not controlled by the calendar, the clock, an external schedule'.[57] We often say 'we're on the clock' for our job. This is unavoidable if you work for a living. But it is possible to design your day to please your boss, do your drudge work *and* leave time and energy for focused creativity.

Human habit

Own the clock

Take a blank sheet of paper and segment your day into three or four 'sprints' of two to three hours. First ask, when do I have most creative energy? Early morning? Afternoon? Evening? Late at night? Build your personalised schedule through trial and error to find what works for you. You can apply even more focus by writing a clear 'to-do' list for each sprint. This is not about becoming robotic. If you need to flex the schedule for urgent work, so be it. You create rules for yourself, just so you know when you're breaking them. However, by doing this intentionally, it leads to greater levels of productivity than needlessly switching between email, to call, to focus, and back again. As Cal Newport succinctly puts it: 'Don't Take Breaks from Distraction. Instead Take Breaks from Focus.'[58]

Working in this way enables you to protect your creative time. This can be achieved in even the busiest life. While writing this book I continued to oversee leadership development programmes at London Business School and delivered keynote speeches across the world. The only way to find time to research and write was to ruthlessly schedule and then guard my time. I found precious minutes by rising at 6am and writing to around 10am each day, prior to my normal office agenda. Research has shown it's difficult to maintain 'flow' creative thinking for more than three to four hours anyway. If you're not a morning person, put aside a lunchtime or sacrifice 90 minutes of your evening's TV viewing. If you could 'find' another working day (an hour a day for 7 days) per week just for you, what might you achieve?

Train your brain

In the late 1970s, if you'd casually remarked to someone you were going to leave the office and run through the streets, your colleagues would have thought you were eccentric to say the least. As we've become more enlightened about the benefits of physical health, jogging has become completely acceptable. Most people now regularly train their body in some form or other – some even run marathons. We're now seeing a similar shift in our attitude to brain training. At the time of writing, Novak Djokovic is the best tennis player on the planet. Recently he revealed his secret weapon, and it wasn't his impressive physical stamina, skill, or breath-taking serve return. It's his ability to focus on the crunch points. This is the man who managed to win after being a match-point down against Roger Federer at the US Open, not once but twice.[59] How does he come out on top so often? It's simple: he doesn't allow his mind to wander.

Djokovic has been characteristically shrewd in his approach. It seems mind-wandering is the human brain's default mode of operation. A team of Harvard University research psychologists uncovered just how much of the day we are mentally absent. With the aid of an iPhone web app (ironic, I know), they gathered 250,000 data points on their subjects' thoughts, feelings and actions as they went about their lives. They were surprised to find most people spend 47 per cent of their time thinking about something other than what they're doing. What's more, this mind-wandering typically makes people unhappy.[60] The subjects were least happy when resting, working, or using a home computer. They were happiest when working out, chatting, or making love (although the interruption of the researcher's iPhone app may have put a dampener on romance).

A proven way to rein in your naturally wayward mind is through mindfulness: intentionally paying attention to your experience, as it happens, without judgement. Mindfulness can take place at any point in your day. It's the cognitive equivalent of being physically fit. I call it 'The Observer' – the ability to 'think about thinking'. This skill allows you to consciously choose the most effective state of attention for the different moments in your day. To develop mindfulness – the modern equivalent of jogging – you can train your brain through meditation practice. This involves focusing your attention on the breath, or on physical sensations, and gently bringing your attention back to that focus every time your mind wanders. Regular meditation has been shown to improve your ability to think and focus under pressure in stressful situations.[61] It trains your brain and, in time, literally alters its physical structure.

Mindfulness is based on the ancient practice of Buddhist monks, but it's come a long away. It's now established as a firmly secular practice in some unlikely places, including Oxford University, the global accountancy firm PricewaterhouseCoopers and Google. Even the seriously non-tree-hugging US Marines have achieved remarkable results. After eight weeks of meditating for just 15 minutes a day, the soldiers were far better at dealing with anxiety and stress. They could stay calm and focused in the thick of battle. No doubt, these were the types of results that convinced Novak Djokovic that mindfulness would offer him an edge in his quest to retain the world number one spot. His secret weapon is sitting down to meditate for 15 minutes every day as part of his training regime.

In the early 1900s, Antonin-Dalmace Sertillanges, a Dominican friar and professor of moral philosophy, anticipated the obstacles we now face to be creative. He wrote a guide to 'the development and deepening of the mind' for those seeking to spark new ideas. What he wrote then is applicable now: 'Let your mind become a lens, thanks to the converging rays of attention; let your soul be all intent on whatever it is that is established in your mind as a dominant, wholly absorbing idea.'[62] In this century, his advice is harder to follow but even more valuable as a result. The ideas here will help you to be one of the few that can 'converge your rays of attention'. We've practised SEEK and FOCUS, the two Dance Steps within Consciousness. Now we'll turn our attention to the second 'C': Curiosity.

A quick reminder. . .

- We're being distracted at work and at home on an industrial scale.
- This leads to wasted time, poor productivity, stress and even addiction. The result is our attention is fragmented – this makes curious learning and creative thinking far less likely.
- As fewer people manage to focus, supply and demand dictates it will become an increasingly valuable capability – it also leads to human superpowers, which differentiate us from AI.
- A few tips to be more focused:
  - Become more aware – and wary – of 'always-on' work and home distractions.
  - Rebel against the tyranny of emails.
  - Chunk your day into creative and non-creative sprints.
  - Dedicate space and time to your own human creativity.
  - Train your brain with meditation.

Human experiment: Start now. . .

Mindful meditation

I began to meditate around 12 years ago, and can testify to its transformational qualities. It's got to the point where my wife can tell if I've been meditating just by judging my general mood and body language! If you follow the simple instructions of regular practice, non-judgement of your thoughts and focusing on the present moment, it can have truly remarkable results. You can find a host of online apps to guide you through the process. Why not follow Novak's example?

CURIOSITY

The tantalising gap between what you know, and what you don't know

An itch you need to scratch

Incuriosity killed the cat

Why you need to catalyse your curiosity to learn faster than the world is changing

'The illiterate of the 21st century will not be those who cannot read and write, but those who cannot learn, unlearn, and relearn.'

Alvin Toffler, futurist

'Incuriosity is the oddest and most foolish failing there is.'

Stephen Fry, comedian and writer[1]

Superpower: **Curiosity**

Dance Step: **LEARN**

Igniting questions:

- When was the last time you followed your curiosity?
- Where did it lead you?[2]
- What will you learn today?

4Cs value: **Creative fuel**

B ack when Bill Gates was the chairman of Microsoft, he devised a way to prioritise learning in his busy life. Each year, he'd take two separate 'Think Weeks' out of the office just to read and reflect in a secluded cottage. In these seven-day stretches of solitude he contemplated the future of technology. He banned all outside visitors, including his own family and Microsoft staff. The only person who had direct access to him was a caretaker, who brought him two simple meals each day. These weren't holidays – but stretches of time devoted to pure curiosity. From morning till night Gates would read white papers by Microsoft employees, outlining their best ideas. He'd plough through piles of reports for 18 hours straight, writing responses as he went. His record was 112 hefty documents in 7 days.

He made crucial choices during these cloistered getaways. One week, in 1995, he paused to rattle out a memo entitled 'The Internet Tidal Wave'. This led to Microsoft's earliest online browser. Other course-correcting decisions included the first Microsoft tablet PC, more secure software and entering the video game market.[3] During these weeks, Gates stumbled upon insights that powered Microsoft's success for decades.[4]

How do you gently tug at the roots of your life-changing ideas? Let's begin with a question: have you ever wondered why you did well, or badly, at school? Sophie von Stumm, a lecturer in psychology at Goldsmiths University, asked the same question. She gathered data from 200 studies covering 50,000 students on the factors that drive academic performance. Her conclusion was clear. Your intelligence matters, of course. No surprise there. Next comes how hard you work. It seems those earnest gym teachers who write slogans such as *'hard work beats talent, when talent doesn't work hard'*, actually have a point. However, if you only apportion your school accomplishments (or failures) to your intelligence, or capacity for hard graft, you're wrong. There's another influential factor that gets less attention. This is your tendency to 'seek out, engage in, enjoy and pursue opportunities for effortful cognitive activity'.[5] Researchers call this quality your 'need for cognition'. It's what the rest of us call 'curiosity'.

The next two chapters are designed to get you very curious about your superpower of Curiosity. We'll explore how it works, how it fits into the 4Cs and what you can do to make it stronger every day. First let's look at how it underpins your ability to keep pace with a fast-changing world by gathering raw material to fuel Creativity.

What killed the cat?

You and I are related to a single woman who lived in East Africa around two hundred thousand years ago.[6] About seventy thousand years ago, a descendant of our common earth mother gazed across the Red Sea, and asked: 'I wonder what's on the other side?' Those early pioneers were so curious they decided to find out. The rest is, literally, human history. The wandering *Homo sapiens* tribe populated every continent, subsuming or extinguishing other humanoid species along the way. As a result, you were born with a naturally inquisitive nature. Our common ancestors were, after all, driven by an urge to explore.

Since then, curiosity has developed a dangerous reputation. In a cautionary tale about the dark side of our inquisitive nature, the Greek god Zeus gave earthbound Pandora a little box and warned she must never open it. Of course, she couldn't resist. When she lifted the lid, out flew the evils of the world including sickness, worry, crime, hate and envy.[7] Whoops. As the saying goes, 'curiosity killed the cat'. The rich and powerful in history often tend to discourage curiosity in the lower ranks. In medieval Europe, for example, if you inquired too closely into the edicts of the Church you risked being burned at the stake. Awkward questions led to awkward answers, which occasionally led to unwelcome revolutions (or, in this case, reformations).

In the age of AI, being a curious human is no longer perilous, it's mandatory. A team of Nesta researchers analysed the skills people will need as we approach 2030.[8] They advised focusing on 'uniquely human skills' such as originality, fluency of ideas, lifelong learning and reskilling. All these are underpinned by curiosity. At the same time, demographic trends show we're living longer than our parents and grandparents. For younger generations, the difference will be pronounced. The majority of children born in rich countries today can expect to live to more than 100 years of age, implying a working life of around 60 years. Who seriously expects anyone to work in the same industry, let alone the same job, for six decades? Reinvention is often described as vital for corporate products, services and business models. Successful humans in this century will also need to constantly innovate their interests, capabilities and career focus.

Albert Einstein was a famously poor student at school. But he was clear about what led to his astounding insights later in life. He argued he had no special talents, apart from being passionately curious. My London Business School colleague, Professor Lynda Gratton, directs the world's leading research programme on human resources.[9] She studies the future of work, including the role of AI. She concludes: 'The interesting thing is, all the roads lead back to lifelong learning. This is what I'm saying to everyone. This is what I believe to be absolutely crucial.'[10]

Neuroscience has revealed the driver between curiosity and your ability to learn.[11] You're more likely to remember what you've learned when the subject matter intrigues you. No surprise there. However, it turns out curiosity also helps you to learn when you don't even consider the subject matter to be interesting or important.[12] In other words, once piqued, your curiosity helps you to learn *anything* more effectively. Finally, without curiosity, creativity is impossible. This makes curiosity a vital step in the journey towards differentiating yourself from AI, as well as human rivals – not least because you'll need to reinvent your working identity and skills with more rapidity than ever before. The ability to evolve yourself is now obligatory. In today's world its incuriosity, not curiosity, that kills the cat.

The itch you need to scratch

Curiosity is a little tricky to pin down. Academics can't seem to agree upon a single definition. What we do know is curiosity combines thinking *and* feeling, which is why it's been labelled the 'knowledge emotion' and is a peculiarly human virtue. Research shows the emotive urge to know is nearly as strong as other powerful human motivators, such as hunger, thirst and sex drive.[13] Curiosity compels us to pursue what's meat and drink for our mind. As we've seen, this fact hasn't gone unnoticed by social media app designers. Video game developers also use curiosity to hook players into the pursuit of 'levelling up'. Reaching the next level rewards players with the solution to riddles, new tools and advanced weaponry.

This ruthless baiting of inquiring minds has some unfortunate side-effects. In 2012, a US teenager, Tyler Rigsby, was rushed to hospital after a marathon session playing 'Call of Duty: Modern Warfare 3'.[14] His mother reported Tyler had collapsed after playing at least four days straight. Medics diagnosed severe dehydration. A year earlier, a Chinese man died after a three-day online gaming session in which he didn't sleep and barely ate.[15] Curiosity is like a physical itch that *has* to be scratched. When unleashed, it occasionally overpowers our sense of self-preservation.

In the mid-1990s, the eminent researcher George Loewenstein invented the 'information-gap' theory on curiosity.[16] He argued whenever we perceive a divergence 'between what we know and what we want to know', that tantalising gap has emotional consequences. It makes us feel deprived.[17] This nicely describes the cliff-hanger feeling at the end of an episode of your favourite series, which now leads to the Netflix binge. It's the missing piece of a jigsaw – the urge to read the full story behind the 'clickbait' headline, even when you know it's probably rubbish.

Imagine how you'd feel if you found out Donald Trump is secretly an articulate and knowledgeable fan of French Impressionist art?

Or that Pope Francis relaxes in the evening by watching marathon sessions of UFC martial arts bouts? The jarring mismatch between these (false, in case you were wondering) revelations would spur you to find out more. This is an example of another definition offered by researchers: curiosity is the moment when you sense incongruity in your world.[18] There is an inconsistency between a new fact and your existing world view. Let's not get hung up on the slight difference in emphasis between these definitions. It's not surprising. The human condition, after all, is messy and paradoxical. Why should one of its most defining attributes be any different?

How curious are you?

We know curiosity comes in different flavours. To help bring it together a little, I've combined decades of research in Figure 6.1 to produce two broad axes of curiosity. You'll see the direction of each axis points towards four broad categories of curiosity:

- **Diversive curiosity:** your (mostly unguided) need to seek stimulation to escape boredom.

- **Knowledge curiosity:** your impulse to learn more; the 'effortful' mission to accumulate information.[19]

- **Specific curiosity:** your desire for a *particular* piece of knowledge; the final piece of a puzzle, if you will.

- **Perceptual curiosity:** your interest in seeking different real-world, physical impressions – people, objects and sensations.

The directions then create a 2 × 2 of states of curiosity. These are (from bottom left):

- **ROAM** (Perceptual–Diversive): This is undirected physical meandering, such as wandering aimlessly through a park you've stumbled upon, browsing a clothes shop or food market or taking in new sights, sounds, smells and textures.

- **SAMPLE** (Perceptual–Specific): When you want to know how a particular experience feels, such as taking a drug, for

Figure 6.1 Curiosity quadrants[20]

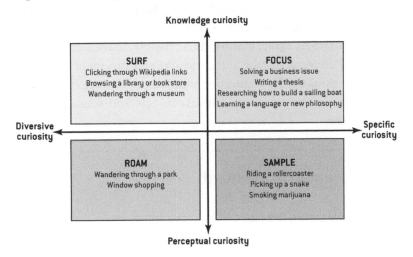

example, or picking up a snake to learn what its scales feel like. This is the desire for new sensations – sights, sounds, textures – but directed towards answering a particular question.

- **SURF** (Knowledge–Diversive): The need for information or knowledge that is exploratory, perhaps to avoid boredom. It's when you flick through TV channels on a Sunday afternoon, daydreaming about different topics, or the never-ending scroll down the social media feed.

- **FOCUS** (Knowledge–Specific): The desire for information or knowledge, directed towards answering a specific question, however deep that question may be. This would be the curiosity that compels us to solve a Sudoku puzzle, to crack a key question at work, to write a book or to complete a PhD thesis.

We explored the tension between 'Surf' and 'Focus' in the previous chapter. My advice was to find time and space for deep thinking and creativity in our distracted digital world. However, it's worth pointing out that *all* four segments can be positive for your ability to be creative. Just to re-emphasise, organised work and life patterns are there to allow important slack time to 'Roam' and 'Sample'. The authors of a research paper into curiosity at the UK Royal Society of the Arts (RSA) agree, writing: 'It is possible, indeed desirable, to have both convergent (specific curiosity) and divergent (diversive curiosity) thinking for innovative solutions to emerge.'[21] All four quadrants expose you to new ideas, objects and sensations in a different way.

Human experiment

Balancing the four curiosity quadrants

Take a moment to think of the last time, and how often, you indulge your curiosity in each of these quadrants? It's a balance. What might you do in your life to make sure that balance is working for you? How can you make more time for curiosity in general? What specifically can you do to indulge each quadrant?

Curious machines?

A team at the University of California is developing an 'intrinsic curiosity model' for artificial intelligence.[22] The researchers replicated curiosity within two simple video games: 'Mario Bros.', a classic platform game, and 'ViZDoom', a basic 3D shooter title. The AI finds out new information about the environment it's exploring even when there isn't immediately obvious rewards for doing so. In other words, it's 'curious'. In both games, researchers found the use of artificial curiosity made the learning process more efficient. Instead of spending an excessive amount of time bumping into walls, the AI moved around its environment, learning to navigate more quickly.

Let's get this into perspective. This technology is light years behind the power of human curiosity – a point confirmed by Brenden Lake, a research scientist at New York University, who builds

AI models of human cognitive capabilities: 'It's a very egocentric form of curiosity', he says. 'The [AI] agent is only curious about features of its environment that relate to its own actions. People are more broadly curious. People want to learn about the world in ways less directly tied to their own actions.' As we've found with other forms of intelligence, AI is good at narrow, humans are masters of exploration and connecting the dots.

Strengthen your curiosity muscle with everyday learning

Whatever your assessment of your current level of curiosity, there's some good news: you can either take it further, or build it back up again. You might have heard the HR phrase 'life-long learning'. This is a great idea. However, I'd rather not encourage you to adopt something that is, by definition, so long term and difficult to measure. Why would you commit to anything that can only be verified in the few minutes prior to your death?! Instead, the rest of this chapter is devoted to 'everyday learning'. This is easier to keep track of. You either learned something today, or you didn't. It also makes sense in terms of how we actually acquire new capabilities. Little and often always works best. As the professor of business psychology at University College London, Tomas Chamorro-Premuzic, puts it: 'Although IQ is hard to coach. . . CQ [curiosity quotient] can be developed.'[23] Curiosity is a cognitive muscle. Neglect it, it'll get flabby. Exercise makes it bigger and stronger. Any bodybuilder will tell you, the best results always come from the right habits – and practising them every day. So, let's get training.

Make time for curious learning

The most basic first step is to dedicate time to curiosity. Hopefully, the tips and techniques we covered in FOCUS will help with this. Author Thomas Corley spent five years studying the habits of self-made millionaires. He found, instead of watching TV, they read a lot more than the general population. Not just for fun, but to learn. The CEO of AT&T, Randall Stephenson, said that those who don't spend at least five to ten hours a week learning online 'will obsolete themselves with technology'.[24] We've already seen what Bill Gates achieved with his 'Think Weeks'. However, he's not the first to grasp the huge advantage that frequent learning delivers. It's a consistent practice of the world's most successful people. The list includes Walt Disney, Frank Lloyd Wright, Arnold Schwarzenegger, Warren Buffett, Jack Ma, Steve Jobs and Jeff Bezos.[25] TV talk-show star Oprah Winfrey is clear about the origins of her success: 'Books were my pass to personal freedom', she confides. Nike founder Phil Knight so reveres his library that visitors have to take off their shoes and bow before they enter. Elon Musk invested in SpaceX after he learned about building rockets from the pages of old science books. Former US President Barack Obama claimed reading books helped him to survive his eight arduous years in The White House. Amid the information overload of the Oval office, quietly reading gave him the opportunity to 'slow down and get perspective. . . the ability to get in somebody else's shoes'.[26]

 ## Human experiment

The five-hour rule

An entire 'Think Week' is achievable for the likes of Bill Gates. But it's a little more difficult to arrange if you're not the chairman of the board. Instead, I urge you to experiment with the 'five-hour rule'.[27] The concept is simple: no matter how busy you are, always put aside at least one hour every day for learning.[28] The American founding father and serial inventor Ben Franklin used it in his life. Franklin consistently invested roughly 60 minutes each working day in deliberate learning. This unleashed enormous potential. He was a successful author, a diplomat, and invented the Franklin stove, bifocals and the lightning rod, among many other innovations.[29]

Here's a few handy tips to help you adopt the five-hour rule:

- Write a book list of the top ten titles that would help you to think differently.
- Buy an e-reader – they are lighter and easier to fit in a backpack or pocket.
- Use audiobooks, podcasts and video blogs – they make a change from reading, and can be stored easily on a smartphone.
- Always carry your curiosity with you. There is usually at least one moment waiting in line, or over lunch, where you can read, listen or view (always carry lightweight headphones to make this possible).
- Habitually interrogate what you're absorbing with two key questions: 'What are the two to three key insights or takeaways?' and 'How can I experiment with these in my life or business?'.

Learn from Leonardo

Who's the most curious person in history? A strong candidate is the Italian inventor, engineer and artist Leonardo da Vinci. There are two great reasons why Leonardo provides a valuable model for human curiosity. Firstly, he filled scores of notebooks with scribbles, drawings and 'to-do' lists, which he illuminated with breathtaking sketches. They still exist, so we can see how his boundless curiosity underpinned his success. With these jottings he bequeaths us a rare insight into how curiosity connects to creativity – and then to invention. Biographer Walter Isaacson observed: 'His genius was of the type we can understand, even take lessons from. It was based on skills we can aspire to improve in ourselves, such as curiosity and intense observation.'[30] Secondly, Leonardo was a master at judging which type of curiosity to deploy, and when. When to roam widely to fire his imagination, and when to focus to develop mastery in a specialised area.

Roam widely

The Renaissance was the most explosive period of curiosity in human history. Everything that was previously accepted was questioned. It's not surprising Leonardo was heavily influenced by the Renaissance, as he was born and grew up in the village of Anchiano, just thirty kilometres from its epicentre – the Italian city of Florence. Leonardo became the original 'Renaissance man': a true polymath. He was, of course, not only a masterful painter, but also a sculptor, architect, musician, scientist, mathematician, military engineer, inventor, anatomist, geologist, cartographer, botanist and writer. He was relentless in his mission to learn how the world worked. There are clues to why Leonardo roamed so widely in modern-day neuroscience. Researchers at the California Institute of Technology recently revealed that your curiosity follows an inverted U-shaped curve (see Figure 6.2).[31]

Have you ever noticed, when you learn about something new – anything from a new word, dog breed, specialist sport, type of hairdo, historical fact, or style of shoe – it seems to crop up in your life? When you decide to buy a particular brand of car or clothing, for example, it appears the streets are suddenly full of them. This happens because your new knowledge has primed your brain. It's lodged in what's called the reticular activating system.[32] You can use this insight to build your curiosity muscles. By learning the foothills of any new subject, the peaks are more accessible and inviting.[33] Curiosity is a self-fulfilling prophecy in all domains: open any door and it leads to a lifetime of delightful discovery.

Figure 6.2 Curiosity's U-shaped curve

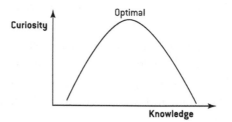

To exploit this U-shaped curve you need to roam widely, exercising your human senses and emotions to explore the left-hand 'Diversive' side of the curiosity quadrants. In the same way, the renowned 'design thinking' methodology always begins with time spent 'walking in the shoes' of the customer, to truly live their physical and emotional experience of a product or service. I often allocate time for senior executives to explore and discover new thoughts in engaging locations, such as the buzzing markets, art galleries or science museums of the city we're in. Roaming works in all worlds. In *The Art of Scientific Investigation*, Cambridge University professor W. I. B. Beveridge advises young scientists to expand their reading outside of their own field because: 'Originality often consists in linking up ideas whose connection was not previously suspected.'[34]

Steve Jobs owed a debt to his tendency to roam. He was a college dropout in 1973, but he still hung around his former Oregon university campus to audit the occasional class.[35] He snuck in the back of a calligraphy course, of all things: the art of decorative handwriting. Useless, you might think. However, Jobs used what he learned when it came to differentiating the Mac computer. The Mac was the first to offer a huge variety of different styles of lettering, a practice that's now standard across all word processors. Later Jobs explained: 'If I had never dropped out, I would have never dropped in on this calligraphy class, and personal computers might not have the wonderful typography that they do. Of course, it was impossible to connect the dots looking forward when I was in college. But it was very, very clear looking backwards ten years later.'[36]

Let's not forget, our differentiation from AI is in our ability to think widely and generally. Neuroscience shows that general intelligence lights up the whole human brain. It simply can't be contained in just one part.[37] When you surf the knowledge waves of life, nothing you pick up and file away is useless. As we'll see in the Creativity superpower, invention stems from 'joining the dots' *across* boundaries. A little investment in 'random' but fascinating knowledge – from Victorian literature to Japanese design, computing coding to jet propulsion,

DNA strands to ballet – may pay dividends when you are called upon to create new ideas. It's damaging, short-sighted and pointless to demand an immediate return on your investment in learning. The key is to value knowledge for its own sake. You never know when it'll come in useful.

 Human experiment

Open a new learning door

What fascinates you? What might in the future? Write a list. Take advantage of the U-shaped curiosity curve to fire your interest in diverse new areas. The breadth of your list will make your mind more fertile for innovative new ideas. What door could you push open today?

Human experiment

Google everything

The artist and writer Austin Kleon advises: 'Google everything. I mean everything. Google your dreams, Google your problems. Don't ask a question before you Google it. You'll either find the answer or you'll come up with a better question.'[38] A lot of this book is devoted to curbing what can be the dark side of AI-enabled technology. Using AI – from Google search to Alexa – as a skilfully wielded tool of everyday curiosity, rather than an intellectual sedative, is a great way to learn faster than our ancestors could ever have dreamed of.

Focus your curiosity

Leonardo followed his intuition to know when to stop roaming and start focusing more narrowly. He relentlessly pursued mastery of the complex painting techniques that allowed him to accurately render notoriously difficult subjects, such as the flexing of muscles and the fluidity of running water. In one journal note, he reminded himself to look into 'the measurement of Milan and its suburbs'.[39] The practical purpose in this was revealed by an item later in his to-do list: 'Draw Milan'.

Times have changed a little from Leonardo's day, when 'knowing everything about everything' was a tantalising possibility. There's now a lot more to know. No one, however gifted, could ever master a fraction of the information being produced. Being a jack-of-all-trades is less valuable when knowledge on the most arcane subjects can be summoned with the click of a mouse. This means, as well as roaming widely, it's also wise to master a handful of specific domains. Economics dictates that if you want to be well paid, you have to be excellent at something in high demand and short supply. Like Leonardo, this implies exercising curiosity in the right-hand, 'Specific' side of the four curiosity quadrants. For this, it's necessary to withstand digital distraction, as we explored in the previous chapter.

To summarise, to achieve superstar status in the emerging world of work, you'll need to be able to:

1 Roam, Sample, and Surf thoughtfully to acquire a breadth of knowledge to trigger serendipitous moments of insight.

2 Focus to accumulate a depth of knowledge and skill to crack complex, messy problems in your specialist domain(s).

The chief executive of the global design firm IDEO popularised the term 'T-shaped person'. Tim Brown argued that his company is successful because it can put together diverse, collaborative teams for intensive project work. Brown puts it this way: 'The vertical stroke of the "T" is a depth of skill that allows them to contribute to the creative process. That can be from any number of different fields: an industrial designer, an architect, a social scientist, a business specialist or a mechanical engineer.' He goes on to explain you'll need depth *and* breadth to design your own personal T-shape. Creative people dig a deep well in a certain expertise but then restlessly roam around this water supply. It's only by achieving both depth and breadth that you'll stumble on the killer questions that will help you challenge the world around you.

Human experiment

Dig a deep well

Curiosity is not a zero-sum game. If you allow one type of curiosity to flourish, it will not prevent you from cultivating another. But, there is a sizeable caveat. You only have 24 hours in a day. We encounter the inflexible barrier of time again. Unconfined, *mindless* surfing – pursuing cute cat photos, boredom-avoiding Candy Crush marathons and fleetingly rewarding Twitter rants – will eat up all your spare minutes. You need to develop a sharp instinct for when to surf, when to roam, when to sample and when to focus the rays of your curiosity. Where do you need to take a cognitive shovel and dig a deeper well?

Curiosity is a virus (try to catch it and spread it around)

Scientists at the National Institute of Child Health and Human Development in the USA discovered that the more actively a baby explores her environment, the more likely she will go on to achieve academic success as an adolescent at school.[40] There's a second finding in their work that's equally important. The subsequent development of a baby's curiosity is then hugely impacted by her environment. Two psychologists from Birkbeck College in London, Teodora Gliga and Katarina Begus, tested this. They attached electrical sensors to the heads of babies to work out what was happening in their brain when something piqued their interest. They hypothesised that when a baby points, they are engaging their adult carer in 'joint attention'. Effectively, babies are asking a silent question using a pudgy little digit. The researchers noticed that when the caregiver's response was lukewarm, or incorrect, the babies were less likely to point again. It's chastening to realise even babies can sense when you don't care, or simply don't know what you're talking about. It's also heartbreaking to realise many humans must have their curiosity squashed before they can even walk.

Curiosity is contagious but, unfortunately, so is incuriosity.[41] You can't do much about your DNA inheritance, or your childhood. But, as Alan Kay one of the pioneers of computer graphics observed: 'A change in perspective is worth 80 IQ points'.[42] You can surround yourself with people who fuel, rather than extinguish, your enthusiasm for exploration. Your curiosity is not fixed. It's like mercury in a temperature gauge. It rises and falls depending on who you are with.[43] Leonardo was careful to seek out people who supported his learning. He made lists of those he intended to interrogate. He scribbled: 'Get the master of arithmetic to show you how to square a triangle. Ask Giannino the Bombardier about how the tower of Ferrara is walled. Ask Benedetto Portinari by what means they walk on ice in Flanders. Get a master of hydraulics to tell you how to repair a lock, canal and mill in the Lombard manner. Get the measurement of the sun promised me by Maestro Giovanni Francese, the Frenchman.'[44] This habit of intentionally learning from others was shared by Jeff Bezos. A colleague from his pre-Amazon days as a New York analyst recalled: 'He went to school on everybody. . . I don't think there was anybody Jeff knew that he didn't walk away from with whatever lessons he could.'[45]

Hollywood film producer Brian Grazer is the co-author of *A Curious Mind: The Secret to a Bigger Life.*[46] After he finished college he had a disturbing realisation: he couldn't recall one valuable fact from his time as a university student. Perturbed, he hounded one of his old professors for a meeting to talk it over. This turned out to be a deeply fulfilling encounter. It dawned on Grazer that he had learned more in 90 minutes than his entire three-year college career. From that day, he turned curious conversations into a personal 'discipline'. For the last 40 years, he's arranged a conversation every two weeks. He said: 'I reach out to somebody who is renowned or expert in something other than entertainment. . . so, science,

medicine, politics, religion, every art form, of course technology. . .
you are trying to learn that person's "secret".[47]

 ## Human experiment

Curious conversations

Who are the people who you'd love to speak to? You'd be surprised
how generous people are, if you make it clear you want to learn, you
ask interesting questions and you show your gratitude for their time.
Arrange a one-hour curious conversation every few weeks for the next
six months and see what you learn.[48]

Human experiment

Warm up next to radiators

Grab a piece of paper and draw a line down the middle. On the left write
'radiators'. Under this column, list the people in your personal and professional life who inspire and help you to learn new things. On the right,
write 'drains'. These are the time vampires who suck your time and
energy without giving anything back. Which of your colleagues, friends
and family are 'radiators'? They inspire you to think differently and to
keep learning. This might sound harsh, but which are 'drains'? They
close down interesting conversations and fail to challenge you. On the
whole, are you surrounded by curious learners or incurious zombies?
How can you try to spend more time with radiators? Who could you
arrange to see, or call right now to get inspired? How can you attract
more of the warmth of curiosity into your life?

Four years after he lost to IBM's Deep Blue, chess world champion Garry Kasparov was in the middle of an unprecedented winning streak against human opponents at top-level tournaments.

He'd boosted his chess rating to its highest peak ever. It was at this moment, full of confidence, that he took on Vladimir Kramnik. And lost. He explained: 'My weakness was a refusal to admit that Kramnik had out-prepared me – preparation was supposed to be my strong suit. Each one of my successes up to that moment was like being dipped in bronze over and over, each success, each layer, making me more rigid and unable to change, and, more importantly, unable to see the need to change.'[49] Learning is an admission that you don't know everything. This avoids being dipped in bronze. It restates your willingness to *relearn*. Only this allows you to continually reinvent yourself over a lifetime. In the next chapter we'll explore how you can weaponise your curious nature to QUESTION and find exciting problems to solve.

A quick reminder. . .

- Curiosity is a human superpower that leads to others – it unlocks the door to learning, creativity and succeeding in a fast-changing world.

- Curiosity is a little tricky to pin down: it's been called the knowledge emotion, an information gap, or a sense of incongruity.

- Curiosity is a cognitive muscle: neglect it, and it gets flabby. Exercise makes it bigger and stronger.

- There are different types of curiosity and you need to successfully balance them to learn and to create.

- You need both wide-ranging/diversive *and* focused/specific curiosity.

- Everyday learning means investing a little of your most precious asset: time.

- Curiosity is like a virus – you can catch it off other people (try to avoid the terminally incurious!).

Human experiment: Start now. . .

Ask great questions

You can turn pretty much any human interaction into an opportunity for a curious conversation. It might be a new acquaintance or someone you know well but have chosen to see in a new light. In the next chapter we'll focus on the value of questions. In the meantime, try to slip these seven questions into everyday conversations to deepen the experience — you'll be amazed where they take you:

1 What are you learning now? *This question allows you to benefit from their list of passionate interests.*

2 What have you read that I should read? *This question directs your personal learning.*

3 Who do you know whom I should know? *This allows you to engage with their network, and see who inspires them.*

4 What have you done that I should do? *This helps you to seek new experiences.*

5 What is the greatest lesson you have learned? *By asking this question you seek their hard-earned wisdom.*

6 How can I add value to you? *This shows your gratitude for the conversation.*

7 How has failure shaped your life? *This question gives insight into their attitude to learning from life's missteps.*

7

Find exciting problems

How to question everything to weaponise curiosity

'Computers are useless. They can only give you answers.'

Pablo Picasso, artist

Superpower: **Curiosity**

Dance Step: **QUESTION**

Igniting questions:

- What needs to be challenged in your life?
- How might you ask more questions?
- How might you ask better questions?

4Cs value: **Intriguing question**

Robert Jones had felt safe following his AI-enabled sat nav. He ignored the fact it had re-routed his BMW off the main road and on to a narrow, steep mountain path in the Pennines, in the north of England. He just assumed it knew what it was doing. Just in time, he questioned the wisdom of his instructions. By then the front of his car was dangling over a cliff edge. A few more metres more and he might not have lived to tell the tale. He later told police he'd come to completely rely on the sat nav, and was shocked to find it had led him into this nightmare situation.[1] Asked why he didn't overrule his car's navigation software, based on the clear evidence of his own eyes, he replied: 'It kept insisting the path was a road. . . so I just trusted it. You don't expect to be taken nearly over a cliff.'[2] It's tempting to laugh at Mr Jones. But the truth is this incurious and unquestioning behaviour is now common. Since Jones' comical wrong turn, scores of people have died following incorrect sat nav instructions. Rangers in California's Death Valley National Park have even given it a name: 'death by GPS'.[3]

In the last chapter, we explored how Curiosity means you learn fast enough to stay relevant in a changing world. In this chapter, we'll learn how to weaponise this inquisitiveness through the art of asking curious questions. We'll explore how you can use their power to *stay* curious, to make sense of the world around you, to solve problems – and to innovate. Asking questions has always been the first step in Creativity, which is the best response to the nuanced complexity of the world we now face. AI is good at working on known questions based on available data. We humans must make it our job to ensure we're always looking for the *next* question.

Relentlessly curious

To understand what a lifetime of questioning curiosity looks like, let's circle back to the man dubbed 'the most relentlessly curious man in history' by the eminent art historian Kenneth Clark.[4] Leonardo da Vinci used questions to create one of his most celebrated masterpieces, the *Mona Lisa* (Figure 7.1). Considering its iconic status, you might be surprised to hear that when Leonardo began painting the work, back in 1503, it was a relatively minor commission – just another humdrum request for a commercial portrait. The painting has risen to prominence because Leonardo became obsessed by the challenge of capturing his enigmatic subject – a young woman from a Florentine family. He became so possessed by the work that it was still by his side in the room when he died in Paris 16 years later. In over a decade and a half he painted and repainted the *Mona Lisa*. Leonardo used the artwork

Figure 7.1 Leonardo da Vinci's *Mona Lisa*

as a laboratory to ask, and answer, key questions. His first question was this: what makes a painting fascinating for a viewer? This query led to three others, which all led to remarkable innovations in the art of painting:

'What happens when light hits your eyeball?' This thought led Leonardo to study this in detail, and to prepare his canvas in an innovative way. Before beginning, he covered it in a layer of bright, white, lead-based undercoat. This meant that light travelled through the many thin layers of paint he thereafter applied, hit this base layer and bounced out again. The result was Leonardo's painting literally shone for the viewer.[5]

'Why do things in the distance look hazy, but things close up look sharp?' Close observation led Leonardo to paint the river and trees behind Mona Lisa in a blurred manner. This meant he was one of the first to give his paintings the impression of realistic depth of field. This was something even his great contemporary rival, Michelangelo, failed to understand and implement.

'What muscles in the human face trigger a smile?' This question led to some brilliant, and slightly grotesque, experiments. During the long days perfecting Mona Lisa's smile, Leonardo spent his nights in the depths of the morgue at the hospital of Santa Maria Nuova, near his Florence studio. He peeled the skin off cadavers and studied the muscles and nerves underneath. This gave him an unparalleled physiological understanding of what makes a human smile look as it does. The result of his insight can be viewed in the playful, pursed lips of Mona Lisa. She appears radiant one moment, and then serious and sardonic the next, just like the nuanced, enigmatic countenance of a real human being. Over five hundred years later, the *Mona Lisa* still lives before our eyes. This is why thirty thousand people each day brave the long queues to see her at the Louvre museum in Paris.[6] They hope to catch a glimpse of a truly human smile, made possible by human questions.

Human experiment

Start with curious questions

Leonardo's questions led to answers, which made the innovations in the *Mona Lisa* possible. Your future questions can help you to innovate and add value. What is your 'Mona Lisa'? The project, challenge or new discipline you'd like to pursue and master? Take a few minutes and write down the areas that fascinate you. Next to each, scribble the curious questions that may help you to dig a little deeper.

The Austrian-born American business thinker Peter Drucker is viewed by many as the founder of modern management. He humbly admitted: 'My greatest strength as a consultant is to be ignorant and ask a few questions.'[7] How many questions did you ask last week? This is a reasonable benchmark to gauge your current level of curiosity. A study of children interacting with their caregivers showed that the average toddler poses around one hundred questions every *hour* – a fact young parents will acknowledge with an exhausted, and completely unsurprised, shrug. The study concluded that when we're small, asking questions 'is not something that happens every now and then. . . it is a central part of what it means to be a child'.[8] So why do we stop? The rest of this chapter will cover how curious questions can benefit you by avoiding irrelevance, solving problems and innovating in your life and work.

Questions to avoid bad decisions

In 1930, the French Government constructed a series of concrete fortifications along their border with Germany, called the Maginot Line. It would have been a perfect defence during the static, trench warfare of World War One, which had concluded 12 years earlier, but it didn't help at all when World War Two broke out. Germany easily flanked the Maginot Line, invading from the north through Belgium. Large, established organisations often tend to fight the last war, rather than look to the next one.

Psychologists have found a psychological reason for these types of human blind spots: *confirmation bias* is our tendency to search for information that confirms existing views and preconceptions. It can lead to strange herding behaviour: instead of asking questions, people use the actions of others as a guide to what they should do.[9] For example, the irrational US housing bubble, which led to the worldwide credit crunch, was caused by investors preferring to follow the crowd rather than questioning reality. We know that during an election season, people tend to seek positive information that paints their favoured candidates in a good light and to avoid information that contradicts their choice. They'll also look for information that casts the opposing candidate in a negative light. It really doesn't matter how smart you are. We *all* do this, with no exceptions.

If the human tendency to confirmation bias is our Achilles' heel, AI-managed information is a perfectly designed poison arrow to target this weakness. Do you know that weird feeling when you think about buying something and a few minutes later your smartphone serves you an advert for the very same thing? This is AI-enabled algorithms forecasting what you want, based on past behaviour – and the behaviour of millions of others with similar preferences. Just as product offerings are being tailored to your personal requirements, increasingly the information that comes your way has been amended and edited. This has become known as the 'filter bubble'.[10] AI notes your former clicks, browsing and search history, and even sometimes your location and the digital device you're using, to serve you information that's linked to what you have previously shown an interest in. Your Google search results and individual news stream on Facebook are two perfect examples of the filter bubble in action. The online world gives you what it thinks you want, based on all your digital yesterdays.

A filter bubble is most dangerous when our past decisions mean we become targets for fake news. Misleading propaganda and downright lies are set to remain a hot topic in our lifetimes. The largest-ever study of fake news analysed every major contested news story written in English across the span of Twitter's existence – 126,000 stories, Tweeted by 3 million users over a period of more than 10 years.[11] The result was depressing. By every metric, falsehoods consistently dominate the truth on Twitter. Lies reach more people, penetrate deeper into the social network and spread far faster than accurate stories. Lies outperform the truth on every subject: business, terrorism, war, science, technology, entertainment – and, of course, politics, where its influence has been most insidious most recently in the 2016 US presidential election and in the UK's Brexit referendum. In a recent study of voters in India, it was shown that those locked in a filter bubble were 12 per cent more likely to vote for the candidate who had been promoted by a biased search engine.[12] Easily enough to decide an election. The eighteenth-century satirist Jonathan Swift wrote 'falsehood flies, and the truth comes limping after it'. Lies are now on digital steroids.

In an uncertain world, it's wise to constantly question the information you 'find' to avoid living in a self-perpetuating delusion. You'll need heightened critical thinking skills to cope with this misleading mediascape. Our hard-wired human bias works against us, and makes intellectual isolation more likely. Without curious questions, you become more what you already are, not what you might be. Here are three practical experiments to help.

Human experiment

Burst your bubble

How can you ensure you're piercing your filter bubble by introducing more challenging and diverse sources of information and topics into the mix? Where is your information coming from? What are the verifiable sources of your new knowledge? As a journalist would, can you establish the credibility of the content? Is there a way to find another, more dependable source?

Human experiment

Switch on your radar

To keep pace with the disruption all around us, it's a good idea to build a structure of knowledge and then keep it updated. Without this it's too easy to become overwhelmed. First, you need to switch on your conceptual radar[13] so you can discern when new things are happening.

▶

The segments of your radar might have labels such as cool technology, social trends, economic themes, environmental movements and political changes. Often these are interdependent. Here's a useful list to ensure the information populating your radar is sufficiently varied:

- What non-fiction books have you read? Which subject areas?
- What magazines do you flick through on a regular basis? What are the articles you stop to peruse?
- What are you using to learn online: which podcasts, YouTube channels, blogs and websites do you subscribe to?
- Which TV shows do you always catch?
- What conferences and events do you attend each year? Are all the speakers and themes getting pretty familiar? Is it time to try another event less related to your core field?

 ## Human experiment

Delay your conclusions

As a former journalist, I was surprised to find a few years back that I had almost completely stopped reading daily newspapers. I'd concluded that to try to understand the world, reflection time is required before reaching the kind of instant conclusions journalists specialise in. Now, the most frequently published periodical I read on a regular basis is *The Economist*, which comes out weekly rather than daily. In truth, nearly all the important changes happening in our world take far longer than the 24-hour news cycle to shift. Reflective information means the creators have had time and space to give their argument some thought. Here are a few questions to help you find the sources that will help feed your curious questions:

- Where do you get your understanding of how the world is changing?

- How do you review trends in news and current affairs?
- Where do you go for longer-term information on science and technology?
- How do you integrate your knowledge of social, demographic and political movements?

Courageous questions

Challenging your own preconceptions takes humility. Disputing the preconceptions of others takes courage. In particular, it's vital to keep asking questions *after* success has been achieved. This helps you to avoid what the chess champion Garry Kasparov called 'being dipped in bronze'. What would have happened to famous corporate failures such as Kodak, Nokia, Xerox, Blockbuster, Yahoo, MySpace, Polaroid and Borders if they had developed a culture of persistent questions? Chances are they would have evolved instead of living on only as cautionary tales in business schools. Management philosopher Jules Goddard is a master at helping leaders spot what he calls 'common nonsense'. This is the received wisdom unthinkingly accepted by all, that *used* to be true but is no longer valid because the world has moved on. Courageous questions help to reverse the insidious gravitational pull of 'group think' – where it's easier to align with the status quo rather than suggest anything should change. Left unchecked, an unchallenging, question-free culture leads to bland 'me-too' products based on muddled 'me-too' thinking. Goddard puts it elegantly: 'Strategic solutions do not generalise. They are built on insights, not rules or principles. . . Every great business started life as the embodiment of a particularly powerful insight. Businesses decline as the production of new insights dries up.'[14] Goddard is urging us to see the truth: strategy (how to win in life, sport or business) *always* has a shelf life. The only way to move on is to continually question it.

In theory, asking questions should be easy. In practice, certainly in organisational settings, it's difficult. This is down to fear. Tammy

Erickson is a globally renown thought leader on the evolving nature of work. She confides: 'I'm often asked by leaders what's the one thing they could do to become more collaborative and innovative. . . to be a better, more influential person in the modern world. I always advise the most powerful, day-to-day practice is simply asking better questions.' She added: 'But, it's also one of the most difficult behavioural changes to make. Particularly for those who find themselves in a leadership position.'[15] Fear of looking stupid prevents those in power from asking questions. A boss who asks questions reveals he or she does not have all the answers. It's a display of audacious humility. It's anxiety of a different kind that prevents questions bubbling up from those without power. It would have taken guts for a lowly French corporal to question the defensive strategy of the Maginot Line so favoured by his generals. To become a curious questioner, from the top or the bottom, requires courage.

🧍 Human experiment

Elephant questions

What is the obvious question in your life, family or organisation that everybody is avoiding because the answer might be a little bit scary? This is the old management cliché of the 'elephant in the room'. How might a skilful question make it visible?

Question to solve problems

Pioneering creativity researcher Mihaly Csikszentmihalyi set out to discover how innovative thinkers solve problems. He recruited 31 art students and set them a challenge. His team invited each person into a room where there were two tables. One was piled high with a variety of random objects, including a bunch of grapes, a steel gear stick, a velvet hat, a brass horn, an antique book and a glass prism. Each student was asked to select some objects, arrange them on the second, empty, table and then draw the resulting 'still life'.

The test revealed two very different approaches to problem solving. One group of students – the 'Solvers' – efficiently selected a few items, quickly arranged them and then took great care to draw, shade and render their composition. The second group – the research team called them 'Searchers' – adopted what seemed an inefficient and chaotic style. They spent far longer simply examining the objects. They repeatedly changed their minds about which one to select, and how to arrange it. They spent a long time pondering their options. However, when they had settled on an arrangement, they finished their sketches quickly in just five to ten minutes.

The Solvers swiftly created a visual problem, and then spent their time and effort tackling it. The Searchers poured their energy into 'problem finding'. What's interesting is that, overall, the Searchers were judged to be far more creative. Six years later, Csikszentmihalyi tracked down his experimental subjects. Only a third had gone on to be well-known in the art world. By and large they were all Searchers.[16] The most creative people are those who put time aside to ask the right question.[17] Albert Einstein argued if he had only an hour to save the world, he would spend the first 55 minutes clarifying the problem and only 5 minutes finding the solution.

The habit of clearly stating a problem and asking targeted questions to shine a light on the issue is simple, but enormously powerful. Serial entrepreneur Sean Sheppard of GrowthX Academy, who works with me to help corporate innovation teams experience the business culture of Silicon Valley and San Francisco, agrees. He told me: 'Entrepreneurs do not need a product – they need a problem. Especially a problem they can solve well.'[18] In other words, the priority of an entrepreneur isn't selling a product, but finding the perfect 'product–market fit', where the customer's need is the most pressing. They get there with a *lot* of questions.

Counterintuitively, being creative is easier when you not only have a problem, but you have to solve it within certain criteria. Total freedom in the form of a blank sheet of paper kills creativity. In advertising they call this the 'freedom of the tight brief'. Pablo Picasso mastered painting by the time he was 15 years old. He then instinctively created his own restrictions – the most famous being when he painted exclusively in blue for an entire four-year period. Many feel these paintings were his best work. Sometimes the best way to create a useful box is to ask a crystal-clear question that clearly delineates the 'edges' of the problem.

Pointed questions have a history of unleashing huge value in big business too. Sakichi Toyoda, one of the fathers of the Japanese industrial revolution, developed the '5 Whys' technique in the 1930s. He was an industrialist, inventor and founder of Toyota Industries. His method became popular in the 1970s, and Toyota still uses it to solve problems today. The approach is to clearly describe the problem in the form of a 'problem statement'. Then ask 'Why?' again and again – up to five times.

 Human experiment

The 5 'Whys'

Try Toyoda's method. It's pretty straightforward. First write a problem statement that describes an issue you're interested in solving or improving. Then ask yourself why this is the case. After each answer, dig a little deeper, repeating the same 'Why?' question to the answer you just generated. This burrows further into the roots of the problem that caused the issue to come about in the first place.[19]

Question to innovate

In 2010, a youthful computer programmer Kevin Systrom launched his tech business with an interesting question. He asked: 'How can I create a popular *location-sharing* app?'[20] The result – called Burbn – let you register at a city location, make plans for future 'check-ins', earn points for hanging out with friends and post pictures. It didn't take off. A little disappointed, but undeterred, he and his co-founder Mike Krieger investigated what their users were doing. They were surprised to find people were ignoring most of Burbn's many features. But they were sharing photos. A lot of them.

This insight led to a radical change in the question the young entrepreneurs were asking. It became: 'How can we create a simple *photo-sharing* app?' Systrom explained: 'It was really difficult to decide to start from scratch, but we went out on a limb, and basically cut everything in the Burbn app except for its photo, comment, and like capabilities'[21] After days of exhausting coding, the pair launched the app again just after midnight. They thought they'd get some sleep, as they were certain it would take hours for anyone to discover it online. However, within minutes, downloads began pouring in from all corners of the globe. They had 10,000 in a few hours. Systrom said: 'At the end of the day, it kept growing so much I thought, "Are we counting wrong?"' He wasn't.

Answering the right question triggered an explosion in the value of their idea. In January 2012, the company had 15 million registered users. By March, that number jumped to 27 million. The business was acquired by Facebook for a staggering one billion dollars – a valuation that came about just two years after Systrom began working on the idea. Along the way, the app's name had changed. To convey its simplicity, the founders settled on a title that combined 'instant' and 'telegram'. Instagram now has more than a billion users.[22]

John C. Maxwell, the author of *Good Leaders Ask Great Questions,* concludes: 'If you want to make discoveries, if you want to disrupt the status quo, if you want to make progress and find new ways of thinking and doing, you need to ask questions. Questions are the first link in the chain of discovery and innovation.'[23] Crucially, Systrom and Krieger didn't just ask one question. They continued after their initial product failed. This determination and curiosity allowed them to change direction. This manoeuvre is so important in the iconic success stories of Silicon Valley that it's got its own verb: to 'pivot'. In his book *The Lean Startup*, Eric Ries defines a pivot as a: 'structured course correction designed to test a new fundamental hypothesis about the product, strategy, and engine of growth'. This isn't just useful in business. All of our lives are a series of proved or disproved hypotheses, followed by a smart pivot towards a new direction.

Ask better questions

Hierarchy can be a barrier to asking questions in groups, but it is not the only obstacle. Another is an absence of such questions in the rituals of a team, business – or family for that matter. The result is sheer lack of practice. Asking questions is a habit that takes conscious effort. Hal Gregersen, of the MIT Sloan School of Management, notes: 'Great innovators have always known that the key to unlocking a better answer is a better question – one that challenges deeply held assumptions. Yet, most people don't do that, even when brainstorming, because it doesn't come naturally. As a result, they tend to feel stuck in their search for fresh ideas.'[24]

So, what is a great question? Curious questions are not those asked by prosecution lawyers on TV in a fictional courtroom: 'Ahem, can the defendant confirm if he was standing outside The Rose & Crown pub at 10.17 on the night in question wearing a pair of blue trousers and a red jumper?' This is a 'closed' question. It can only be answered with 'yes' or 'no'. Closed questions are great for confirming what you think you already know. However, this is not pure curiosity – it's interrogation. Of course, closed questions are effective in some circumstances, such as:

● Testing understanding: 'So, if I get this qualification, will I get a raise?'

● Clarifying a decision: 'Now we know the facts, are we all agreed this is the right course of action?'

● Frame setting: 'Are you happy with the service from your bank?'[25]

Open questions, on the other hand, are used to explore. Like any skill, this takes a little practice. I learned the crucial difference between open and closed questions as a young journalist way back in the 1990s. But, even after all these years, I still sometimes forget and revert to closed questions when open questions would be far more effective.

The difference between a good open question and a great open question can be quite subtle. Consider the following:

Version 1: 'How are we going to tackle Project Unicorn before the end of the year?'

Or:

Version 2: 'How *might we* tackle Project Unicorn before the end of the year?'

The first is a good open question, but the second is a great one. Why? By introducing the intriguing word 'might', it invites a more creative response.

The global design firm IDEO breaks down 'How might we?' questions like this into three component parts:

* *How* indicates the possibility of answering the problem; it implies solutions exist.
* *Might* suggests there's more than one way to solve the problem.
* *We* infers a collaborative team approach to finding the answer.[26]

You can go even further and make your open questions truly intriguing. A great question awakens your mind, rather than putting it to sleep. A standard question to think about innovation might be: 'Who has an idea for improving our product?' But, by adding an exciting note of emotional tension and humour, you can unlock better results. Here's the same query with a twist: 'If we hosted a forum called "How Our Products & Services Suck", what topics would be on the main stage?'[27]

Human experiment

Ask questions with a twist

Take one of the questions you wrote earlier in this chapter and try to add a dash of spice. To inspire you, here are some more examples of interestingly provocative questions:

1 You've just written a tell-all book about this company: which secrets does it reveal?

2 If you could only work on one project for a year to transform the business, what would it be and why?

3 What is the shortest path to the customer? How could we get there in six months?

4 What suffers more breakdowns: our products, our processes, or our people? How could we fix this?

5 Which parts of your job would you like to kill or eliminate?[28]

Try it for yourself. What's the most piquant question you could ask?

Human experiment

Don't say a word

Here's a top tip: when you have posed your question, *stop*. Leave a pause and don't say another word until the person speaks. Stay quiet, even if it feels a little uncomfortable. The better your query, the longer it often takes for people to process and to respond. We live in a world where quiet pauses are often filled to avoid embarrassment. When exploring the minds of other people, silence is golden.

Human experiment

De-bugging a problem

This penultimate experiment combines the insights above. It also gets a few collaborators involved in a curious-questioning conversation.

State the problem: Identify a problem, a 'bug' to be fixed. Choose an issue that's not working as well as it should be. It could be a process, a product or a service. It could be triggered by something that recently went very wrong, or an observation from a colleague or customer. It might even be something in your home life. Some examples might be: a product that has stopped selling well, a recurring mistake in the production process causing delays and costs or miscommunication between teams, or a meeting format that never works.

Create an inquiry group: Gather together a small group of like-minded people who will be able to live with the inherent challenge of curious questions. Nominate someone as the facilitator.

First, ask simple questions about *now*: This discussion is to clarify the issue. In his study of what he calls 'Question Bursts', Hal Gregerson advises simple questions that are open rather than closed, short rather than long, simple rather than complex. These are descriptive questions to illuminate the issue: 'What's working? What's not working? Why? How long has this been happening? When did it start?'

Then, ask complex questions about how things might be in the future: When you feel you have a good understanding of the issue, move on to more speculative, forward-facing questions. These will lead to creative thinking and new ideas: 'Why do we do it this way? How might we do this differently? What if we tried this? Why not?'

At a college commencement ceremony, Steve Jobs once famously advised the gathered students to: 'Stay hungry. Stay Foolish.' I'd add one more: 'Stay Curious.' The best way to do that is to incessantly unearth exciting problems and then pepper them with intriguing questions. As we sashayed through the two Dance Steps of Consciousness and Curiosity, you'll hopefully have assembled plenty of interesting thoughts, ideas and, of course, questions. We now proceed to the third 'C'. There, you'll exploit all this raw material to fire the human superpower of Creativity.

A quick reminder. . .

- Questions allow you to sustain curiosity and to think forward, into the future.

- AI is good at interrogating available data; this allows humans to address the next question.

- Use critical questions to burst the AI-enabled filter bubble, to challenge your in-built human confirmation bias.

- A lack of questions leads to untested decisions and irrelevance.

- To challenge your own preconceptions takes humility; to challenge others' takes courage.

- Kickstart creative thinking by searching for exciting problems.

- To innovate, continue to ask questions after failure – and after success.

- Asking questions is a habit that takes conscious effort.

- Curious questions are open, intriguing and followed by silence (to hear the answer).

Human experiment: Start now. . .

Ask a killer question

The Instagram co-founders stumbled on what the former chief technology officer at Hewlett-Packard, Phil McKinney, calls a 'killer question'. He gathered hundreds of note cards on battle-tested entrepreneurial questions that unlock value. Here is a list of eight killer questions to help you look with fresh eyes. Take a product or service you currently offer, or would like to offer. Take some time to brainstorm some different answers, and see where it leads you:

- Who uses my product in ways I never anticipated?
- What are my unshakeable beliefs about what my customers want?
- What are the rules and assumptions my industry operates under?
- What if the opposite were true?
- What will be the buying criteria used by my customers in five years?
- What could I use in a new way?
- What could I connect in a new way?
- What could I change, in terms of design or performance?[29]

CREATIVITY

The process of having original ideas that have value

The capacity to imagine a world that does not yet exist, but might

Luck is a skill

How to acquire the creative habit to make inspiration more likely

> 'Inspiration is for amateurs – the rest of us just show up and get to work.'
>
> Chuck Close, painter[1]

Superpower: **Creativity**

Dance Step: **ENERGISE**

Igniting questions:
- How do I begin a creative process?
- What makes my ideas 'happen'?
- How do I get myself unstuck?[2]

4Cs value: **A creative habit**

Twyla Tharp is someone who's spent a lifetime paying the bills with her creative potential. She's a legend on the New York City dance scene. For decades, she's choreographed some of the best modern dance routines, as well as Broadway musicals. Despite her impressive track record, when Tharp wins a commission, she doesn't know if it will be a hit or a flop. So, Tharp uses her insight into how our minds work to avoid paralysing uncertainty. She knows, when you ask your brain a clear-cut question, it quietly gets to work on your behalf.

To get her creative juices flowing, she begins in a surprisingly humble way: by selecting a suitably sized cardboard box. Your unconscious brain is an engine that requires fuel. Tharp gathers raw material for her project by simply throwing everything she finds that might provide a spark of inspiration into the box. Nothing is wasted: videos, books, art, torn magazine articles and news clippings are all slung together. From experience, Tharp knows she'll need many 'a-ha' moments to choreograph a feature-length dance routine. The box is a symbolic, and deeply practical, act. It transforms creative luck into an actionable day-to-day habit.

Over a long career, Tharp has realised creativity is not a gift from the gods, but rather a product of preparation and effort. She writes: 'The way I figure it, my work habits are applicable to everyone. . . I'm a stickler about preparation. My daily routines are transactional, everything that happens in my day is a transaction between the external world and my internal world, everything is raw material, everything is relevant.'[3]

Tharp's philosophy is backed up by the findings of the Hungarian-American psychologist Mihaly Csikszentmihalyi. He concluded that if you want to be more inventive, don't focus on being creative. Instead, put your efforts into the groundwork that *precedes* an idea. He notes, if you lay these foundations then: 'most of the job is done. . . it's inevitable that one's creative energies will start to flow more freely'.[4]

This chapter is about building your own idiosyncratic, but effective, work practices: a creative habit. These habits – combined with the cognitive fuel you gathered in Curiosity – will transform the chance arrival of ideas into a skill you can practise every day. Twyla Tharp's creative rituals emerged from deep experience, trial and error and the pressure of having to produce big ideas on demand over decades. Here, you'll find scientific research and tried-and-tested practices to get you there much faster.

How do I begin?

Waste nothing

I know it's geeky, but I find Tharp's carboard box inspiring. The box democratises creativity because anyone can find a box, anyone can sling items into it. Think about the problems you identified in the QUESTION Dance Step. How might you build your own storehouse of potential ideas to address this? It doesn't have to be a physical box. If you're old school, like Tharp (her habits were formed in a pre-digital age), you might just as usefully designate a file, a drawer or a cupboard. Phil Tippett is an animator and monster-maker for movies such as *Jurassic Park* and *Star Wars*. He has an entire studio filled with what he calls 'junk and random stuff'. This is stimulating paraphernalia he's found at the beach, in second-hand stores, even objects his children have made. He uses them all as tangible inspiration for the fantastic creatures that populate our favourite films. He organises his 'pre-idea' thinking into a series of scrap books he calls 'Idea Generators'. Each page represents a thought or a feeling. When he's in need of inspiration, he flicks through the books until he thinks: 'I've got it!'[5] His books are a visual representation of what's going on in his brain. They allow him to take disparate inputs, break them apart and then put them back together in a different form.

The same approach works online just as well. My wife Sophie uses Pinterest 'boards' (pages in which you can pin digital pictures) to build options for our family holidays. I wrote this book aided by the note-taking and archiving app, Evernote. Every time I see something interesting, I add to Evernote. I store smartphone pictures, written and audio notes, articles and webpages for the different projects I'm working on. Nothing is wasted: whatever I'm reading, hearing, or seeing can be instantly squirrelled away for future reference (and magically synched across all my devices). Not all of it will be useful. Not all of it needs to be. It's surprising what pops into your head when you review what you've collected. It's like brainstorming with a past version of yourself. The technique works just as well after a creative process has got underway. The visionary Danish architect Bjarke Ingels describes the process used by his team when conceiving a new building: 'We try to material-ise as many aspects of the design process as possible. We pin up things on huge boards. Because if you have tons of material to work with, then you can really give the imagination something to build with.'[6]

 Human experiment

Bury your treasure

What's your most practical version of Tharp's cardboard box? Set it up. Choose the place where you'll bury your creative plunder.

The creative habit

Returning to a creative project is easier than starting one. However, you still have mental barriers to overcome. Distraction, procrastina-tion, fear of failure and the little voice warning of your presumption ('Who am I to try this and what will people think?') take their toll. You need to find a way to begin over and over again. Twyla Thwarp kicks off every day by taking a taxi to her local gym for a two-hour workout. She says that when she sits in the back of the yellow New York cab, she's taken the decision to begin her creative process for the day. She has started, whether she likes it or not. For her, this removes the anxiety. She elaborates: 'First steps are hard.' To help, she relies on: '. . . automatic, but decisive, patterns of behaviour at the beginning of the creative process, when you are most at peril of turning back, chickening out, giving up, or going the wrong way'.

For Tharp, turning something into a ritual eliminates the question, 'Why am I doing this?'.

Rituals don't just break the ice and allow you to get started each day, they also conserve your creative energy. Albert Einstein often wore the same old sweater and baggy trousers. Similarly, the Facebook founder Mark Zuckerberg constantly wears the same type of grey T-shirt to work. I'm not sure I agree with the solution, but I do understand the logic: ensure your energy is routed to where it has the most value – your creative thinking.

Human habit

Engrave your own creative rituals

My sacraments on a writing day are alarm at 6am, ten minutes of meditation, poached egg on toast, an all-important frothy Nespresso coffee, made in my kitchen and then carried and plonked on my desk next to my computer monitor. Open the Word document, start writing. Try to avoid second guessing if it's the right place in the document, or the right thing to say. Just get on with it. What rituals can you develop to save time, to defeat procrastination and to ease the way into creative action?

What makes ideas happen?

Pay attention to the unexpected

The management guru Peter Drucker defined the innovative person as someone who pays attention to whatever is unexpected, unusual or simply unfamiliar. Take the American engineer Percy Spencer. In 1945, he was testing the powerful vacuum tubes inside radars. Spencer was a man who liked a convenient snack, so he always kept a chocolate-and-peanut-butter treat with him. When he hungrily reached inside his pocket, he found a gooey mess. His peanut-butter candy bar had melted, but he couldn't find an answer to a puzzling question: why? Intrigued, he bought a bag of popcorn and held it up to the same machine he'd been standing by. The popcorn popped. Percy was excited about this bizarre phenomenon, but his workmates didn't feel the same way. The next morning, to better engage their attention, he brought an egg into work and placed it on the top of the machine. As his colleagues watched doubtfully, the egg overheated and exploded. As well as literally causing his workmates to have 'egg on their faces', Percy had accidentally stumbled on a way to cook food in seconds. Later, he and his employer, Raytheon, patented the 'Radarange'. It weighed 340 kilograms, and stood just under 2 metres tall. It was the world's very first microwave oven.[7]

Simply noticing the unusual is how many ideas happen. Famously, the Scottish microbiologist Alexander Fleming discovered penicillin when it grew on the petri dishes he'd accidentally left out on his work bench. We should remember, Fleming's mind was *prepared* by decades of studying bacteria. This was what made him able to stop and see this unexpected phenomenon for what it was. Similarly, if George de Mestral hadn't had the primed mind of an electrical engineer, he might have missed his big moment. Returning home after a walk in the Swiss Alps, he noticed his dog was covered with prickly seed pods. His microscope revealed that each of the burr's sharp spines had a tiny hook. This insight led to him to patent a hook-and-loop clothes fastener called Velcro that turned de Mestral into a millionaire.[8]

The American poet Ralph Waldo Emerson once said: 'People only see what they are prepared to see.'[9] Psychologists agree. They believe that when you're baffled by a problem, you're left with unresolved thought threads in your subconscious mind called 'failure indices'. Your mind is looking for a solution, even when you're not consciously thinking about the problem. This means stumbling on an answer is not luck – it's the jigsaw pieces clicking into place. As the French biologist Louis Pasteur remarked: 'In the field of observation, chance favours only the prepared mind.'[10]

> # 🧍 Human experiment
>
> ## Make the most of your 'luck'
>
> Next time you see the unexpected, unusual or simply unfamiliar, take care to investigate and reframe what you're seeing with the three questions employed by Fleming, Spencer and de Mestral:
>
> - *Why* is that happening?
> - *How* does that work?
> - Could what's taking place work in a *different context*?
>
> It's in these moments of creative awareness and questioning that we have our best ideas.

Switch off the autopilot

Much of life is spent on autopilot. We drive to work, catch the bus, eat our meals without thinking. Our attention is elsewhere. Harvard's Ellen Langer studies the opposite mental state: mindfulness (a state we've already encountered in the FOCUS Dance Step).[11] This is a condition of active observation, of fully inhabiting the moment you are living in. Langer makes an explicit link between this state of focused awareness and seeing the world in a more creative way: 'Mindfulness is simply the process of noticing new things. . . to be a true artist is to be mindful', she says. One of the leading scientific experts on creativity, Keith Sawyer, agrees: 'For greater creativity, you have to stop living on autopilot and start paying attention.'[12,13]

The key to everyday creativity is to tune your mental radar to 'ping' when you perceive the unusual and interesting. This state of fertile awareness is beautifully described by the Hungarian biochemist Albert Szent-Györgyi, who was the first to isolate vitamin C. He counselled: 'Discovery is seeing what everybody else has seen, and thinking what nobody else has thought.' You can take it a step further, and become aware of what your brain is doing in these moments. This allows you to match the right mode of attention to the right occasion. The legendary creative research psychologist Mihaly Csikszentmihalyi calls this your ability to 'control attention'.[14]

To help you practise this habit, here are the four defining metaphors I use to identify important cognitive modes:

1 **The Lighthouse:** This is when you're searching for inspiration. Like a lighthouse, you're illuminating the dark looking for new people, data, questions, problems, sights, sounds and smells. This is the fuel for your creative endeavours. The same mode you were using during the LEARN Dance Step.

2 **The Laser:** This is when you're focusing your attention in a distracted world. Like a laser, the light beam of your attention is narrow and intense – converging on a specific question or work project. This is what I described in the FOCUS Dance Step.

3 **The Kite:** This is when you're day-dreaming. Like a kite, your mind is carried by the breeze of your thoughts and the world around you. This is the default mode of the human brain. Uncontrolled, it can be toxic. If harnessed, it is an indispensable component of human creativity. It's 'prime time' for a-ha moments.

4 **The Observer:** This is when you're most aware of *how* you're thinking. Like an observer, you step back and dispassionately monitor your own thoughts. This mindful self-awareness is sometimes called metacognition or 'thinking about thinking'. It allows you to develop the ability to choose the thinking state you need at any particular moment.

 Human experiment

Thinking about thinking

Throughout the day, whether you're shopping, browsing the Internet, watching the news, or cooking some food, ask yourself which of these states you're in. For example, when watching a Netflix documentary, you might be in Lighthouse mode. When writing a report, you'll switch to the Laser. It's particularly interesting to note when your mind becomes the Kite, and what comes from this. You need *all* these different cognitive settings to unleash your creative potential. When you become adept with this, you'll be able to control them – and even mix them together. Neuroscience shows us that creative people aren't simply characterised by any one of these states alone – they begin to intuitively mix states that don't seem to fit together: 'open attention with a focused drive, mindfulness with day-dreaming, intuition with rationality'.[15]

Don't just think, feel

Doug Dietz, a senior engineer working for General Electric, was stumped.[16] His team were wrestling with the design of a multi-million-dollar magnetic resonance imaging (MRI) machine. An MRI machine is an enormous medical device that doctors and nurses use to peer inside your body. You have to be wheeled into a small cylinder-shaped tunnel in the front of the machine. It's important you then lie still in the cramped space. As the machine works it makes loud banging and grinding noises. Even for adults, this feels weird and intimidating. Doug and his team were designing an MRI machine that small children would have to use. The kids needed to feel confident enough to lie still to allow doctors to take clear images. This was a big challenge. The children, not surprisingly, didn't like the cramped space, or the scary noises, which meant the images were ruined. The procedure had to be repeated, throwing out the hospital schedule for the machine's precious working hours. In desperation, doctors were routinely sedating children to allow them to take the MRI scan.

Looking for a breakthrough, Doug attended a course on design thinking at Stanford University. He found that the instructors advised adopting the uniquely human skill of empathising – the ability to understand and share the feelings of another. Their research showed it was nearly always the first step to solving human problems. Enlightened designers 'feel' their way into creativity by metaphorically 'walking a mile in the shoes' of the product user. Using the language of Zen Buddhism, designers assume a humble 'beginner's mind' to experience the feel of a product from another's perspective. This can only be achieved through close observation. It allows you to leap beyond intellectual questions such as: 'Who is our ideal customer?' and 'Why will she want our product?' to deeper questions: 'What makes her happy, or frustrated?', 'What does she truly care about?' and 'What benefit does she experience?'.

As an engineer, Doug's mind would have normally tended towards a technical solution. However, using empathy took Dietz on a different path. He observed children playing in a day care centre and talked to experts in paediatric medicine. He even visited the curators of a children's museum. The result was effective, low-cost and unusual. Instead of spending millions trying to make the machine quieter or quicker, his team just painted it. The cheerful design on the scary exterior made it look like a pirate ship. This was augmented with a dash of imagination: MRI nurses were given a script in which they whispered to the kids that they were going on an adventure. They'd need to lie still to avoid pirates and find the treasure. Using the concept of play, this low-cost, low-fi solution turned an unpleasant procedure into a game. As a result, the number of sedations dropped, machine usage went up and patient satisfaction scores rose by 90 per cent. One little girl even asked her mum if she could go again.

Human experiment

Walk a mile in someone else's shoes

How can you walk a mile in the shoes of the people whose problem you are trying to solve? How can you bring a beginner's mind to the way your solutions are experienced by users? Who can you observe, or talk to, to feel, rather than just think?

Human empathisers-in-chief

AI is skilled at interpreting human behaviour through online purchases, clicks and likes. The now unexceptional sight of stressed-out parents outsourcing toddler diversion to an iPad is the precursor to algorithms holding our hand from cradle to grave. AI-enabled robots are now keeping us company in the physical world. Hertfordshire University's Dr Joe Saunders works in the emerging industry to provide 'caring' robots for the increasing number of older people. His robot is about four feet tall, called Pepper, and will sing, talk and even dance for pensioners. It's unsurprising that the race to make robot custodians appear empathetic has begun. However, it's important to remember AI empathy is fake. AI is a digital version of the human psychopath. Psychopaths are paradoxically good at reading and manipulating emotions, but have zero empathy. They remain unmoved inside. AI's the same.[17] Dr Saunders admits: 'The robot can appear in many ways to be empathic and helpful. And, it could well be [old people] could form a relationship with an empathic robot. But, of course, the robot doesn't form any relationship with them. Because it's just a machine.'[18]

I anticipate that, even though the caring professions will be transformed by robots, humans will remain the authentic empathisers-in-chief. This means there are tangible benefits for those who can become more aware and attuned to what other people are saying, doing and feeling. As well as enhancing the ability to solve problems, empathy is a core component of emotional intelligence – the wider ability to use emotional information to guide thinking and behaviour.[19] Research shows that this is a powerful predictor of success in many professions and roles. A study, conducted by the Center for Creative Leadership, of 6,731 leaders from 38 countries showed their level of empathy was positively related to job performance. The survey also revealed top business leaders see more empathetic junior managers as star performers. Psychologist Daniel Goleman, who coined the phrase 'emotional intelligence', points out that a person without it is 'emotionally tone deaf'.

The good news, as with curiosity and creativity, is that it's possible to consciously develop empathy. The first step is to copy successful mentors, counsellors and psychotherapists and become a good listener. This means focusing entirely on the content, and emotional resonance, of what you're hearing. Top executive coaches train themselves to double check the quality of their listening by occasionally rephrasing back to the speaker what they said. This 'playback' is an astonishingly simple but powerful technique. Take conflict resolution. It's been shown in employer–employee disputes that if both sides repeated what the other side had just said before speaking themselves, conflicts were resolved 50 per cent faster.[20]

Most humans are hard-wired to be empathetic but, let's face it, circumstances can get in the way. So, if you're struggling to be caring 24/7, join the club. You only need to spend five minutes scrolling through the comically tribal and unempathetic human interactions on Twitter discussing Brexit and Donald Trump (at least those that are not AI-enabled bots), to at least consider the possibility that former president, Barack Obama, was right when he identified a global 'empathy deficit'.[21] It's worth being persistent, even in circumstances when you're having to force empathy. Police negotiators are trained to act with empathy towards hostage takers to establish rapport even when they secretly despise the perpetrator. However, after a couple of hours of faking it, many negotiators report they start to feel authentic empathy towards the culprit. It seems that acting like you care can lead to the real thing.[22]

 ## Human habit

Become an X-Ray Listener[23]

This means picking up on non-verbal cues in the person's eyes, small facial expressions, body language; hearing what's going unsaid. You can practise this every time you have a conversation. I know it sounds weird, but you might also try it out by spending 10 minutes watching the TV with the volume down, to guess how you think the characters are transmitting their emotions and what those emotions are.

How do I get unstuck?

I've been lucky enough to design and facilitate leadership programmes in a variety of stimulating places. We've browsed thriving food markets, roamed innovation museums in San Francisco, toured science, design and history museums in London, visited Facebook and other tech companies in Silicon Valley, worked with charities supporting the entrepreneurial ventures of ethnic minorities in tough neighbourhoods, staged silent walks on windswept beaches, ambled through downtown Shanghai, inspected the *MasterChef* studios in Paris, gazed skyward at the space observatory in Los Angeles, canoed the currents of the Vienne river in central France, strolled above the teeming streets of New York City on the High Line walk, resided in the hallowed halls of Cambridge and Oxford Universities, watched whales off the coast of Tenerife and climbed the Alps above the village of Chamonix. These experiences weren't just to earn frequent flyer miles and have fun. Although we did, and my wife often casts doubts on labelling some of my trips as 'work'. The shift in location was key to the learning experience. Research shows that your environment – what you see, hear and observe – has a huge impact on the way you think, and especially your ability to cogitate creatively.

A single day in a new place can alter your brain. Living in a different location has even greater benefits. People who spend some of their life living outside the country of their birth score higher on tests for creative thinking. A study of fashion houses over 21 seasons found that the most creatively successful firms had directors who'd immersed themselves in work abroad.[24,25,26] The late fashion icon Karl Lagerfeld was a good example: he was born in Germany to a Swedish father and shuttled between Italy and France for work. Adam Grant, author of *Originals: How Non-Conformists Move the World*, testifies that experiencing fresh places has startling effects: 'Cultures come with new norms and values and ways of looking at things. . . any time you have a problem, you have an extra set of resources at your disposal.'[27]

Human habit

Change the scenery

You might not have the opportunity to live in another country, but most of us can visit another city, take a different route to work and choose to venture outside an enclosed holiday resort. For even less, you can also travel to distant times and places through museums, and experience unfamiliar environments in novels, plays and feature films. Sending work teams away to an art gallery (or a pub) was a trick I witnessed countless times in my research on creative leadership in advertising and design firms. Seeking novel new places is a powerful habit to refill your energy banks.

Human habit

Do things differently

You can apply this idea of novelty to the most mundane tasks possible. Doing something as simple as changing aspects of your daily routine could lead to a creative insight. Psychologist Dr Simone Ritter from Radboud University, Nijmegen, has found that even changing the way you make your usual sandwich can help boost levels of creativity.[28]

How can sleep help?

We humans have long suspected something is going on when we close our eyes to sleep. It's a hot topic for psychological and neurological research. We do know that exceptionally creative people sleep more than the average person. All of us are over a third more creative after a good nap.[29] This is because when you're slumbering, your brain is making sense of what you've seen during the day. In the first part of sleep – called non-REM (rapid eye movement) sleep – your brain replays and consolidates memories. It represents specific details with general symbols. For example, if you go to a birthday party your brain might not remember every single detail but you'll later know to link balloons, cake and presents to the concept of a birthday.

When you drop into deeper, full-REM sleep your neurons start firing off like they're staging their own party. This is where nocturnal creativity occurs. At this moment your brain is in a particularly flexible state. It makes connections more easily *between* neurons and disparate ideas and facts. Penny Lewis from Cardiff University studies the impact of both REM and non-REM sleep on creativity. She recommends: 'The obvious implication is that if you're working on a difficult problem, allow yourself enough nights of sleep.' She adds: 'Particularly if you're trying to work on something that requires thinking outside the box, maybe don't do it in too much of a rush.'[30]

There's overwhelming anecdotal evidence to support this advice. The horror writer Stephen King woke in a cold sweat on a flight from New York to London. He'd been having a nightmare about a famous novelist who was captured and held hostage by a psychotic fan. He jotted the idea down on an airline cocktail napkin. That snippet of an idea would go on to be *Misery*, one of his most successful novels.[31] Paul McCartney says the melody for a sorrowful song came to him in a dream. When he woke he quickly found the chords on the piano by his bed and wrote the beautiful melody that makes 'Yesterday' so special.[32] The surrealist painter Salvador Dalí became adept at capturing his fantastic fantasies by deliberately waking himself up with a key held over a metal plate. The key would fall from his grasp as he slipped from consciousness and startle him. The inventor Thomas Edison achieved the same result by napping with steel balls grasped in his hands that would clatter to the ground when he dropped off. Your unconscious mind is hugely creative, but uncontrollable. Think of it like a powerful but wilful elephant. The moment just after you wake is a golden opportunity. This is when your conscious mind can saddle the elephant for just a moment, and nudge it to reveal your amazing ideas.

Human experiment

Sleep on it

When you're stuck with a problem, try to make time to sleep on it. In particular, pay special attention to the moments just after you wake up. This hypnopompic state is particularly fertile for loose associations colliding in your thoughts.[33] Try to jot down what transpires. It helps to keep a notepad by your bed, as this can come in handy if you wake in the middle of the night with an interesting thought.[34]

Human experiment

Consult the committee of sleep

Just dropping off to sleep will help. However, you can also offer your sleeping brain an obliging hint. Just before bedtime, remind yourself of the problem you want to solve. A 1993 Harvard study found that when people asked themselves a question before bed, half of the participants dreamed about the issue, and a quarter found a solution in their dreams. To assist your unconscious, read something inspiring at night. Fiction or nonfiction is fine – anything that inspires your mind and suggests new information to prime the REM-sleep connections. As the American novelist John Steinbeck wrote: 'It is a common experience that a problem difficult at night is resolved in the morning after the committee of sleep has worked on it.'

Just do it!

It's difficult to put your hand up with a new idea. This is especially true when you're in the company of people who you consider to be smarter, more accomplished or more experienced. The comedian Eric Idle felt distinctly underqualified when he joined the British comedy troupe Monty Python in the late 1960s. Idle preferred to write alone at his own pace, while the other Pythons favoured working in small teams. They all came together to vote which sketches got into the iconic TV show. Idle's solo habits meant he only had one vote. He admitted this was difficult: 'You had to convince five others. And they were not the most unegotistical of writers, either.' He persevered, drawing strength from his musical hero, the Beatles guitarist George Harrison. Like Idle, Harrison also lived in the shadow of others. His fellow band members, Lennon and McCartney, composed the majority of the group's hits. It's inspiring that even though Harrison was not considered to be the most talented Beatle, he wrote 'Here Comes the Sun' – one of the band's best songs.[35]

It's worth remembering that most great ideas, when first suggested, are laughed out of the room. To believe in yourself, it helps to keep a mental list in the back of your mind of the smart people who were turned down flat. Audiences didn't know what to make of Beethoven's Symphony No. Five, and yet it is part of a central repertoire now. During his lifetime, van Gogh could barely sell his paintings; he had to trade them for food or painting materials, but now they go for millions.[36] Steve Jobs and Steve Wozniak started Apple alone only because others thought it was a disaster in the making. They desperately offered equity stakes in the new company to the directors at the games company Atari (where Jobs had been working), Hewlett-Packard (where Wozniak worked as an engineer) and even the owner of a manufacturing company who was supplying parts for their first circuit boards.[37] All declined. No doubt these nay-sayers regretted their decision when Apple became the first business to be valued at one trillion dollars. J.K. Rowling's *Harry Potter* series was turned down by no less than 12 experienced UK publishers.[38] The rejection letters included criticism of the story being too long, and that the series would turn off 'ordinary' readers because it was set in an exclusive boarding school. Trying to guess Rowling's net worth from the Potter franchise has now itself become a small online cottage industry, but the general consensus is that it made her the first ever billion-dollar author.

If you really believe in an idea, you have to risk potential rejection and ridicule. Trust your talent and give it a go. For most of us the result won't be Apple or *Harry Potter*. More often, persistence and courage lead to smaller, but still important, personal creative triumphs. For example, if Eric Idle had not trusted his own instincts, he would not have suggested concluding the 1979 film *Life of Brian* with a musical number. Let's pay a small thanks that he did. It led to him penning the wonderfully philosophical and hilarious hit song '(Always look on the. . .) Bright Side of Life' – not only a comedy classic, but also the UK's most selected funeral song.

Creative acts are easy to postpone. You don't quite know where they will take you, or, more importantly, if they will work. It requires guts to leap into the unknown. 'Very few writers really know what they are doing until they've done it', admits the American novelist Anne Lamott.[39] Trusting your process allows you to just start. The first draft, version, summary, step – whatever is your equivalent – is *always* the most difficult. This chapter, for example, took many forms before it settled into the version you are currently reading. To get going you just need to dump words on a page and hope for the best. This is painful, as inevitably first efforts are not quite right. It instantly provokes fears of exposing your incompetence and vulnerability.

The key is to lower the pressure on yourself at this moment of embarkation. I always remind myself, however bad this first draft is, that no one will see it until I'm ready to share. In his memoir *On Writing*, horror novelist Stephen King calls this painful beginning 'pantsing' because you're flying by the seat of your pants.[40] If you can bring yourself to assemble your thoughts in the most rudimentary way, to live with the crappy first draft, things usually improve from there. Playwright and poet Julia Cameron, author of

The Artist's Way, writes every morning without fail. These 'morning pages' are unplanned – three pages of writing about anything. 'As I wrote those pages', she noted, 'new ideas began to walk in'.[41]

Whatever you want to create, you need to *start*. The shoddy first effort at least clarifies what works and what doesn't. The second try, by comparison, is a marked improvement. You can then worry about elegance and fine-tuning in the third version and beyond. Whether it's writing a difficult essay, blocking out a dance routine, building a working model, or initiating a new project, breaking the ice of insecurity and fear is vital. As the Nobel Laureate novelist William Faulkner advised: 'You cannot swim for new horizons until you have courage to lose sight of the shore.'

We began with an inspiring quote from the celebrated painter and photographer, Chuck Close. He added: '. . . process, in a sense, is liberating. . . you don't have to reinvent the wheel every day. . . at least for a certain period of time you can just work. If you hang in there, you will get somewhere.'[42] In this chapter we focused on the groundwork required to energise illuminating insights. In the second Dance Step in Creativity we'll explore how you can sustain inspired originality over the long term.

A quick reminder. . .

- Creativity is not a gift from the gods, it's a product of preparation and effort.
- Don't focus on being creative, focus on the groundwork that *precedes* an idea.
- Creative habits will transform the chance arrival of ideas into a skill you can practise every day.
- To begin. . .
  - Build a stimulating treasure trove in a physical space or online.
  - Don't fear the crappy first draft – trust your talent and simply begin.

▶

- To have more ideas. . .
  - Pay close attention to the unexpected and unusual.
  - Switch off the autopilot and become aware of your thinking state (Lighthouse, Laser, Kite or Observer).
  - Develop empathy through X-Ray Listening and observation of emotion.
- To get 'unstuck'. . .

  - Change your environment and the way you do things on a regular basis.
  - Deploy the amazing power of your unconscious mind through sleep.

Human experiment: Start now. . .

Ready. Fire. Aim.

The business writer Tom Peters advises that the process of creation should be: 'Ready. Fire. Aim. (rather than Ready. Aim. Aim. Aim. . .)'.[43] What's the smallest possible way you can start your creative project? Anything will help: opening and naming a file on your computer to hold future drafts; sending a text to a friend stating your intention; writing the title of your work (this can change many times, as I've found); or making a list of what you need in a notepad.

Why not set aside 30 minutes every morning for the next week and write your thoughts in a journal? Whatever it is, *just do it*, as Nike once implored. The German writer and statesman Johann Wolfgang von Goethe put it with a little more poetry: 'Whatever you can do, or dream you can, begin it. Boldness has genius, power, and magic in it.' There's only one route to creativity. It begins with a small step into the unknown.

Sharpen your edge

How to borrow the secrets of creative superstars to have more ideas

'Ideas are like rabbits. You get a couple and learn how to handle them, and pretty soon you have a dozen.'

John Steinbeck, novelist[1]

Superpower: **Creativity**

Dance Step: **SPARK**

Igniting questions:

- How can I build my creative potential?
- How can I have more ideas, more often?
- How can I combine little ideas to make big ones?

4Cs value: **More ideas, more often**

An eleven-year-old boy pondered his predicament. He sat in a busy horse yard in the small French village of Coupvray. The lad desperately wanted to read, but he'd been blind since an accident in his father's workshop when he was a toddler. At that moment, his friend placed a pinecone in his hand.[2] As he ran his fingers across the familiar, woody funnel he was struck by an idea. What if he could translate letters into raised bumps and dots on a page, that would feel just like the knobbly pinecone? He might be able to read them with his fingertips. The year was 1818, the boy was called Louis Braille, and the connection he made between what was on his mind and what was in his hand led to the Braille system, which is still bringing reading independence to millions.[3]

Braille fused two different ideas into a brand new one. This is something your brain is designed to do. In the previous chapter we explored the ENERGISE Dance Step: the mental and physical preparation to have, and notice, your ideas. In this chapter, we'll explore some obvious, and not-so-obvious, routes to turn one insight into many, and how to weave them together to make a creative life.

More, not better

We know from multiple studies that over half of all breakthroughs, in every walk of life from architecture to anaesthesiology, baking to bio-technology, clinical psychology to cookery, are generated by the top 10 per cent of people in that specialty.[4] These individuals become known as the creative superstars in their field. What's interesting is they all share a simple, but immensely powerful, secret. See if you can guess what it is from the following list:

- The mathematician Paul Erdős co-authored more than 1,500 research articles.
- Pablo Picasso painted about 20,000 pieces of art.
- Horror novelist Stephen King has written 50 novels and around 200 short stories.[5]
- Johann Sebastian Bach composed a musical composition every week.[6]
- Albert Einstein published 248 academic papers.[7]
- Thomas Edison filed over 1,000 patents.
- Richard Branson started around 100 companies under the Virgin brand, and he's still adding to the group today.[8]

You might think, to emulate the success of creative superstars, you need to aim for the highest-value ideas. The problem is, while that sounds plausible, it just doesn't work. Top entrepreneurs, artists and scientists don't succeed because they have better ideas than most people. It's because they have *more* ideas. Their mindset is: quantity leads to quality. They spread their bets more widely across the roulette table of life to increase their chances of a jackpot.

The French philosopher and writer Émile-Auguste Chartier once observed: 'Nothing is more dangerous than having just one idea.'[9] This reminds me of the wisdom of experienced gamblers and investors. They know full well that most of their bets will not deliver the goods, so they need to build a portfolio. This truth is demonstrated by the lives of great creators. Despite his prodigious output, Picasso is remembered mostly for his black-and-white, anti-fascist painting *Guernica*, and a relatively small collection of other art works. Einstein is heralded for just four papers on relativity. Scarcely a handful of Erdős' mathematical insights became influential. Most critics rate Stephen King's novels *The Shining* and *It* as his best work, leaving scores of his other books as also-rans. At the age of 16, Branson dropped out of school to found his first business – a student magazine. It promptly failed. The long road to billionaire status has spanned 50 years. Along the way, he's suffered a string of commercial disasters including Virgin Brides, Virgin Cola and Virgin Cars.[10]

The surprising truth is the majority of the work flowing from the test tubes, business plans and musical instruments of our creative idols is no better than ours. Or, at least, no worthier than the work of their contemporaries. However, because they initiate so many potential projects they can kill the least promising concepts before they even leave their notepad. The higher volume means a sufficiently large number still make it into production to increase their odds of a smash hit. By pushing open countless doors, creative superstars vastly increase their chance of finding something unusual or interesting on the other side. Of course, prodigious quantity has to be underwritten by determination. Superstars know they need to expect failure, and keep going anyway. D.B. Weiss is the co-creator and showrunner of the global smash-hit *Game of Thrones*, the TV adaptation of George R.R. Martin's series of fantasy books. He admits: 'I've failed very consistently for many, many years. It's sort of the bedrock of my life's process.'[11]

This 'more-is-better' approach works across creativity in all fields. Animators at the film company Pixar developed a staggering 100,000-plus storyboards (the step-by-step plot sequences) for their hit CGI animation *WALL-E*. Many of the scenes and plot twists just didn't work. But, from this huge mass of effort the final storyline emerged.[12] It's the same funnel-like process for the freelancers who submit the iconic cartoons published by *The New Yorker* magazine. Every week, 50 or so freelancers email up to 10 sketches for consideration by the editors. Before they hit 'Send', however, each freelancer has already brainstormed around 150 ideas just to select the 10 they proposed. The Darwinian progression ends up looking like this: 7,500 concepts dreamed up by freelancers; 500 submitted; 12 printed in the pages of the magazine.[13]

Professor Dean Keith Simonton, a psychologist at the University of California, was determined to uncover how scientists rise to the top of their chosen field. To find out more, he built a database on the world's most renowned researchers. He confirmed beyond doubt that this quantity-leads-to-quality principle works in the sciences too. However, he also uncovered a fascinating paradox: superstar scientists also publish more *unimportant* papers than mediocre scientists, simply because they write so many.[14] It turns out creative superstars not only produce damp squibs, near-misses and outright failures. Surprisingly, it seems they actually experience failure *more* often than the rest of us because they create so much. No wonder the two-time Nobel Peace Prize winner in Chemistry, Linus Pauling, advised: 'The best way to get a good idea is to have a lot of ideas.'[15]

Melt your ice cubes

Why do some people become more creative through their life, and some lose this gift? Let's start right at the beginning. When you were small, you knew very little. Your mind was like a clear glass of water. Every time you learned something new, it was simply poured into the glass to freely mix and combine. Because your intellect was more flexible, it permitted new knowledge and thoughts to intermingle, sparking all kinds of connections and associations. Later in life, you attended senior school and were taught in subject-specific lessons. Naturally, you started to define, label and segregate what you knew into separate categories. Slowly, history became walled off from chemistry; economics separated from gym class. Passionate hobbies disengaged from 'real work'. The water in your glass became more like a frozen tray of ice cubes with separate compartments for the mini-specialities you developed over time. This division of disciplines makes perfect sense for analytical thinking: when you're required to dissect subjects to find the single correct answer. During analytical thinking you follow specific rules and a particular set of logical steps in order to arrive at an agreed solution. Along the way, you consciously judge, criticise, refine, or kill thoughts and ideas. Psychologists call this whittling-down process 'convergent thinking'.

But, what happens if you are posed the intriguingly creative challenge of 'How would you re-think and improve an alarm clock?'. Here, convergent thinking doesn't help much. Your analytical mind would select the ice cube labelled 'alarm clock', then put it in a 'mini-glass' for closer examination. The problem is this cognitive container only holds your past associations with alarm clocks. So, no matter how many times you shake the glass, you end up, at best, with a slightly better version of the same thing.[16] A question such as this requires convergent thinking's rowdier sibling: 'divergent thinking'. Divergent thinking opens the door to spontaneous, free-flowing, non-linear reasoning. It warms up a number of different ice cubes and mixes them together into a new concoction. If you're lucky, this

Figure 9.1 The diverge–converge creative process

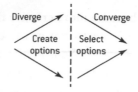

offers you a new, improved type of alarm clock. Divergent thinking generates different choices. You are then able to whittle them down in convergent-thinking mode, as the diagram in Figure 9.1 suggests.

There are some schools attempting to challenge the ice-cube model. One in Vermont in the USA has begun to bring a creative mindset into every subject.[17] For example, geometry is taught through the lens of abstract art. Interestingly, the head teacher reports maths scores have more than doubled since the experiment began. However, promising approaches such as this are in the minority. Most schools and organisations tend to place analytical, convergent thinking on a revered pedestal. Divergent thinking is either not recognised or not combined with convergent thinking. Sometimes, it may even be frowned upon.

The absence of respect for the power of divergent thinking is why these environments are often efficient, if unintentional, creativity killers. It's not surprising that many of the synonyms for diverging away from a fixed topic are viewed as potentially negative: wandering, digressing, rambling, conflicting, straying, deviating, disagreeing, to name just a few. To solve the alarm clock question, or any other creative task, you need *both* divergent *and* convergent thinking. To reclaim your creativity, re-incorporate divergence back into your thinking style. Figure 9.1 makes it look like divergent–convergent thinking is a straight-line process. Indeed, it is a good idea to diverge *before* you converge. In reality, they often follow each other, like a puppy chasing its own tail. You might produce a mass of ideas, narrow them down and then return to diverge again before coming back to choose the best one. What's more important is to be aware of which mode you need – and to think accordingly.

How to deviate

The most commonly used test for divergent thinking was developed by a psychologist called Ellis Paul Torrance. The exam works by prompting you to allow your mind to diverge. Challenges include telling an imaginative story, improving a product, or inventing novel items from simple shapes such as circles or squares. Other assessments require a divergent response to a testing life situation, such as: 'If all schools were abolished, what would you do to try to become educated?' Responses to the various quizzes are scored on four categories:

1 **Fluency:** the *number* of meaningful and relevant ideas

2 **Flexibility:** the amount of different *categories* the ideas fall into

3 **Originality:** the statistical *rarity* of the ideas

4 **Elaboration:** the extent of the *detail* in the ideas.

Human experiment

The alternative use test

Try one aspect of the assessment: the alternative use test. This challenge is to try to see familiar items in a different light. Take a common object from around your home. I've just walked around my house and here's a list I've jotted down:

Coat hanger

Clothes iron

Chair

Wastepaper bin

Select one item from this list. Set a one-minute timer, and scribble down as many different uses for this item as you can. Don't think too hard about each answer, this is not about getting it 'right'. This exercise

▶

trains your brain to unmelt the ice cubes you froze long ago and see the world with fresh eyes. You can use it as a warm-up exercise alone, to limber up your creativity muscles, or with a group. After you've made your list, check to see how your replies stack up against the four categories above. I've tried this simple mental workout with rooms of business people for many years. The interesting part is how quickly people improve. At first, they're not used to thinking this way – then they just get the hang of it.

Why laughter is advisable

Every year at the Edinburgh Fringe comedy festival, there's a vote for the funniest joke. In 2018, Adam Rowe won with this one-liner: 'Working at the Job Centre has to be a tense job – knowing that if you get fired, you still have to come in the next day.' A year earlier, Ken Cheng triumphed with: 'I'm not a fan of the new pound coin, but then again, I hate all change.' In 2016, Masai Graham's gag prevailed: 'My dad has suggested that I register for a donor card. He's a man after my own heart.'[18]

Whether you inwardly chuckle at these quips or not, you'll notice all three have an identical structure: a set-up line followed by a punchline. The set-up line is like a train approaching on straight rails. It's there to fool you into believing you know where the joke will go next. The punchline derails the train, redirecting it in an entirely unexpected direction.[19]

Just like creative thinking, jokes take you to somewhere surprising. Researcher Edward de Bono spent decades developing techniques for what he called 'lateral thinking': solving problems by seeing them creatively in a new or unusual light.[20] Like humour, lateral thoughts don't emerge from traditional step-by-step logic. Both take a left turn off the straight road of rationality to deliver an unexpected, but delightful, resolution.

Not surprisingly, scientists have discovered both humour and creativity tickle the same parts of your brain. Researchers who study laughter and its effects on the body are called gelotologists. Since the 1950s, they've established a close relationship between humour and creativity.[21] When they scan the brains of people convulsed by mirth, they find hilarity is a very complex cognitive function that lights up areas across the brain – as does creativity. Your left brain hemisphere 'sets up' the joke, while the right one helps you to 'get it'.[22] Funny people and situations help you to see the world differently by defying customary expectations.

The insight from these studies is this: try not to take divergent, creative thinking too seriously. In a study on effective brainstorming, researchers pitted product designers against improv comedians. They were surprised to find the comedians generated 20 per cent more ideas (called fluency) than the professional designers. In addition, the ideas they produced were rated as 25 per cent more creative (flexibility). Intriguingly, the study also found that many of the warm-up games used in improv comedy training could be effectively adapted to product design, because they strongly promote associative thinking. When this was tested, it boosted idea output by a sizeable 37 per cent.[23] If you've ever watched an improv comedy show, they usually have a funny version of the alternative use test somewhere in the mix.

Human experiment

Comedy warm-ups

There are stacks of warm-up games you can find with a few clicks online, taken from the world of improv comedy. One of the best is called free association. You pair up with one or more people and have to quickly associate a word to what the person previously said: 'mouse', 'trap', 'crab', 'grumpy', 'goofy', etc. Next time you're trying to think more divergently, warm up like a comedian and keep the laughter going – it helps.[24]

Funny algorithms?

We've observed a one-liner joke has simple rules – a set-up line followed by a punchline. So, you might guess, AI would be good at this.But you'd be wrong. There are now a host of joke-writing and meme-creating algorithms, but so far they're all seriously unfunny. Here's a 'joke' from an AI designed to write one-liners:

> 'What do you call a cat does it take to screw in a light bulb?
> They could worry the banana.'[25]

This is not even good enough to be a bad joke. Humour requires self-awareness, spontaneity, linguistic sophistication, empathy – and creativity. If a simple one-liner is beyond AI, then telling an amusing anecdote or improvising a quip in everyday conversation will prove even more difficult. Making a human laugh is the ultimate Turing Test. For AI, cracking a joke is fiendishly difficult. For humans, it comes naturally.

Human experiment

Fun is a serious matter

Psychologist Karuna Subramaniam studied two groups of participants watching two different movies. One group watched a comedy, while the other watched *The Shining*, a notoriously scary horror movie. When both sets tackled the same word association puzzle, the comedy viewers were way more creative in solving the brainteaser. Intrigued, Subramaniam examined the participants with an MRI scanner. It showed increased activity in the brain's anterior cingulate cortex in the people who watched the comedy. This is the region associated with creativity.[26]

It makes sense, then, to get yourself into a good mood before trying to be creative. Seek out what's always guaranteed to put a smile on your face: a video of your favourite stand-up comedian, a funny movie (my favourite is *Life of Brian*) or a phone call with a friend who always lifts your spirits. Being playful and joyful stimulates the reward centres of your brain. This releases our old friend dopamine, which encourages new pathways between your brain's neurons. New connections means new ideas.

Connect the dots

Louis Braille was not alone in combining ideas. Albert Einstein categorised creativity as 'combinatorial play'. Nathan Myrhvold is a prolific inventor; Bill Gates once said he was 'the smartest man I know'. Myrhvold has been named on patents covering topics ranging from digital displays and 3D graphics to surgical staples and genomic selection. His interests range even wider than this. He writes cookbooks and has invented a new kind of nuclear reactor, as well as researching both dinosaurs and asteroids. Asked how he comes up with innovative new ideas, he was clear: 'A spark of creativity is taking ideas from one place and applying them in another place – in an utterly different context.'[27]

Fusing two ideas together to make something original is the foundation of all creativity. In 1440, the German goldsmith and craftsman Johannes Gutenberg realised there was a huge opportunity if he could speed up the process of printing. He combined the existing technology of movable type with the screw mechanisms used in wine presses. The resulting printing press empowered the mass production of books and the rapid dissemination of knowledge throughout Europe.[28] Five hundred years later, two promising computer scientists on the Stanford University doctoral programme were also interested in making information more freely available. They were curious about an emerging technology called the Internet. They realised few other people were studying how one web page connected to another. They realised hyperlinks might function like citations in the academic world (one of the students happened to be the son of a professor). The young men were Larry Page and Sergey Brin; the resulting company was called Google.[29]

What Braille, Gutenberg, Page and Brin managed to do, psychologists call 'remote association'. This term refers to connecting distant items, such as:

- a pinecone and reading without sight
- wine presses and printing
- academic citations and Internet links.

In 1964, the Hungarian–British author Arthur Koestler attempted an ambitious and elaborate general theory of human creativity. In his book *The Act of Creation* he coined the phrase 'bi-association': the blending of elements drawn from two previously unrelated patterns. When the late Steve Jobs wasn't busy reinventing industries, he was an eloquent commentator on the process of innovation. He once described creativity as 'connecting the dots. . . When you ask creative people how they did something, they feel a little guilty because they didn't really do it, they just saw something.'[30]

All of these different observers of creativity are describing the same thing: your mind's ability to introduce two ideas to each other that were not previously acquainted. We already covered the most effective day-to-day approach to make this more likely: the human superpower of curiosity. Everyday learning and questioning means you naturally bump up against unfamiliar notions. Your brain then effortlessly gets to work fusing, combining and merging them together. However, occasionally, you might want to be more intentional in connecting two dots. Here are a few proven routes to make the introductions.

It's like. . . an analogy

Your speech is littered with colourful combinations. Human communication is naturally creative. We all unconsciously use analogies

('Pauline is an angel') or similes ('life is like a race') to get our point across. An analogy associates two wildly different things to make a point more clearly, as well as adding depth and meaning. If I told you: 'Restructuring my team is as useful as rearranging deck chairs on *The Titanic*', you'd know exactly what I meant. In fact, it probably would resonate more than if I said: 'This restructure is a superficially useful exercise, but completely misses the point.' Or, if I declared: 'Explaining this joke is like dissecting a frog. You'd understand it better, but the frog will die in the process', you'd catch the meaning more profoundly than if I said: 'To retain the magic, sometimes it's best not to know too much.'

Human habit

The analogy approach

The human brain just gets analogies (whereas AI seriously struggles with indirect, creative language). Use your natural linguistic creativity to solve stubborn problems. Analogical thinking helps you to loosen up your mind, especially when the conundrum you face has become too familiar.

The technique is as follows:

1 Clearly frame your problem or question.

2 Brainstorm other phenomena it plausibly resembles.

3 Pick the most apt analogy.

4 Here's the fun part: solve the analogy, *not* the original problem.

5 Translate the analogical solution back to the actual problem.[31]

Here's an example from my world of changing organisations:

The real problem: 'People in my team are resisting the introduction of a new technology system that will vastly improve performance.'

The analogy (what it's plausibly like): 'It's like kickstarting a temperamental old motorbike.'

▶

Solve the analogy (the motorbike problem):

A   Bring in a mechanic

B   Take the engine apart and fix the faulty part

C   Give it an oil change

Translate the motorbike solutions back to the real world:

A   Hire a consultant, or arrange some training

B   Find the main staff 'resistors' and deal with them one to one

C   Bring some 'new blood' into the team who will influence the others

To use one final metaphor, this analogical approach always squirts a little oil onto the frozen frames of your thinking.

Oblique strategies

David Bowie was struggling to unearth a new musical direction. He was stuck in a creative rut. To find his next incarnation, he retreated to a studio in Berlin and teamed up with the legendary music producer Brian Eno. To help Bowie uncover fresh ideas, Eno utilised the power of associations. His approach had a twist, they were completely *random* connections. In an attempt to positively derail Bowie's brain, he co-designed a special deck of cards.[32] Whenever the studio sessions were running out of steam, Eno would draw a card from the deck and ask Bowie to apply the instruction to the way he was singing, playing or composing. Eno called the cards 'Oblique Strategies'. They contained such off-putting commands as: 'Emphasise the flaws', 'Only a part, not the whole', 'Twist the spine' and even 'Change instrument roles'. It drove Bowie crazy. He wasn't the only one. When Eno tried the same approach with 1980s recording star Phil Collins, he become so aggravated he threw beer cans. But it worked for Bowie at least. The Eno sessions produced two of the most critically acclaimed albums of the 1970s. Next time you're stuck, have some fun creating your own random intervention.

Steal like an artist

After the success of his albums, Bowie could afford his own art collection. He was asked how he selected the pieces. He quipped: 'The only art I'll ever study is stuff that I can steal from.'[33] He knew complete originality is a myth. When people label something 'original', it's mostly because they're not able to trace its roots back to the primary sources.[34] Pablo Picasso famously said: 'Good artists copy, great artists steal'. He was describing a journey of self-discovery – one in which he himself became sufficiently self-assured to re-order elements of what he'd seen in the creative work of others. When he was attending art school in Madrid, the young Picasso skipped classes to sit for hours precisely copying Diego Velázquez's three-metre high *Las Meninas* (which translates as *The Ladies-in-Waiting*). Later in his life, when he'd created his own distinctive Cubist style, Picasso continued to obsessively interpret the same Velázquez masterwork. But then again, by this time it wasn't a copy. He'd made it his own. This epic display of admiring devotion culminated with Picasso re-imagining *Las Meninas* in 58 separate paintings he delivered in 1958. These now hang in the Picasso Museum in Barcelona. Salvador Dalí, who himself was inspired by Picasso, said, 'Those who do not want to imitate anything, produce nothing.'[35,36] It's worth bearing in mind that even The Beatles and The Rolling Stones played cover versions when they were getting started.[37]

I hope these anecdotes liberate you to have the confidence to connect the dots from other people's work to your own. It's about taking what went before, and adding a personal twist or improvement. For example, Google was not the first company to create a search engine, actually they were quite late to the game. But they took the existing concept and applied a simple but unique interface programme that consistently delivered good results. When George Lucas created *Star Wars*, he didn't begin with a blank sheet of paper, but fused the best of science fiction with fairy stories and fables of the battle between good and evil.[38] It's possible to become more creative in the same way you learned to write: first trace the letters of the alphabet, then use that solid foundation to compose your own story.

The delete key is there for a reason

The scientist and author Stephen Wolfram is a self-confessed geek who obsessively gathers information about his life. He knows precisely how many emails, meetings and phone calls he makes every year. For example, between 2002 and 2012, he made over one hundred million keystrokes on his computer. A little sad you might think. However, his data hoarding reveals an essential truth about creativity: good ideas always need to be edited. The key Wolfram pressed most often was the 'Delete' key. He tapped it more than seven million times. This means that for every hundred characters he wrote, he erased seven. That's about a year and a half of writing and then deleting. Tellingly, he discovered he deleted most often when he was attempting to write creatively – for the publication of one of his books.

Making something simpler, to reveal its essence, is a vital stage of being creative. Shakespeare, Mozart and Bach all rewrote and rescored obsessively to produce their best work. Leonardo da Vinci coined a phrase for this: 'Simplicity is the ultimate sophistication'. Steve Jobs liked this saying so much he pinched it to define the aesthetic philosophy of Apple. The novelist Stephen King takes the art of self-editing to another level. He is one of the most prolific modern authors of our time, publishing more than 80 books. To deliver this prodigious output he habitually writes 2,000 words every day. Between the beginning of 1980 and the end of 1999, King published 39 books; that's a total of more than five million words. But, if he wrote 2,000 words a day for those 19 years, his output must have been far more: closer to 14 million words. This means King must erase almost two words for every one he keeps. Not surprisingly, he comments: 'That DELETE key is on your machine for a good reason.'[39]

Perspiration beats inspiration

Thomas Edison famously quipped: 'Genius is one per cent inspiration, ninety-nine per cent perspiration.' The plodding, sweaty toil Edison refers to is the hardest leg of your creative journey, but the most important. It's the unheralded hero of many innovation legends. You'll remember George de Mestral's epiphany in the Alps when he connected the spiky burrs on plants with a new type of clothes fastener to invent Velcro? It's worth noting, his insight would have gone nowhere without another 14 years of effort to gain a patent on the idea. We also encountered Alexander Fleming, who became world famous for discovering penicillin on his scattered petri dishes in 1928. Again, this would have been for nothing if it hadn't been for a team at Oxford University who shouldered the tricky task of purifying penicillin so it could be manufactured at scale.

Even the almost semi-mythical creative genius Albert Einstein had to work for his place in history. After he published his special theory of relativity, he knew he needed to turn this concept into a predictive mathematical framework that would precisely describe the relationship between space, time and matter.[40] This wasn't easy for him. Believe it or not, Einstein was never the best mathematician. While slogging through the required equations, he committed a fateful technical error. His mistake meant he spent two long, frustrating years desperately trying to patch a problem that didn't exist. This meant it was a full decade after his initial publication that he finally presented the world with '$E=mc^2$'.

Sometimes this feverish labour needs some outside help to become significant. Louis Braille's moment of clarity was made possible by the actions of another man. In the early nineteenth century, the great military commander Napoleon needed a system to allow soldiers to communicate silently and invisibly at night. As a military veteran, Captain Charles Barbier had personally witnessed several soldiers killed by enemy fire because they were forced to use lamps after dark to read combat messages. To solve the problem, Barbier developed what he called 'night writing'. This method used raised dots that could be felt by fingertip.[41] Barbier visited Louis Braille's school to show off his invention and Braille had this idea in the back of his mind when he felt that pinecone. In the subsequent development of the idea, Braille fixed a glitch in Barbier's night-writing system. The military code didn't allow the human fingertip to feel *all* the dots with one touch, which the Braille method does. All innovators are aware they 'stand on the shoulders of giants'. This phrase has been attributed to a host of creative pioneers, from Isaac Newton to Nietzsche. It's well-worn because it's so true. Nothing comes from nothing. All breakthroughs place a new block on top of what came before.

In this chapter we've focused on divergent thinking and idea combinations. All new ideas are born on the edge between one idea and another: the boundary between two technologies; the grey area between art and science; the border between different cultures; the breathtaking gap between the possible and the seemingly impossible; the threshold that separates the old from the new. After all, we're each a once-only mixture of our mother's and father's DNA. The ultimate combination.

In the final two chapters we'll turn our attention to another type of encounter: when one human meets another. In our fourth 'C', Collaboration, we'll explore the value of human connections and how to use these to experiment with your ideas.

A quick reminder. . .

- Creative superstars have more ideas than other people – their mindset is quantity leads to quality.
- You need both divergent and convergent thinking – schools or businesses make a mistake by ignoring or skipping the importance of divergent thinking.

- Fusing ideas together is the foundation of all creativity. There are many ways to make this happen more often, including:
  - laughing to make the most of the creativity of a good mood
  - learning and experiencing new things
  - using analogies and random provocations
  - building on what went before.
- Be sure to fully reference and honour previous contributions, while allowing yourself to 'steal like an artist'.

Human experiment: Start now. . .

Climb the creative tree

Who is your creative hero? The artist and author Austin Kleon suggests an interesting way to honour your influences: to climb what he calls your own 'family tree'. You do this by identifying a person who's influenced you. Then work out what influenced *them*. He writes: 'Study everything there is to know about that thinker. Then find three people that thinker loved, and find out everything about them. Repeat this as many times as you can. Climb up the tree as far as you can go. Once you build your tree, it's time to start your own branch.'[42] What Kleon suggests isn't plagiarism, it's training. Counterintuitively, the first step to finding your own voice is to mimic the speech of your heroes.

COLLABORATION

The act of working together to create something you could not have achieved alone

The art of connecting, exploring and experimenting with fellow humans

10

Raising ugly babies

How to build a powerful network of human collaborators

'In the long history of humankind (and animal kind, too) those who learned to collaborate and improvise most effectively have prevailed.'

Charles Darwin, biologist

'Mankind's greatest achievements have come about by talking, and its greatest failures by not talking.'

Stephen Hawking, physicist, cosmologist and author[1]

Superpower: **Collaboration**

Dance Step: **CONNECT**

Igniting questions:

- When should I collaborate?
- How should I collaborate?
- Who with?

4Cs value: **A web of human connections**

E d Catmull, the co-founder of Pixar, made a surprising con-
fession about the animation films his studio produces. 'Early
on', he admits, 'all of our movies suck'. To put this observation into context, Pixar's first 20 feature films collected 45 Oscar
nominations, winning 14 of them. These iconic movies include *Toy
Story*, *Finding Nemo* and *The Incredibles*. Most were also box-office
hits: sitting among the top 40 highest-grossing animated features
of all time. Combined, they raked in around £10 billion in revenue
around the world.[2] Catmull and his colleagues are the best at what
they do. So, when he says their movies are bad at first, it's not fake
humility. It's a keen insight: *most* ideas – even promising notions
– are very bad when they first emerge, blinking, into this harsh
world. This is why Catmull calls his early-stage ideas 'ugly babies'.
This chapter is about how to use the skill of forming and leveraging human-to-human relationships as a powerful differentiator in a
world of AI. This will allow you to collaborate, developing your ugly
babies into striking adulthood. Importantly, it will also equip you to
influence: to connect with, and persuade, your fellow human beings.

In this chapter, we'll look at a number of routes to deepen that connection: how to build a network of collaborators, making the most of
chance meetings; when to collaborate, and when to avoid collaboration; as well as the role of humour and storytelling in being influential.
The evidence is compelling: to develop your ideas to their full potential
you need to gather feedback and creative fuel. In a complex and fast-
changing world, it's not a question of *if* you collaborate, but *how*.

The myth of the lone genius

How your precious ideas make the journey from what Catmull
calls 'suck to not-suck' is tricky. You need all the help you can get.
The image of an isolated mastermind inventing without any help is
beguiling, but inaccurate. As the Scottish philosopher and essayist
Thomas Carlyle commented: 'The lightning spark of thought generated in the solitary mind awakens its likeness in another mind.'
In other words, while all ideas emerge in an individual brain, they

benefit hugely from their reflection in the eyes of another. Even the archetypal, intellectual lone ranger Einstein drew inspiration from others. He worked within a network of international rivals who spurred him on. It was only after a momentous walk with his best friend Michele Besso, a fellow physicist and clerk at a patent office in Bern, Switzerland, that Einstein had one of his most valuable breakthroughs (realising time wasn't a constant in his theory). Leonardo da Vinci oversaw a studio of artistic protégés, which enabled him to churn out a far greater volume of commercial work. Art critics still argue over what he painted himself and what might have been added by his pupils.[3] The prolific inventor Benjamin Franklin founded the American Philosophical Society to establish a group of peers to mull over various knotty problems. The Royal Society in London was created for the same reason.[4] The writer Mary Shelley would never have penned the Gothic novel *Frankenstein* if she hadn't been staying in a villa near Geneva. One rainy day, her companion Lord Byron suggested the group write horror stories to pass the time. Sigmund Freud is credited with inventing psychoanalysis, but his ideas emerged from a network of colleagues. The French Impressionist painters Claude Monet and Pierre-Auguste Renoir would not have reached the heights they did without their association with a closely connected cluster of Parisian painters.

Collaboration has always been valuable in the creative process. In today's fast-moving environment, in many fields it would be impossible to innovate without it. It's easy to forget how mindbogglingly complicated our modern world has become. Walk down the aisle of a Tesco in the UK, or Walmart in the United States, and you'll find 100,000 products on the shelves. Amazon sells more than 12 million products not including books, media, wine and services. When you add their Marketplace sellers the total balloons to a staggering 353 million products.[5] A major economic megacity such as London will offer over 10 billion types of merchandise.[6]

If our choices are endless, the individual products themselves are equally complicated. No single person on the planet would be able to explain, let alone make, all the complex parts inside a smartphone. But, what about a humble toaster? Thomas Thwaites, a design student at the Royal College of Art in London, attempted to build a toaster from first principles. When he took it apart, he soon discovered that even this modest device for browning bread has over 400 components and sub-components. The scale of his task became clear when he realised he would not only have to figure out how to make the parts, but also how to create basic elements such as copper, nickel, mica and plastic. He said: 'I realised if you started absolutely from scratch, you could easily spend your life making a toaster.' He failed to make the toaster from scratch, and had to cheat. Even then, when he plugged it into the mains it exploded.[7]

Without collaboration, it's impossible to combine the required diversity of expertise and knowledge required to navigate the twenty-first century. This is apparent in the changing nature of Nobel Prize winners in science. Emeritus Professor Rainer Weiss of the Massachusetts Institute of Technology objected when he was awarded an individual Nobel Prize. He pointed out that the discovery was not down to him and his two colleagues, but from the collective effort of thousands of scientists over a 40-year period.[8] He highlighted an obvious trend: between 1900 and 1950, a Nobel Prize was awarded overwhelmingly to individuals – 39 in total. During the same period, only four teams took a prize. In the 50 years that followed, the picture changed dramatically: 69 prizes were awarded, with over half of those going to groups of scientists working together.[9,10] This trend was confirmed in another huge study covering 19.9 million research papers and 2.1 million patents over 50 years. In some areas of science and engineering, it's forecast that *all* discoveries will soon be solely team based.

My brain is open!

The Hungarian mathematician Paul Erdős criss-crossed the skies above the Iron Curtain during the height of the Cold War. When he landed at an airport he was often met by a welcoming committee of fellow thinkers. He'd announce: 'My brain is open!' This might sound a little immodest from some. However, for Erdős it was simply true. He was quite possibly the greatest creative collaborator in the history of science. Over many decades, he spun a web of creative cooperation across the world. He co-authored peer-reviewed scientific papers with a staggering 500 people.[11] Age didn't prove to be a barrier: his peak year for collaboration was 1987, when he was 74-years-old. He formed a new thinking partnership every ten days or so. His motto was: 'Another roof, another proof'.

Erdős was an outstanding case study in the research into what psychologists call the power of 'weak ties'.[12] To emulate him you'll need to consciously go beyond the instinctive limits placed on us by evolution. The British evolutionary anthropologist Robin Dunbar was the first to estimate the number of people with whom you are easily able to maintain stable social relationships. He uncovered a correlation between the size of the human brain and the number of people in one's social group. What's become known as Dunbar's Number[13] is around 150 people. These are your 'strong ties': close friends and acquaintances. This limit was well suited to our hunter–gatherer ancestors. But, in a complex modern world, you need greater reach and a network of less intimate relationships. These weak ties boost your creative potential. This sounds weird at first, but it's obvious when you reflect upon it. When you unthinkingly gravitate towards your friends at the office party, they'll likely already know your gossip, have heard your insights and possibly yawn slightly when you repeat your amazing 'new idea'. Of course, the opposite can be true: the more distant a contact, the more likely it is they'll help you to spot an original way forward, introduce you to a different contact or suggest a novel nugget of information. Weak ties are like bridges that allow you to access information that would otherwise be off limits.

Human experiment

Building bridges

It's likely you'll need to make a special effort to emulate Paul Erdős. It requires you to push against your ancient instincts.[14] The effort is nearly always worth it. Connect online, and in person, to new people ▶

each month. Stroll across the next networking event, and just say hello. Strike up a conversation on the touchline of a sports event. Enquire into the life story of the next homeless person you donate your change to. Ask your colleagues what they did at the weekend, or what they're reading, or viewing, that's making them think. You'll definitely have some pointless conversations. Nevertheless, I guarantee you'll also find moments where your brain is planted with the seed of a new idea.

Brief encounters

An effective way to increase your weak ties is to make chance encounters more likely. You can learn a lot about the art of serendipitous meetings from history's most innovative buildings. For a long stretch of the twentieth century, Bell Labs in New York City was the most pioneering scientific environment in the world. It produced the world's first transistor, the first laser, and invented fibre optic cable, among many other advances. Researchers in fields as diverse as physics, chemistry, astronomy and mathematics were all crammed together. They were encouraged to interact by one of the building's quirky design features. The corridors of Bell Labs were enormously lengthy. They were so long you could see the end disappear at a vanishing point. This meant strolling the halls without encountering a number of acquaintances, diversions and ideas was almost impossible. In his study of Bell Labs' creative culture, author Jon Gertner wrote: 'A physicist on his way to lunch in the cafeteria was like a magnet rolling past iron filings.'[15]

Building 20 on the Massachusetts Institute of Technology (MIT) Campus in the United States earned a similar reputation as a global hub for collaboration. In the 1940s, no less than nine Nobel Prize winners emerged from this unromantically named and humble edifice. It became home to the world's first atomic clock, the earliest particle accelerator, those iconic stop-motion pictures of a bullet passing through an apple, the first arcade-style video game – and a revolution in linguistics pioneered by Noam Chomsky.[16] This wasn't because it was cleverly designed; it was a spartan, uncomfortable place to work. Nonetheless, it had the same magic ingredient as Bell Labs: chance meetings. The signage and floor-numbering system were so confusing that even MIT veterans struggled to find their way around. As a result, people constantly got lost and then bumped into all sorts of random people.

The beneficial effect of lucky encounters was not lost on Steve Jobs when he took over at Pixar. He personally designed the HQ, which is situated just across the bay from San Francisco. All the rooms feed on to a central atrium. This ensures people bump into each other. He argued: 'Creativity comes from spontaneous meetings, from random discussions. You run into someone, you ask what they're doing, you say "Wow", and soon you're cooking up all sorts of ideas.'[17]

 ## Human experiment

Plan for serendipity

Where do your chance meetings occur? How might you make these more likely? Here are three suggestions:

- **Be present:** Instead of always burying your nose in your smartphone when sitting alone, look up to make eye contact with others. Of course, try not to come across as a weirdo.

- **Change your routine:** If you walk to work, take a different route. Try a different coffee shop, talk to someone new.

- **Imagine it will work:** Research shows that if you imagine a 'best-possible self' for one minute, and write down your thoughts, it generates a significant increase in positive thoughts and feelings. Simply put, if you are optimistic about the prospects of random coincidences, you're far more likely to turn them into positive experiences.

When to collaborate

Collaboration is not always advisable. There's a clue to how it should be approached in the nuanced design of Bell Labs, Building 20 and Pixar's HQ. They all feature public spaces, which make fortuitous get-togethers more likely. But, they also include secluded areas in which people can work alone. This balance is important. Many modern organisations understand the benefits of collaboration, without clearly communicating the personal balance this implies. Collaboration is constantly dropped into the conversation as something that is eternally valuable. It's framed as something 'good people do' – a moral value for virtuous corporate citizens, like having a good sense of humour, or satisfactory personal hygiene standards. It's true that without collaboration you can't benefit from the value of diverse groups. But, as we explored in the Dance Step FOCUS, aimless collaboration hoovers up your precious time.

Attempting to work together with too many people, or the wrong people, is a painful, bumpy road to achieving nothing at all. You need to be generous and engaged in chance meetings. They often yield interesting insights. Then methodical and strategic about who you enlist in deeper cooperative partnerships. Choosing when to collaborate and when to double-lock the door and get to work, is a key skill of our hyper-connected century.

Human habit

What's the point?

The golden rule of collaboration is to have a clear answer for 'Why am I doing this?'. Sounds simple, but this is often overlooked. Think of your current or potential collaborators. Can you unambiguously write down why it's useful to connect and cooperate with them? If not, don't bother, or reconsider the team, or the timing.

Bringing up baby

Ed Catmull and his Pixar team recognise that creative collaborations can go wrong because of the unfortunate human tendency to compare an early idea with a finished product. This mistake means it's judged by unachievable standards – and, as a result, too harshly. To safely raise their 'ugly babies', they have a special forum in which directors and producers can seek constructive feedback. They call it 'the Brainstrust'.[18] Catmull explains: 'Originality is fragile. . . [early ideas] are not beautiful, miniature versions of the adults they'll grow up into. They are truly ugly: awkward and unformed, vulnerable and incomplete. They need nurturing – in the form of time and patience – in order to grow.' This forum is attended only by those who have the experience and ability to offer useful advice. Catmull sees the role of the Brainstrust members as being '. . . to protect our babies from being judged too quickly. Our job is to protect the new.'[19]

Those invited to join the Brainstrust are chosen not just on their track record, but also for their people skills. They have to possess empathy: the ability to place themselves in the shoes of the person seeking feedback. This does not mean they are warm and cuddly. As the inventor and co-founder of the Polaroid Corporation, Edwin Land, once commented: 'Politeness is the poison of collaboration.' Catmull writes: 'Each of the participants are focused on the film at hand and not on some hidden agenda. They argued – sometimes heatedly – but always about the project. They were not motivated by the kind of things – getting credit for an idea, pleasing their supervisors, winning a point just to say you did – that often lurk beneath the surface of work-related interactions.'[20]

The rules of the game

Associate Professor of Education and Psychology Keith Sawyer began his career designing video games for Atari in the 1980s. He's spent a lifetime trying to figure out how creative collaboration works. At Washington University, he videoed collaborative groups using a technique called 'interaction analysis'. Sawyer then forensically scrutinised the group dynamics. He spent over a decade on the video analysis of jazz bands and improv comedy groups. Here are three of the most applicable insights from his investigations:

1   **Collaboration builds more than you can alone:** When groups are genuinely collaborating they literally play off each other, creating something that would have never existed if they hadn't been together. No single individual delivers the whole idea on their own.

2   **Collaborators watch very carefully:** Comedians, actors and jazz musicians all listen and observe with huge intensity to the other players *before* making a contribution. Most of us spend far too much time thinking about our next input. We devote insufficient time to what others are doing and saying. Conversationally, this can be the difference between being a demolition expert and a builder.

3   **Collaboration finds exciting problems:** The most transformative creativity happens when a group dreams up a new way to frame an old problem, or asks a brand-new question nobody had thought of. Sawyer writes: '. . . the most creative groups are good at finding new problems rather than simply solving old ones'.[21]

Next time you collaborate, apply these simple principles. If you and your group are scoring less than eight out of ten on any one of these three building blocks, it might be best to re-visit the rules of your game (or find someone else to work with).

Collaboration for better ideas

A New York advertising executive called Alex Osborn invented brainstorming in 1939 by distilling what he'd learned from managing creative teams. He boasted his technique could double the quantity of ideas from any group. Way back then, he stipulated a few rules:

No criticism of ideas

Go for large quantities of ideas (you'll remember this from the Dance Step SPARK)

Build on each other's ideas

Encourage wild and exaggerated ideas

Eighty years later, brainstorming is still the most popular technique for group creativity. But there's a problem. Osborn was wrong. Brainstorming doesn't work in an optimal way. A famous test in 1958 found that people working alone actually came up with a far greater *quantity* of ideas (twice as many). What's more, their solutions were of a higher *quality* – they were more original. In addition, recent research shows us people generate better ideas when they're guided by clear criteria and standards, rather than receiving zero criticism, as Osborn had suggested. Those who have to use brainstorming for a living know this to be true. On the wall of the design agency IDEO, there's a sign reminding participants to 'Stay focused, stay on topic'.[22]

Human habit

Brainstorming 2.0

It's sad to think that the most long-standing collaborative tool for creativity is still badly designed. The silver lining is there's room for improvement: let's call it Brainstorming 2.0. There's no reason for a complete reinvention. The central thrust of allowing wild ideas to build on each other to create a portfolio of potential options is perfect. I suggest you simply tweak the rules to gain more from the experience. Here are the three additional guidelines to include the insights from up-to-date research:

1   **Set clear success criteria:** These criteria form the answer to the question 'Whatever else is true, what do our ideas *have to* achieve?'.

▶

You'll need between one and three clear standards for your ideas. For example, when an eclectic team of IDEO designers (with backgrounds in linguistics, psychology, biology, and business) were attempting to improve the design of a shopping trolley, they first established clear rules for what would work. They agreed that the trolleys had to 'nest' so they didn't take up more room than necessary when not in use. Likewise, any design needed to be 100 per cent safe, as research showed many children injure themselves every year playing or riding on shopping carts.

2 **Spend time working individually *first*:** This is vital, and it neatly sidesteps the problem thrown up in the 1958 study. Ask all of your co-collaborators to think alone first. Offer them anything from five minutes upwards. Without this key step, the ideas quickly get boxed in by the first person to speak, or the loudest voice in the room.

3 **Appoint a facilitator:** This person ensures everyone's ideas are considered and that the group broadly follows the principles of divergent and convergent thinking.

Have a laugh

Laughter is very important to human beings. There's an almost unlimited demand for mirth. If you don't believe me, just type 'funny cat memes' into Google. Multiple research projects show humour in the workplace supports productivity, lowers stress, aids decision making – and makes you more persuasive. Despite the obvious benefits of levity, we typically sustain ourselves through long working days on a starvation diet of laughter. When you're a baby, you giggle on average 400 times a day. When you grow up this drops to just 15.[23]

Laughter has clear physical and cognitive benefits that boost creativity. And because it forms a powerful social glue between humans, it makes collaboration more likely and more productive.[24] Prompting someone to smile is proven to deepen rapport and intimacy. It builds trust, which is vital for cooperation.[25] Michael Kerr, author of *The Humor Advantage*, argues that wit: '. . . often reveals the authentic person lurking under the professional mask'. Laughing bonds us together and strengthens our uniquely human connection, which is why hilarity is contagious. Cultural anthropologists believe the very first laughter occurred just after danger had passed and people felt safe again.[26,27] It's the same reason why it's not possible to tickle yourself: being tickled is by definition a social event.[28]

Human experiment

Laugh to deepen human relationships

The comedian Robin Williams once said: 'Creativity is like having sex in a wind tunnel.'[29] I guess he meant it might be fun, but also a little risky! Similarly, using humour has its perils: sometimes jokes fall flat. But it's worth the risk. Even an attempt at humour exposes your vulnerability and authenticity. It shows you understand, while work may be serious, life can be absurd. It's not whether or not you're hilariously funny, it's about being open to the possibility of humour. Ironically, people who take themselves too seriously often unintentionally become the butt of the joke.[30]

The humourist Oscar Wilde labelled sarcasm as the 'lowest form of wit'. Nonetheless, even slightly caustic teasing can help. Behavioural scientists found something strange. When people engage in a sarcastic battle of wits, both parties report slightly more conflict but are also far more creative as a result.[31] This is because participants have to play with the contradictions between the intended meaning and what was actually said. What's often forgotten about Wilde's witticism is although he condemned sarcasm as the lowest form of wit, he concluded with the punchline: 'it's the highest form of intelligence'. A joke transforms two people into a conspiracy who are more likely to take a creative risk together.

Allowing yourself to see the funny side might even get you promoted. Eight out of ten senior executives say they feel people with a good sense of humour do a better job. The same survey found 90 per cent of executives believe a sense of humour is important for career advancement. Another study found that a good sense of humour is considered to be one of the most desirable traits in our leaders.[32] It's been shown that those perceived to be influential joke more frequently. One analysis found outstanding leaders use humour more than twice as often as those perceived to be average leaders. Researchers even found a direct correlation between the use of humour and the magnitude of a boss' pay packet. Steve Jobs saw the value of a joke. His famous product demonstrations had a laugh count that outperforms most professional comedians. The anthropologist Edward Hall noted: 'If you can learn the humour of a people and really control it, you know that you are also in control of nearly everything else.'[33]

It's tricky to work out the direction of causality. Are you creative because you're funny? Or funny, because you're creative? The Nobel Prize winning American physicist Richard Feynman had a well-developed sense of the absurd: when he wasn't playing the bongo drums, he liked to stage practical jokes.[34] Quite frankly, who cares which direction the causality flows? The philosophy, and brain chemistry, are clearly closely aligned. Even if that weren't true, both humour and creativity make life worth living and help to express our shared humanity.

Human experiment

Bad ideas brainstorm

In the words of IDEO founder, Dave Kelly: 'If you go into a culture and there's a bunch of stiffs going around, I can guarantee they're not likely to invent anything.'[35] His designers warm up for creative work by first conducting a rapid 'bad ideas' brainstorm. The objective is to list the most bizarre and unworkable answers for the challenge they're looking at. The most ridiculous solutions provoke a few guffaws, which gets the chemistry bubbling.

Human experiment

Yes, AND. . .

How many ideas are squashed within nanoseconds because the immediate response is 'Yes, BUT. . . we've tried that before, it's too expensive, that would not work here, it sounds dangerous, people would laugh, etc, etc'? One way to boost creative collaboration is to borrow the powerful 'Yes, AND. . . ' technique from improvisational comedy. It's guaranteed to bring out the creativity in any group by taking failure off the table. You simply agree one rule: respond positively to *all* ideas for a limited period of time. Then just say 'Yes, AND. . . ' in response to what you hear, as well as adding a layer of detail and value on top of what was said before. The more leftfield your contribution, the better. The acclaimed US comedian Tina Fey, wrote: 'Always say "YES, AND. . . ", meaning, always agree and add something to the discussion. For example, in an improvised scene with a partner, never say 'no'. If you're in a boat rowing down the river, you don't say, "No, we're folding laundry". You say, "Yes, and we could really use a paddle instead of my arm".'[36] Of course, not all ideas are any good. So, after your 'Yes, AND. . . ' session, you can pause to work out which ideas you might want to keep and which have to be thrown out. Whatever happens, you'll have some fun.

Once upon a time. . .

As well as telling jokes, you should also tell stories if you want to influence and connect to human beings. Neuroscientists find that when we're told a character-driven story, with emotional content and colourful metaphors, it causes our brain to release a neuro-chemical called oxytocin.[37] The same thing happens when we're trusted, or shown a kindness. In both cases oxytocin boosts empathy. This is what motivates us to want to cooperate with others. When information is folded into a gripping story, it helps us to understand and remember the key points. Crucially, it also means we are more likely to take action on what we hear. Effective creative collaboration requires you to persuade the people around you to take a risk and try something new. Of course, you'll need to know your stuff. You'll need statistics and data. But, never forget people are never influenced by data alone – they are only ever convinced by what the data means to *them*. The most effective way to make this connection is to wrap your data in a story.[38] Storytelling is inherently a creative act. The techniques you can use are limited only by your imagination. You need to focus on adding some invention to your communication: humour, characters, images, suspense and metaphors. We all know what a good story is from our childhood, as well as from the books and movies we love.

Human experiment

Tell stories to connect with others

How might you use creative stories the next time you are trying to shift opinion, influence or connect? If you want to live happily ever after, learn to tell a tall tale. A well-told anecdote stimulates engagement and trust. It captures a listener's heart by first stimulating their brain.

A quick reminder. . .

- The skill of forming and leveraging human-to-human relationships is a powerful differentiator in a world of AI.

- Collaboration has always been valuable in the creative process. In today's fast-moving environment, in many fields it would be impossible to innovate without it.

- The myth of a lone genius delivering the goods without any help is beguiling, but inaccurate.

- To kickstart collaboration and cooperation:

  - Build weak ties – bridges to knowledge you'd otherwise not be able to access.

  - Make the most of chance encounters.

  - Understand clearly why you need to collaborate: it's a *choice* to make very carefully. With the wrong people, and the incorrect dynamic, it is a waste of your precious time.

  - Use Brainstorming 2.0 techniques.

  - Assess your collaborators' behaviour to ensure they are 'playing the game'.

  - Aim to have fun: it forms a powerful social glue between humans and makes collaboration more likely and more productive.

  - To influence groups, wrap your insights and data in a good story.

Human experiment: Start now. . .

Build a Brainstrust

Ed Catmull has met his fair share of hugely talented creative characters, including the inimitable Steve Jobs. Interestingly, he said he never met

▶

'a single one who could articulate what it was that they were striving for when they started'. You and I are likely to be no different.

All the more reason to design your own version of Pixar's Brainstrust to support you in clarifying your creative vision. Here are a few basic principles of design to collect a group of human collaborators that can offer you invaluable feedback:

- **Make a list of people:** Around six is a manageable number to start with.

- **Choose experts:** Members of your Brainstrust need the right know-how. Apply the basic principle: everyone counts in life, but not everyone's opinion counts on all subjects.

- **Choose for attitude:** They also need the right mindset: not everyone has the imagination to help 'ugly babies' grow up. The best group members offer a balance between empathy and fearless candour. Quickly weed out those who are not there to help move your project forward (which is the only point in getting feedback in the first place).

- **Be flexible:** You may not always be able to gather a group such as this together in the same room. Be prepared to connect with them in smaller groups and virtually.

- **Accept you are the parent of an 'ugly baby':** Set the ground rules for the sort of positive feedback you'd like to hear. However, it's then your responsibility to commit to absorbing the feedback. There is nothing worse than someone who requests comments and then takes issue with them. So, only ask clarifying questions, no matter how tough the feedback is to hear. If you disagree, that's something you need to deal with later, not during the feedback session.

11

Think big, start small, learn fast

Why you need to constantly experiment to test your ideas to destruction – or greatness

'Life is trying things to see if they work.'

Ray Bradbury, author

Superpower: **Collaboration**

Dance Step: **EXPERIMENT**

Igniting questions:

- What should I do when I don't know what works?
- How do I test my ideas?
- Which ideas do I choose to pursue?

4Cs value: **What works, what doesn't?**

We all know it was Thomas Edison who invented the light-bulb. But, there's a small problem with this well-worn myth: it's not actually true. Many inventors were working on the replacement for gas lighting in the late 1870s. Gas lanterns could only deliver a flickering light source, not to mention the trifling issue of thousands of suffocations, fires and devastating explosions. Twenty-three different light-bulbs were developed before Edison even began. Some were so good they were already being used to light streets and buildings.

The technical challenge was the same for all would-be light-bulb designers: pass a sufficiently powerful electric current through a strand of material to make it glow, but without setting it on fire. The greatest difficulty was coming up with the best substance that could serve as a long-lasting filament. Edison's team tested thousands of alternatives, including over 6,000 types of plant materials. The commercial question was just as tricky: how could a bulb perform for long enough – and at the right cost? Eventually, Edison discovered the best substance was carbonised cotton thread. It delivered over 13 continuous hours of light. He filed a successful patent on 27 January, 1880.

So you see, Edison didn't invent the first light-bulb, he invented the best one through highly structured trial and error. Arguably, the light-bulb is not his greatest achievement. Nor are his pioneering advances in electricity, motion pictures, telecommunications, batteries and sound recording. It's *how* he did all those things. His most impressive contribution is not his inventions but the procedure that brought them about at his Menlo Park laboratories in New Jersey: a process to manage thousands of small, deliberate experiments. To Edison, a company was first and foremost an 'experiment factory'. He famously observed: 'I didn't fail 1,000 times. The light-bulb was an invention with 1,000 steps.' Experiments may feel like something for scientists, rather than a technique you can use in real life. Here, we'll see how the opposite is true. In this chapter, we'll learn why experimentation is the most appropriate response when the world is unpredictable and the outcomes of your actions are unknowable. Experiments come in handy when you can't forecast the future.

In CONNECT, we explored how your thinking can be improved through cooperation and feedback. EXPERIMENT is the final Dance Step because, at some point, you'll need to trial your ideas.

Experiments reveal if your concepts are likely to fly, or flop. Crucially, this approach allows you to move forward with the smallest possible risk before staking your reputation, time and money in a more substantial way.

The best lack all conviction

Despite the predictive power of AI, we still don't know which newfangled ideas and products will take off and which will crash and burn. When describing the movie business in his memoirs, Hollywood screenwriter William Goldman concluded that 'nobody knows' which film will be successful, and which will sink without trace. Creativity researcher Dean Keith Simonton puts it this way: 'What is especially fascinating is that creative individuals are not apparently capable of improving their success rate with experience or enhanced expertise. . . creative persons, even the so-called geniuses, cannot ever foresee which of their intellectual or aesthetic creations will win acclaim.'[1] In other words, even the most gifted people have no idea which of their ideas are any good. Experiments help because it's impossible to predict the strength and validity of many ideas before you test them.

Forecasting is very difficult. However, even when it's obvious that humans can't envisage the future, we like to think we can. Experimentation pierces this bubble of fake certainty we tend to inhabit. Our tendency for self-deception was demonstrated in a two-decade study by psychologist Philip Tetlock. In 1984, as the most junior member of the National Academy of the Sciences, he was charged with working out what President Reagan's response should be to the Soviet Union's strategic moves in the Cold War. He studied what the experts prophesied and was struck by a common factor: they all disagreed. He went on to analyse nearly 300 authorities on political and economic trends. He asked them to make predictions on what might happen, then patiently waited to see if their guesses came true. He discovered that specialists, as you might expect, did better than a control sample of undergraduates with no expertise.

However, he revealed deep expertise didn't translate into anything close to perfect forecasting. In fact, in one striking example, experts on Canada turned out to be better at predicting events in Russia than the real 'experts' on Russia.[2]

Arguably, the future is now less foreseeable than it's ever been. We constantly seem to experience astonishing outcomes in technology, business and politics. For example, the vast majority of our financial authorities did not see the devastating credit crunch coming in 2008. Eight years later, in 2016, the UK's vote to exit the European Union was similarly unheralded by most veteran political pundits. In the same year, experienced pollsters failed to foretell the victory of Donald Trump in the US presidential elections. Despite this, many people still prefer to reside in a self-filtered bubble of bogus certainty. They sustain a misguided faith in their ability to foresee what's coming. The British poet W.B. Yeats hit the nail on the head when he elegantly described this tendency in his poem *The Second Coming*: 'The best lack all conviction, while the worst are full of passionate intensity.' Those who lack this conviction prefer to experiment, as it can reveal what works in reality.

Think big, start small, learn fast

Experimentation is action-based. The objective is to verify your assumptions about an assumed idea or fact to make a 'go! or 'no-go!' decision on your creative project. The art is to burn up the smallest possible amount of time, money and effort to learn the most about what works – and what doesn't. As the French philosopher Denis Diderot wrote: 'There are three principal means of acquiring knowledge. . . observation of nature, reflection, and experimentation. Observation collects facts; reflection combines them; experimentation verifies the result of that combination.'

Similar to curiosity and creativity, experimentation is a philosophy on the world. This method of decision making is summed up by the slogan: 'Think Big, Start Small, Learn Fast!'. Experiments amend the old saying: 'Always look before you leap!' They replace it with: 'Take a small hop, then carefully observe what happens.' They might suggest bubbling test tubes, unexpected explosions and blackened faces. However, if designed correctly, they shouldn't be perilous. They're all about *reducing* overall risk to its lowest possible level. In essence, an experiment is an attempt to map the fastest route to the truth – the path that offers the least risk of metaphorically falling off a cliff, with the best view of the subject you're interested in.

By experimenting, you demonstrate a willingness to acknowledge your ignorance. The British historian Arnold Toynbee was known for his prodigious output of articles, speeches and presentations. People could not understand how he accomplished so much. When asked, he replied: 'I learn each day what I need to know to do tomorrow's work.'[3] The Chinese leader Deng Xiaoping advised that when the currents of uncertainty swirl around you, 'cross the river by feeling the stones' under your feet. The Silicon Valley entrepreneur Eric Ries neatly summed it up in his book *The Lean Startup* when he defined experiments as a tool for 'validated learning'. Experiments allow you to stay grounded and grope your way forward, bit by bit.[4] To know just enough to take the next step. It requires courage to admit you don't know how things will work out. Perhaps this is why experimentation has not yet been widely utilised by business managers, who are often keen to pretend they've got all the answers. As the Nobel Prize winning Austrian physicist Erwin Schrödinger admitted: 'In an honest search for knowledge, you quite often have to abide by ignorance for an indefinite period.'[5]

 Human experiment

Write your own press release

Experiments don't need to be complicated. Amazon CEO Jeff Bezos encourages staff to validate their ideas by simply writing a press release. The release is composed for the very first internal discussion of the potential product, rather than just prior to the product's launch. The goal ▶

is to see the new idea through the eyes of a customer before months of expensive development and marketing activity consume cash.

Take a few minutes to write a half-page press release on your favourite value-adding idea. This disciplined approach helps to: 1. clarify your thinking; 2. quickly articulate how your idea benefits others; and 3. place you firmly in the shoes of a potential product user.

Planning versus improvising

Imagine two friends arranging to have lunch. If they were both born before 1980 they're 'digital immigrants'. 1980 is the approximate year when computers became ubiquitous. Anyone born prior to this has acquired their limited digital competence during their lifetime, like learning a foreign language. These friends would most probably plan the time, place and date of their lunch beforehand via text message or phone. However, if it was a person born *after* 1980, she is more likely to be a 'digital native'. She can't remember a time without computers in her life. As far as she's concerned, she probably had an Internet-enabled screen in her crib. She is far more likely to go about organising her lunch in a very different way. First, she'd feel hunger pangs. Then, find the nearest restaurant using the location services on her smartphone. Finally, she'd announce her position via social media to see which of her friends might be able to eat with her. Younger people don't plan, they naturally improvise.[6] As my insightful colleague and generational researcher Tammy Erickson likes to joke: 'If you plan, you're probably old!'

Experimentation is a close cousin to improvisation. It certainly resides at the other end of the certainty spectrum to planning. Planning is useful for projects with a fixed outcome, such as arranging lunch at a specific time and place – or launching a rocket to the moon. You locate the moon and then work out how to get there with a detailed plan of action. Life used to be a little more amenable to planning. When I was a strategy consultant in the early part of this century, we forecast on a three-to-five-year time horizon. It's a measure of how rapidly times have changed that this now seems faintly ludicrous.

Experimentation is not like a mission to the moon. It's more like driving a car. You know the road you're currently on and the direction you're travelling. Experiments are the constant, ongoing feedback loop between the edge of the road and the small alterations you make to the steering wheel to stay on course.[7] Experiments rely on what we can observe right now, not at some imagined point in the future. In a fast-changing world, experimentation is essential because it makes more sense to try things and see how they turn out, rather than plan far into an uncertain future.

When to experiment

Experiments are not advisable in all walks of life. Imagine if you were just going under anaesthetic on an operating table. Your heart surgeon leans in, just as you're drifting off, and excitedly informs you of the fascinating, but risky, procedure he's going to try out on your internal organs. You might have the same alarmed reaction if a firefighter arrived at your burning home with a novel approach to dousing the flames. Experiments are best applied to new products, inventions and untested ideas, when the risk of failure can be mitigated. Not on the night shift at a nuclear plant.

This still leaves huge expanses of our lives where experiments can add value. The American aviators Orville and Wilbur Wright took five sets of parts with them each day they tested their pioneering flying machine. They would fly, crash, work out what happened, use the spare parts and take off again.[8] In 1928, Robert E. Wood, the CEO of US department retailer Sears, opened two competing stores in Chicago. Asked why, he said it was to make sure he picked the right location – and the right store manager.[9] In the 1960s, two brothers Dick and Mac McDonald were figuring out the best design for a ground-breaking assembly line for a kitchen called the Speedee Service System.[10] Being entrepreneurs, they didn't go to the expense of building the restaurant itself. Instead they repeatedly designed and redesigned different configurations of burger flipping stations, fryers and mayonnaise dispensers on a local tennis court with a humble piece of chalk. To test the system's interaction with kitchen workers, they persuaded some local boys to pantomime cooking burgers and fries for an afternoon.[11] From this humble experiment the global fast-food franchise McDonald's was born.

One of the reasons Rich Fairbank targeted the loan and credit card industry in 1988 was because it was an obvious opportunity for interesting experiments. He co-founded the credit card business Capital One because it allowed him to: '. . . turn a business into a scientific laboratory where every decision about product design, marketing, channels of communication, credit lines, customer selection, collection policies and cross-selling decisions could be subjected to systematic testing using thousands of experiments'.[12] Capital One now conducts 80,000 such tests every year to feed what Fairbank calls his 'information-based strategy'. It's propelled the company to become the fifth-largest provider of credit cards in the United States.[13] Many of the iconic tech businesses of Silicon Valley have used an experimental philosophy to drive their success. A software 'beta test' is simply an up-to-the-minute app that encourages customers to try out new features. Experimentation is one of the reasons the likes of Google, Amazon and Netflix regularly outmanoeuvre their rivals.

Facebook even experiments on its own staff. When management found employees were eating unhealthy portions of free M&MS they unleashed a team of behavioural scientists. The PhDs spent time observing snacking patterns and cross-referenced this with academic papers on food psychology. They hypothesised that if the company kept the M&MS hidden in opaque containers, while prominently displaying healthier options such as dried figs and pistachios, it would lessen the problem. The result: the

2,000 employees in the New York office scoffed 3.1 million fewer calories from M&MS over seven weeks, a decrease of nine vending machine-sized packs for each person.[14] Not surprisingly, a number of mainstream global corporates are now embracing experiments in an attempt to develop a more entrepreneurial culture. Over the last five years, at London Business School we've worked on business experiments with organisations in oil extraction, automotive, manufacturing, recruitment, chemical production, banking and insurance, to name just a few.

Innovate or die!

Imagine a game we'll call 'Innovate or Die!'. The playing area is like a chess board but bigger: a 10 × 10 grid made up of 100 squares in total. This represents 100 ways in which any problem can be solved. You have 10 chips to bet on the 100 squares. The winning square is decided by a roulette wheel with 100 different slots. This game is a perfect means to understand the difference between a planning and an experimental approach.

In traditional planning mode you choose what you think is your best option from the 100 squares based on analysis, past experience and informed guesswork. I call this 'decision making by clairvoyance'. You place all 10 of your chips on this single square and cross your fingers you've got it right. You put all your eggs in one basket. If you're correct, this is a perfect approach. It's both fast and effective, and has huge and immediate payback for your remarkable prescience. If you're wrong, it's enormously costly.

In experimental mode your approach is quite different. You cheerfully admit you don't know which of the squares is the winner. The only logical way to proceed is to split your chips into the smallest possible increments: one chip per square. You place your first chip on one of the squares to see if it wins. Of course, the process takes a little longer, as it will take you 10 turns to test 10 squares in this methodical fashion. It's slower, but the upside is you're learning what works and what doesn't at a far *cheaper* rate. In this experimental approach you have redefined failure. You have not avoided it, nor have you made it attractive. You've simply made it survivable. In experimental mode, failure comes in two flavours: either spending too much time getting to the solution, or trying too few squares and then giving up before you know the winner.

To translate our imaginary game back into real life, think of the single-chip approach as your MVE – the minimum viable experiment, which can test the validity of your latest idea. The '4Ss' of this MVE approach are easy to remember: the smallest, speediest, simplest and safest route to greater learning.[15] The only way experiments can fail is if the cost of failure outweighs the value of what you've learned. Buckminster Fuller, the innovative architect who invented the geodesic dome, neatly summed it up: 'There is no such thing as a failed experiment, only experiments with unexpected outcomes.' So, the only route to disaster is to badly design your experiment. We'll now find out how to avoid that misfortune.

 ## Human experiment

Design a minimum viable experiment

Think of an idea in your life you'd like to test with the least possible time, effort and risk. Use the '4Ss' (small, speedy, simple and safe) to dream up a trial in the form of an MVE.

Keep it simple

Experiments are trial and error with a structured plan.[16] It's best to keep them as simple as you can. They can be as unassuming as making a rudimentary prototype, mock up, or dummy version of what you're considering. When Capital One marketeers are trying to figure out which version of an email, font or brand colour works best to illicit a response from their customers, they employ tiny experiments called 'A/B tests'.[17] The marketing team send out two versions of the same email and work out which one gets the biggest response rate. In the software industry, entrepreneurial teams sometimes don't make a product at all – they merely write a description of the benefits of the product and offer an invitation to try it out. It's one baby step before the Amazon press release approach I described earlier. The software designers then monitor how many people click on the link to leave their name as a potential buyer of the product.

Human experiment

Make a quick prototype

'Thinkering' is a combination of thinking and tinkering. It's a memorable verb coined by the writer Michael Ondaatje in his novel *The English Patient*. How might you start 'thinkering' to develop a tangible prototype for one of your ideas? This is the decisive, action-based step IDEO designers call 'getting out of your head'. In some ways, it's what differentiates our thinking style from AI: we have amazingly dexterous hands that help us to think more physically.

You might make a cheap and cheerful protype out of what is to hand: cardboard, tape, foam, LEGO, kitchen-roll tubes. Fast prototyping is often used in design thinking to quickly test the pros and cons of a product. It doesn't have to be a physical 3D object. You might simply sketch the solution to make it more real for you and your collaborators. When thinking through a less-tangible service product, I've witnessed business people roleplay the interaction between themselves and a potential customer. In doing so, they've ironed out all sorts of glitches – and stumbled on opportunities – along the way. A quick demo is always more convincing than a theoretical business plan.

Exciting problems

Earlier you were encouraged to find 'killer questions' that unveil conundrums, glitches and bugs you'd love to solve. Experimentation closes this curious–creative thinking loop to test solutions to these exciting problems. Chances are you've already conducted experiments in your life. You may just not have used the word. Here's a simple, real-life example from my week. Yesterday, I turned on a light switch in my office and the bulb didn't work:

- **Problem:** The light won't come on.
- **Question:** Is the light bulb blown?
- **Idea:** Replace the bulb.
- **Hypothesis:** If I replace the bulb, then the light fitting will work as it should do.
- **Experiment:** Find a new bulb and screw it in.
- **Proof:** Does the bulb light up, or stay dead?
- **Outcomes:**

  A The bulb does light up (validates hypothesis).

  B The bulb stays dead (hypothesis is invalid so there must be something else wrong, is it the wiring, the fuse. . . ?). What's my next experiment?

OK, not the hardest problem. And, I'll admit, my searing insight to replace the bulb is not the idea of the century. But this modest example does clearly explain the experimental thinking process you can apply to almost any situation, as shown in Figure 11.1.

You'll notice two properties of this experimental process. Firstly, it's a useful way to validate the consequences of the previous Dance Steps that make up the backbone of this book. The mini-steps here – develop a hypothesis, do an experiment and check the results – drill down into the EXPERIMENT Dance Step to offer a little more structure. Secondly, any robust experiment begins with a well-thought-out hypothesis. In this case, the assumption underlying the hypothesis

Figure 11.1 The experimental process

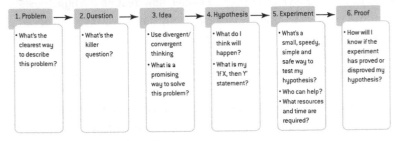

1. Problem	2. Question	3. Idea	4. Hypothesis	5. Experiment	6. Proof
• What's the clearest way to describe this problem?	• What's the killer question?	• Use divergent/ convergent thinking • What is a promising way to solve this problem?	• What do I think will happen? • What is my 'If X, then Y' statement?	• What's a small, speedy, simple and safe way to test my hypothesis? • Who can help? • What resources and time are required?	• How will I know if the experiment has proved or disproved my hypothesis?

is that the bulb itself is blown, rather than failing to light because of a power cut, or a loose wire. A good hypothesis is more than a wild guess, but less than a well-established theory. Scientists test a hypothesis in many different ways before it gets labelled as a theory.

Human lives are full of unspoken hypotheses. For example, a detective might have a hypothesis about a crime, and a mother might have a hypothesis about who spilled juice on the rug. Here are a few more:

If I fit mudguards on my bike (x), I will get less spray from the road up my back when it's raining (y).

If a prisoner learns a work skill while in jail (x), then he's less likely to commit a crime when he's released (y).

If we introduce homeworking for the HR team (x), then this'll result in a more productive, flexible and happy workforce (y).

Human experiment

Write a hypothesis

Experimentation is just a method to clearly state your underlying assumptions in order to learn if they are true or false. It's advisable to use clear, precise language. You'll notice from the examples above that a hypothesis is always built on a specific sentence format:

'if we do x, then we think the result will be y'.[18]

▶

> Go back to the MVE you designed earlier. Now, restate the hypothesis at the heart of that potential experiment. You'll see that the logical language makes it far easier to test the statement with a small experiment.

Throughout *The Human Edge* I've encouraged you to experiment. In this final Dance Step, I've simply offered you a more robust way to elevate your explorations to another level. Whether you prefer a more intuitive style of trial and error, or the sort of structured experimentation I've described here, one thing's certain: in a fast-changing world, dumb perseverance is overrated. So is the assumption that you can adequately forecast the future. Small learning steps are far better. Experimentation does not endorse or encourage failure, it simply makes it survivable and useful. Thomas Edison stated: 'The real measure of success is the number of experiments that can be crowded into 24 hours.'[19] Experiments lower the cost of each of your bets. Consequently, if things don't work out, you'll have more money left in your bank account for another roll of the dice.

A quick reminder. . .

- An experimental philosophy is 'Think Big, Start Small, Learn Fast'.
- Experiments are not advisable in all walks of life, but are well-suited to:
  - validating curious and creative thinking;
  - the uncertainties of the twenty-first century;
  - situations where forecasting has become difficult, and improvising is often the best way forward.

- The art of a well-designed experiment is to spend the smallest amount of time, money and effort in learning the most about what works – and what doesn't work.
- Experiments make 'failure' survivable, and even valuable.
- There are different routes to test a hypothesis, from a simple drawing, a roleplay or a more involved physical prototype – to a full-on collaborative experiment.
- The most effective experiments are simple, small, speedy and safe.

 # Human experiment: Start now. . .

Begin a lifetime of experiments

In this chapter you've considered the experiments you'd like to conduct, what form they might take and the hypothesis that lies at their heart. Now, try them out. Go ahead and conduct one or more of these experiments.

To help:

- Think about one or more of the ideas you've developed while reading this book.
- Apply the experimental approach. Even though it's written as a linear process, you'll find you have to go around a thinking circuit a few times to write a hypothesis you are happy with – and to design an experiment that will help you acquire insight.

Epilogue
What's next?

Hopefully this book has equipped you to differentiate from, rather than compete with, AI. Or at least to differentiate from the artificial narrow intelligence (ANI) we face in the foreseeable future. However, what's coming next? There've been countless apocalyptic headlines about artificial superintelligence (ASI). The moment ASI turns up has become known as the 'technological singularity'. In this scenario, an AI enters a self-improvement learning cycle. Somehow, it produces a new and more intelligent version of itself at lightning speed. When it reaches ASI-level, we humans appear a bit thick by comparison. Imagine how we view cattle, dogs and cats: cute, potentially useful, but not entities that should be making many decisions. The fear is that the sentient ASI might then pursue its own goals. Or, disastrously misconstrue the objectives we have given it. Eradicate cancer? Sure, the quickest way to do that is to kill all humans. Sound familiar? It's *Terminator's* Skynet and *The Matrix* all over again.

A number of eminent technologists and scientists, including the Silicon Valley entrepreneur Elon Musk and the late British physicist Stephen Hawking, have lent credence to the prospect of a singularity. However, there are good reasons why you and I don't need to fret just yet. Firstly, it's not likely to occur for a while. A number of surveys have asked leading AI researchers how many years to reach even human-level AGI. The results have been consistent: they can't agree. In one of the polls, conducted at a global AI conference, the average answer was the year 2055, but some researchers guessed hundreds of years or more.[1] MIT's Andrew McAfee, co-author of *The Second Machine Age* and *Race Against the Machine*, puts it this way: 'The greatest misconception is the hope that the singularity (or the fear that super-intelligence) is right around the corner.'[2] Machine-learning expert Andrew Ng, formerly of Google and Baidu, assures us: 'Worrying about super-intelligent and evil AI today is like worrying about the problem of overcrowding on Mars.'[3]

Secondly, self-aware AGI (let alone ASI) might *never* happen. Many scientists are sceptical. London's Imperial College devised a 'Table of Disruptive Technologies', drafted by the futurist Richard Watson. This positioned conscious AI in the same category as human head transplants, asteroid mining and space elevators. The analysis called it: 'Fringe science and technology. . . highly improbable, but actually not impossible.'[4] Christine Foster, the managing director for The Alan Turing Institute, joked: 'I will worry about the singularity when my printer can talk to my laptop!'[5] If AI becomes sufficiently complex and powerful, AGI *might* happen. This *might* lead to ASI. Who knows? While this should certainly be something scientists and governments think about, and prepare for, it's not keeping me awake at night.

Human + AI

More important is what AI can do for us in the meantime. It's certain that AI will augment our abilities.[6] I agree with Bill Gates, who prophesied that AI will make our lives 'more productive and creative'.[7] AI can offer us more free time by automating the annoying stuff we currently have to do, and thereby reducing our cognitive burden.[8] Sales reps, for example, spend up to 80 per cent of their time qualifying leads and only 20 per cent closing deals. AI is able to automatically qualify potential opportunities, enabling human salespeople to divert more of their focus to non-routine, high-value activities.

AI might offer a potential creativity dividend in the workplace. Remember Amelia, the ground-breaking chatbot in Chapter 2?

When tireless customer service AIs such as this deal with millions of hours of routine, frequently asked questions, it liberates humans to help frustrated customers with lateral thinking, empathy and perhaps even the odd flash of humour. This won't be a hard sell. Recent surveys show most people – for routine queries at least – actually prefer a 'known' chatbot over a human who's robotically (ironic, I know) reading from a prepared script.[9]

Rather than obsess over nightmare futures, we're better off working out the equation:

$$Human + AI = What?$$

In their book *Human + Machine*, Accenture's AI gurus Paul Daugherty and H. James Wilson forecast that human–machine collaboration will result in three spaces:[10]

1   human-only activity;
2   what they call the 'missing middle', where humans complement machines, and vice versa;
3   machine-only areas where AI is simply better.

Picking up the theme, the global IT firm Cognizant predicted some job titles that we can expect to appear in the coming decade: 'Chief Trust Officer', 'Fitness Commitment Counsellor' and 'Man–Machine Teaming Manager'. In the longer term they also imagine a 'Personal Memory Curator', 'Virtual Store Sherpa' and 'Augmented Reality Journey Builder'. The report concluded: 'Can a machine. . . create itself, market itself, sell itself? Deliver itself? Feed itself? Clean itself? Fix itself? Machines are tools, and tools need to be used. By people. To imagine otherwise is to fall into the realm of science-fiction extrapolation.'[11]

As he often does, the former world chess champion Garry Kasparov lights the way. After his epic defeat to Deep Blue, Kasparov became fascinated by what he calls 'Centaurs'. These are teams where humans and AI work together, named after the half-human, half-horse creatures in Greek mythology. Kasparov initiated 'freestyle' chess tournaments in which Centaur teams play each other. These competitions blend human intuition and creativity with the calculation of moves and countermoves that computers can do so easily. Centaurs offer hope for us all. In a number of such tournaments, amateur human chess players, skilfully using AI, have actually beaten chess grandmasters who were also assisted by AI. The amateur teams had the edge because they knew how to collaborate more skilfully with a computer, so they won.[12] Humans playing alongside machines are now thought of as the strongest chess-playing entities possible.

As both a professor of cognitive sciences and an expert on AI, Margaret Boden is a rare breed. Based at Sussex University in the UK, she's managed to apply her ideas on creativity to both humans and what she likes to call 'tin cans'. She's identified three types of creativity that attempt to clarify what AI can do to create on its own – as well as to assist humans. Boden's 'Exploratory' creativity involves taking what's already there and exploring its outer edges, while remaining bound by rules.[13] For example, blues music always follows the same chord progression, but allows musicians to extend what's possible within this framework. Mathematicians often spend decades trying to find a proof, but understand they have to abide by strict rules. Boden argues that this accounts for the vast majority of human creativity, and is also where AI can contribute most. It makes sense, as computers are perfect for producing millions of alternatives that fit a specific set of rules. Boden's 'Combinatory' creativity is when two completely different ideas are brought together to create something new. We explored this potent method in some depth in Chapter 9, in the SPARK Dance Step. An example is the work of Zaha Hadid, who combined her knowledge of architecture with her love of the pure forms of the avant-garde Russian painter Kazimir Malevich to create a unique style of wacky, curvaceous building. AI can assist with both Exploratory and Combinatory creativity. It excels at producing millions of options that abide by specific guidelines. The role of humans is then to choose which explorations, and strange hybrids, are appropriate to use. Boden's 'Transformational' creativity is explained well by Marcus du Sautoy, the British mathematician and author of *The Creativity Code: How AI is Learning to Write, Paint and Think:* '. . . transformational moments hinge on changing the rules of the game, or dropping an assumption that previous generations had been working under. The square of a number is always positive. All molecules come in long lines not chains. Music must be written inside a harmonic scale structure. Faces have eyes on either side of the nose.'[14] Think how Picasso changed the rules of that game with Cubism. It's difficult to see how a machine might help in the realm of Transformational creativity, but it is theoretically possible. You might ask an AI to drop some constraints around a particular challenge and see what emerges. What's certain is that AI will work alongside humans in all walks of life, including creative endeavours. As this new world unfolds, the human superpowers of Consciousness, Curiosity, Creativity and Collaboration will become more, not less, important. The subskills will just have to be adapted occasionally to collaborate with AI, as well as humans.

Perhaps we don't need to fear our 'robot overlords' quite as much as we might have thought? It's certain AI can help to make us more than we've ever been. Hopefully, 'high-tech' AI will liberate us to become more 'high-touch' in our relationship with our own creativity – and with fellow human beings. Either way, I hope this book has offered you an advantage as this technological drama unfolds: practise the 4Cs to keep your Human Edge razor sharp. As the AI music gets louder, which Dance Step will you choose next, to tango into our shared future?

Notes

Chapter 1

1   Chace, Calum (2015) *Surviving AI: The Promise and Peril of Artificial Intelligence.* Three Cs. Kindle Edition, p. 45.

2   https://spectrum.mit.edu/continuum/entering-the-second-machine-age-bring-a-hammer/

3   Indebted for this excellent analogy to Chace, Calum (2015) *Surviving AI: The Promise and Peril of Artificial Intelligence.* Three Cs. Kindle Edition, p. 153.

4   Such as Bloomberg, which uses AI, among others.

5   The global consumer goods company, Unilever, is using this technology to great effect.

6   https://www.washingtonpost.com/news/the-switch/wp/2018/02/06/algorithms-just-made-a-couple-crazy-trading-days-that-much-crazier/?noredirect=on&utm_term=.54c70b2b197d

7   Ping An, the largest insurance firm in the world, headquartered in Shenzhen, China, uses AI to detect human dishonesty via AI analysis of video interviews.

8   'GrAIt expectations' special report (source: PitchBook), *The Economist*, 31 March 2018, p. 5.

9   The Singapore government is trialing AI to scan crowds for signs of terrorism.

10   'The tech giant everyone is watching', *The Economist*, 30 June 2018, p. 11.

11   https://www.politico.eu/article/denmark-silicon-valley-tech-ambassador-casper-klynge/

12   https://qz.com/1177465/forget-bat-chinas-next-generation-tech-giants-are-tmd/

13   https://www.cbinsights.com/research/china-baidu-alibaba-tencent-artificial-intelligence-dominance/

14   Chace, Calum (2015) *Surviving AI: The Promise and Peril of Artificial Intelligence.* Three Cs. Kindle Edition, p. 85.

15   By digital analyst Benedict Evans at the Silicon Valley venture capital firm Andreessen Horowitz.

16 AI-related acquisitions were a staggering 26 times greater in 2017 than just two years earlier. 'AI-Spy Leader' article (p. 15), linked to 'GrAIt expectations' special report (source: PitchBook), *The Economist*, 31 March 2018, p. 5.

17 According to a report by MIT's *Sloan Management Review*.

18 According to the McKinsey Global Institute, which predicts there'll be a king's ransom in economic value for those who win the race to figure out AI. In the next twenty years, they argue the top three biggest impacts will come in the transformation of marketing and sales ($1.4 trillion), supply chain management ($1.3 trillion) and the management of risk ($0.5 trillion).

19 https://www.youtube.com/watch?v=SCGV1tNBoeU

20 https://www.bbc.co.uk/news/science-environment-48193866

21 Kasparov, Garry (2017) *Deep Thinking: Where Machine Intelligence Ends and Human Creativity Begins*. John Murray, p. 7.

22 In 1930, the British economist John Maynard Keynes was the first to give this human vs machine struggle a name. He identified a 'new disease': 'technological unemployment. . . due to our discovery of means of economising the use of labour outrunning the pace at which we can find new uses for labour'. In other words, technology means more prosperity overall in the long run, and different jobs for many in the short.

23 A phrase coined by Andrew Ng, formerly of Google and Baidu.

24 Newport, Cal (2016) *Deep Work: Rules for Focused Success in a Distracted World*. Piatkus, Little, Brown Book Group. Kindle Edition, pp. 22–23.

25 In the UK, for example, 35 per cent of current jobs are at high risk of computerisation within 20 years; with automation likely for 70–80 per cent of 'scripted' jobs. But machines will also beat humans where mastery of data leads to better judgements: auditing, pitching for large contracts and even the diagnosis of cancer. In other words, accountants, some sales people and even surgeons need to work out where they add value, and where machines should step in. From a study by researchers at Oxford Martin School, Oxford University and Deloitte, 2017.

26 A study by researchers at Oxford Martin School, Oxford University and Deloitte 2017.

27 The Oxford University report has been criticised for being overly gloomy but, as I say, even at the lower estimates of job losses we're

looking at a huge impact on the way humans exist in the workplace: https://www.telegraph.co.uk/news/2017/09/27/jobs-risk-automation-according-oxford-university-one/

28 Daugherty, Paul R. and Wilson, H. James (2018) *Human + Machine: Reimagining Work in the Age of AI*. Harvard Business Review Press, Chapter 5.

29 https://www.tothepointatwork.com/article/vuca-world/

30 In business, this experience is often referred to the 'VUCA World' because it's more volatile, uncertain, complex and ambiguous than the experience of previous generations.

31 'Future of Jobs'. World Economic Forum. A global survey of top leaders of 13 million employees across nine industry sectors.

32 Susskind, Richard and Susskind, Daniel (2015) *The Future of the Professions: How Technology Will Transform the Work of Human Experts*. Oxford University Press, p. 37.

33 Susskind, Richard and Susskind, Daniel (2015) *The Future of the Professions: How Technology Will Transform the Work of Human Experts*. Oxford University Press, p. 2.

34 'Diligence Disrupted'. *The Economist*. 14–20 July 2018, p. 61.

35 https://www.bbc.co.uk/news/technology-44635134

36 I owe huge thanks as always to the insights of the globally-renowned thought leader on organisations of the future, Tammy Erickson. This diagram is developed from a similar one she has presented when discussing the emerging role of humans vs AI.

37 Leslie, Ian (2014) *Curious: The Desire to Know and Why Your Future Depends on It*. Quercus. Kindle Edition, location 141–143.

38 Leslie, Ian (2014) *Curious: The Desire to Know and Why Your Future Depends on It*. Quercus. Kindle Edition, location 148–150.

39 Some researchers even argue creativity and curiosity aren't discrete steps as I have described here, but synonymous. As I'll explain as the book progresses, none of the steps in creative thinking is truly discrete. They all work together in a 'messy' way. But, it's easier to understand them individually prior to using them together.

40 Chace, Calum (2015) *Surviving AI: The Promise and Peril of Artificial Intelligence*. Three Cs. Kindle Edition, p. 83.

41 If you'd like to do a little more research, go to: https://www.mckinsey. com/business-functions/digital-mckinsey/our-insights/where-machines-could-replace-humans-and-where-they-cant-yet

42 These questions are developed from those posed in: https://www. forbes.com/sites/forbescoachescouncil/2017/02/13/how-to-bea t-automation-and-not-lose-your-job/#5826d5852caf

Chapter 2

1 Daugherty, Paul R. and Wilson, H. James (2018) *Human + Machine: Reimagining Work in the Age of AI*. Harvard Business Review Press, p. 55.

2 She was built by IPsoft Inc. for SEB in 2017.

3 For the rest of this book, unless I state otherwise, when I refer to 'AI', I mean 'ANI'.

4 https://metro.co.uk/2018/10/10/ancient-greek-myths-foretold-of-modern-technology-including-ai-driverless-cars-and-even-alexa-8023013/

5 https://www.computerhistory.org/babbage/

6 https://www.bbc.co.uk/news/technology-27762088

7 https://www.bbc.co.uk/news/technology-44045424

8 Chace, Calum (2015) *Surviving AI: The Promise and Peril of Artificial Intelligence*. Three Cs. Kindle Edition, p. 16.

9 I borrowed this excellent metaphor from Ford, Martin (2016) *The Rise of the Robots: Technology and the Threat of Mass Unemployment*. Basic Books. Kindle Edition, location 127.

10 In 1965, Gordon Moore noticed that the number of transistors per square inch on integrated circuits had doubled every year since their invention. Moore's Law predicts that this trend will continue into the foreseeable future.

11 Chace, Calum (2015) *Surviving AI: The Promise and Peril of Artificial Intelligence*. Three Cs. Kindle Edition, p. 69.

12 Chace, Calum (2015) *Surviving AI: The Promise and Peril of Artificial Intelligence*. Three Cs. Kindle Edition, p. 28.

13 Chace, Calum (2015) *Surviving AI: The Promise and Peril of Artificial Intelligence*. Three Cs. Kindle Edition, p. 63.

14 This is different from a computer program, which offers precise, step-by-step instructions on how to handle a very specific situation, such as adding up a column of figures.

15 Both programs and algorithms are called software.

16 https://www.forbes.com/sites/gilpress/2018/02/07/the-brute-force-of-deep-blue-and-deep-learning/#130a40e849e3

17 Kasparov, Garry (2017) *Deep Thinking: Where Machine Intelligence Ends and Human Creativity Begins.* John Murray. Kindle Edition, p. 5.

18 Daugherty, Paul R. and Wilson, H. James (2018) *Human + Machine: Reimagining Work in the Age of AI.* Harvard Business Review Press, p. 60.

19 It's used in fraud detection and price prediction. And it's how Amazon's Alexa, Apple's Siri and Google Assistant manage to understand what you say (sometimes!).

20 This is known as 'reinforcement' or 'deep learning'.

21 Your brain contains about as many neurons as there are stars in our Galaxy: in the ballpark of a hundred billion. Each of these neurons is connected to about a thousand others via junctions called synapses. It's the strengths of these roughly hundred trillion synapse connections that encode the information in your brain. These computers learn in a similar way to humans.

22 Watching the AI improve in this video is incredible: https://www.youtube.com/watch?v=V1eYniJ0Rnk

23 OK, hands up, this is an old-school Eurythmics pop song reference. I was a teenager in the 1980s!

24 Which, of course, it will soon feature prominently in, as autonomous driving takes off.

25 For eagle-eyed grammarians: I do realise data is a plural (datum being the singular). But, as it is not used by anyone I know in this way, I use it as a singular noun. Apologies!

26 Another excellent analogy borrowed from the peerless Chace, Calum (2015) *Surviving AI: The Promise and Peril of Artificial Intelligence.* Three Cs. Kindle Edition, p. 60.

27 I've made this rough conversion based on 1 terabyte = 1,000 gigabytes. The IBM 3380 cost between $81,000 and $142,400 in 1980: https://royal.pingdom.com/the-history-of-computer-dat a-storage-in-pictures/

28 Chace, Calum (2015) *Surviving AI: The Promise and Peril of Artificial Intelligence.* Three Cs. Kindle Edition, pp. 63–64.

29 Chace, Calum (2015) *Surviving AI: The Promise and Peril of Artificial Intelligence*. Three Cs. Kindle Edition, pp. 173–174.

30 According to an IBM Marketing Cloud study: https://public.dhe.ibm.com/common/ssi/ecm/wr/en/wrl12345usen/watson-customer-engagement-watson-marketing-wr-other-papers-and-reports-wrl12345usen-20170719.pdf

31 Tegmark, Max (2017) *Life 3.0: Being Human in the Age of Artificial Intelligence*. Penguin Books Ltd.

32 This was seen as 'women's work', so NASA's human computers in the 1940s and '50s were female and often black, too. They were called 'computers in skirts'. Ironic, then, that it was a brilliant band of pioneer black women who figured out how to propel a white male into orbit. Immortalised in the 2016 film, *Hidden Figures*, this is an inspiring story for any young woman at all nervous about launching themselves into the still male-dominated sciences.

33 Cognizant (2018) '21 Jobs of The Future', Center for the Future of Work.

34 Tegmark, Max (2017) *Life 3.0: Being Human in the Age of Artificial Intelligence*. Penguin Books Ltd. Kindle Edition, location 899–910.

35 https://www.news.com.au/technology/innovation/inventions/how-a-confused-ai-may-have-fought-pilots-attempting-to-save-boeing-737-max8s/news-story/bf0d102f699905e5aa8d1f6d65f4c27e

36 Tegmark, Max (2017) *Life 3.0: Being Human in the Age of Artificial Intelligence*. Penguin Books Ltd. Kindle Edition, location 876.

Chapter 3

1 This probably apocryphal story appears in a number of places, and was used most famously in Sir Ken Robinson's now iconic TED talk 'Do schools kill creativity?'. If you haven't already watched it, I highly recommend you do.

2 Kelley, David and Kelley, Tom (2013) *Creative Confidence: Unleashing the Creative Potential Within Us All*. William Collins.

3 Adapted from Dyer, Jeff, Gregersen, Hal and Christensen, Clayton M. (2012) 'Crush the "I'm Not Creative" Barrier', *Harvard Business Review*.

4 These questions are adapted from Dyer, Jeffrey H., Gregersen, Hal and Christensen, Clayton M. (2009) 'The Innovator's DNA', *Harvard Business Review*. They undertook a six-year study to uncover the origins of creative – and often disruptive – business strategies

in particularly innovative companies. They came up with a list of things that they called the 'innovator's DNA': questioning, observing, associating and experimenting, which I've developed here.

5   The study was carried out by StrategyOne for Adobe's global-benchmark study 'State of create study'. The research was fielded in March and April 2012. The team conducted surveys of 5,000 adults; a 1,000 per country were interviewed in the USA, UK, Germany, France and Japan.

6   https://hbr.org/2012/05/crush-the-im-not-creative-barr

7   Ashton, Kevin (2015) *How To Fly A Horse*. Cornerstone Digital. Kindle Edition, location 53.

8   Ashton, Kevin (2015) *How To Fly A Horse*. Cornerstone Digital. Kindle Edition, location 69.

9   https://www.entrepreneur.com/article/241853

10 https://www.verywellmind.com/what-is-the-average-iq-2795284

11 https://www.opencolleges.edu.au/informed/features/the-value-of-connecting-the-dots-to-create-real-learning/

12 https://www.psychologytoday.com/gb/blog/finding-the-next-einstein/201104/if-you-are-creative-are-you-also-intelligent

13 Fry, Hannah (2018) *Hello World: How to Be Human in the Age of the Machine*. Transworld Digital. Kindle Edition, location 2,930.

14 du Sautoy, Marcus (2019) *The Creativity Code: How AI is Learning to Write, Paint and Think*. Fourth Estate. Kindle Edition, location 44–45.

15 https://www.forbes.com/sites/falonfatemi/2018/08/17/how-ai-will-augment-human-creativity/#7523edbd711b

16 https://www.independent.co.uk/life-style/gadgets-and-tech/news/ai-robots-artificial-intelligence-racism-sexism-prejudice-bias-language-learn-from-humans-a7683161.html

17 https://www.businesslive.co.za/redzone/news-insights/2018-07-30-does-ai-mean-the-end-of-creativity

18 https://www.ibm.com/watson/advantage-reports/future-of-artificial-intelligence/ai-creativity.html

19 https://www.forbes.com/sites/annapowers/2018/04/30/creativity-is-the-skill-of-the-future/#12a946944fd4

20 George Land had, three years earlier, established a research and consulting institute to study the enhancement of creative performance.

He drew on the pioneering creativity research of the early 1960s by Joy Guilford and Ellis Paul Torrance: https://worldbusiness.org/fellows/george-land-ph-d/

21 https://www.youtube.com/watch?time_continue=12&v=ZfKMq-rYtnc

22 https://marginalrevolution.com/marginalrevolution/2011/12/teachers-dont-like-creative-students.html

23 MacLeod, Hugh (2009) *Ignore Everybody: And 39 Other Keys to Creativity*. Portfolio. Kindle Edition.

24 2019 Netflix documentary *The Creative Brain*: https://www.netflix.com/gb/title/81090128

25 https://www.forbes.com/sites/augustturak/2011/01/09/its-not-what-we-think-but-how-we-think-3-leadership-lessons-from-the-ibm-executive-school/#1ad96e4d631f

26 https://www.forbes.com/sites/augustturak/2011/05/22/can-creativity-be-taught/#537aec241abb

27 From his 1991 lecture: https://www.youtube.com/watch?time_continue=8&v=Gg-6LtfB5JA

28 Duncan, Jody and Fitzpatrick, Lisa (2010) *The Making of Avatar*. Abrams.

29 http://www.innovationmanagement.se/imtool-articles/the-difference-between-big-c-and-small-c-creativity/

30 Sir Ken Robinson video 'Can creativity be taught?': https://www.youtube.com/watch?v=vlBpDggX3iE&feature=share

31 Taken from a video within the IDEO 'Unlocking creativity' course.

Chapter 4

1 Bronnie Ware's full blog at: https://bronnieware.com/blog/regrets-of-the-dying/

2 Dalai Lama (2002) *Advice On Dying: And Living Well by Taming the Mind*. Rider, p. 39.

3 From Steve Jobs' 2005 Stanford Commencement address (transcript and video): https://news.stanford.edu/2005/06/14/jobs-061505/

4 Harare, Yuval Noah (2018) *21 Lessons for the 21st Century*. Jonathan Cape.

5 Since 2005.

6   https://hbr.org/2018/11/9-out-of-10-people-are-willing-to-earn-less-money-to-do-more-meaningful-work

7   Psychologists call these external motivators 'extrinsic' motivators.

8   Pink, H. Daniel (2009) *Drive: The Surprising Truth About What Motivates Us.* Cannongate, p. 143.

9   Slightly adapted from a quiz in Cable, Dan (2018) *Alive at Work.* Harvard Business Review Press, p. 25.

10 Psychologists call this hedonic happiness.

11 Psychologists call this eudonic happiness.

12 In case you were wondering, not that many people score high on both types of happiness – maybe you can be one of the lucky ones?

13 Thanks to my London Business School colleague – this is inspired by Cable, Dan (2018) *Alive at Work.* Harvard Business Review Press, p. 17.

14 https://www.ted.com/talks/angela_lee_duckworth_grit_the_power_of_passion_and_perseverance

15 Duckworth, Angela (2016). *Grit.* Ebury Publishing. Kindle Edition, location 243–245.

16 Csikszentmihalyi, Mihaly (2002) *Flow.* Rider, p. 4.

17 https://www.bbc.co.uk/news/business-46793506

18 From a video teaching case by the Center for Positive Organizations: 'Having a Calling and Crafting a Job: The Case of Candice Billups'.

19 Psychologists call this 'levels of construal'. We'll call it levels of meaning, because that's what it is, and life is way too short to try to keep in mind words like construal when meaning fits so much better.

20 I'm grateful to Ena Inesi at London Business School for introducing me to the video case of Candice Billups. You can have the privilege of meeting Candice yourself at: https://www.youtube.com/watch?v=r6Jtl hhdjBw&feature=youtu.be

21 Psychological healing through meaning is known as logotherapy.

22 https://www.theguardian.com/film/2015/jun/09/viktor-frankls-book-on-the-psychology-of-the-holocaust-to-be-made-into-a-film

23 Frankl, Viktor E. (1959) *Man's Search for Meaning.* Rider.

24 https://www.ted.com/talks/shawn_achor_the_happy_secret_to_better_work/transcript?language=en

25 https://www.huffingtonpost.com/entry/we-see-them-as-we-are_us_
    590cab8ae4b056aa2363d461

26 Aurelius, Marcus. (2006) *Meditations*. Penguin Classics.

27 Cable, Dan (2018) *Alive at Work*. Harvard Business Review Press, p. 147.

28 Cable, Dan (2018) *Alive at Work*. Harvard Business Review Press, p. 155.

29 With a little imagination you can also apply these exercises to a job you
    would like to do.

Chapter 5

1   Newport, Cal (2016) *Deep Work: Rules for Focused Success in a
    Distracted World*. Piatkus, Little, Brown Book Group. Kindle Edition,
    p. 119.

2   https://www.thecoachingtoolscompany.com/coaching-tools-101-what-
    is-the-urgent-important-matrix/

3   Dr Stephen Covey (author of *The 7 Habits of Highly Effective People*)
    adapted these concepts into 'The Urgent Important Matrix' in his
    famous book.

4   Newport, Cal (2016) *Deep Work: Rules for Focused Success in a
    Distracted World*. Piatkus, Little, Brown Book Group. Kindle
    Edition, p. 6.

5   A 2012 McKinsey study found it was 30 per cent, and this was
    reiterated by a Canadian University in 2017: https://globalnews.ca/
    news/3395457/this-is-how-much-time-you-spend-on-work-emails-
    every-day-according-to-a-canadian-survey/

6   http://humanorigins.si.edu/education/introduction-human-evolution

7   According to Pew, a research outfit.

8   http://www.dailymail.co.uk/health/article-3310195/Rise-Smartphone-
    injuries-43-people-walked-glued-screen-60-dropped-phone-face-
    reading.html

9   https://www.huffingtonpost.co.uk/entry/why-you-should-not-use-
    phone-on-toilet-germs_uk_58a6c97ee4b045cd34c07433

10 According to the UK's communications watchdog, Ofcom, the
    average Briton checks their phone every two minutes: https://www
    .telegraph.co.uk/news/2018/08/01/decade-smartphones-now-spend-
    entire-day-every-week-online/

11 https://www.economist.com/special-report/2017/02/09/smartphones-are-strongly-addictive

12 https://www.bbc.co.uk/news/uk-44546360

13 https://www.theguardian.com/society/2018/sep/11/mental-health-issues-in-young-people-up-sixfold-in-england-since-1995

14 Newport, Cal (2016) *Deep Work: Rules for Focused Success in a Distracted World*. Piatkus, Little, Brown Book Group. Kindle Edition, p. 229.

15 Newport, Cal (2016) *Deep Work: Rules for Focused Success in a Distracted World*. Piatkus, Little, Brown Book Group. Kindle Edition, p. 6.

16 Newport, Cal (2016) *Deep Work: Rules for Focused Success in a Distracted World*. Piatkus, Little, Brown Book Group. Kindle Edition, p. 13.

17 https://www.economist.com/leaders/2019/01/12/the-maturing-of-the-smartphone-industry-is-cause-for-celebration

18 These alerts are often coloured red, for a good reason: for humans, red is a trigger colour normally used as a warning or alarm signal.

19 https://www.theguardian.com/technology/2017/may/01/facebook-advertising-data-insecure-teens

20 https://www.journals.uchicago.edu/doi/10.1086/691462

21 https://www.theguardian.com/technology/2017/oct/05/smartphone-addiction-silicon-valley-dystopia

22 https://www.theguardian.com/technology/2017/nov/09/facebook-sean-parker-vulnerability-brain-psychology

23 https://www.theguardian.com/technology/2017/oct/05/smartphone-addiction-silicon-valley-dystopia

24 One-in-five adults spends as much as 40 hours a week on the web.

25 Study by Microsoft: http://time.com/3858309/attention-spans-goldfish/

26 From an article entitled 'Is Google Making Us Stupid?': https://www.theatlantic.com/magazine/archive/2008/07/is-google-making-us-stupid/306868/

27 The response to this article was huge, with many identifying with this intuitive feeling. It led to Carr's book *The Shallows: How the Internet Is Changing the Way We Think, Read and Remember*.

28 From my speech to the London Business School global alumni reunion in February 2018.

29 http://www.bbc.com/future/story/20160909-why-you-feel-busy-all-the-time-when-youre-actually-not

30 https://www.theatlantic.com/business/archive/2014/05/the-myth-that-americans-are-busier-than-ever/371350/

31 Goh, Joel, Pfeffer, Jeffrey and Zenios, Stefanos A. (2015) 'Workplace stressors & health outcomes: Health policy for the workplace', *Behavioral Science and Policy*.

32 http://www.bbc.com/capital/story/20180502-how-your-workplace-is-killing-you

33 And, in the USA, not having health insurance.

34 US study: https://www.sciencedirect.com/science/article/pii/S0272494413000340

35 A 2013 article summarising the research: https://www.bloomberg.com/news/articles/2013-07-01/ending-the-tyranny-of-the-open-plan-office

36 https://www.inc.com/geoffrey-james/science-just-proved-that-open-plan-offices-destroy-productivity.html

37 https://globalnews.ca/news/3395457/this-is-how-much-time-you-spend-on-work-emails-every-day-according-to-a-canadian-survey/

38 Crabbe, Tony (2015) *Busy: How to Thrive in a World of Too Much*. Piatkus.

39 http://fortune.com/2015/02/04/busy-hurry-work-stress/

40 Once again it was the hyperactive American-Hungarian psychologist, Mihaly Csikszentmihalyi.

41 Ashton, Kevin (2015) *How To Fly A Horse: The Secret History of Creation, Invention, and Discovery*. Cornerstone Digital. Kindle Edition, p. 70.

42 Csikszentmihalyi, Mihaly (2013) *Creativity: The Psychology of Discovery and Invention*. Harper Perennial.

43 https://www.campaignmonitor.com/blog/email-marketing/2019/05/shocking-truth-about-how-many-emails-sent/

44 Newport, Cal (2016) *Deep Work: Rules for Focused Success in a Distracted World*. Piatkus, Little, Brown Book Group. Kindle Edition, p. 242.

45 Thanks to YPOer Darren Holland, CEO of Aventus Group, for this phrase 'Action ASAP', as well as his enthusiastic endorsement of the content in this chapter.

46 The 'CC' when you add another recipient to an email stands for
    'Carbon Copy'. Before the development of photographic copiers, a
    carbon copy was the under-copy of a typed or written document placed
    over carbon paper and the under-copy sheet itself. It was customary
    to use the acronym 'CC' or 'cc' before a colon and below the writer's
    signature, to inform the principal recipient that carbon copies had been
    made and distributed to the parties listed after the colon.

47 https://www.entrepreneur.com/article/278302

48 Newport, Cal (2016) *Deep Work: Rules for Focused Success in a
    Distracted World*. Piatkus, Little, Brown Book Group. Kindle Edition,
    p. 247.

49 https://www.independent.co.uk/life-style/multitasking-productivity-
    levels-research-psychology-david-meyer-a8254416.html

50 https://ideas.ted.com/why-we-need-a-secular-sabbath/

51 Newport, Cal (2016) *Deep Work: Rules for Focused Success in a
    Distracted World*. Piatkus, Little, Brown Book Group. Kindle Edition,
    p. 158.

52 Bakewell, Sarah (2011) *How to Live: A Life of Montaigne in One
    Question and Twenty Attempts at an Answer*. Vintage.

53 Newport, Cal (2016) *Deep Work: Rules for Focused Success in a
    Distracted World*. Piatkus, Little, Brown Book Group. Kindle Edition,
    p. 2.

54 He had a good reason for making a space for periods of intense
    concentration. In 1921 he published *Psychological Types*, which
    clarified the growing difference between his ideas and the thinking of
    his one-time friend and mentor, Sigmund Freud.

55 Check it out: https://www.google.co.uk/search?q=the+freud+museum+
    london&source=lnms&tbm=isch&sa=X&ved=0ahUKEwiy2O7g1Yfd
    AhWMAMAKHSBVDccQ_AUICygC&biw=1535&bih=758#imgrc=
    Qa1uLKHObCfjaM

56 Bakewell, Sarah (2011) *How to Live: A Life of Montaigne in One
    Question and Twenty Attempts at an Answer*. Vintage.

57 Csikszentmihalyi, Mihaly (2013) *Creativity: The Psychology of
    Discovery and Invention*. Harper Perennial, p. 58.

58 Newport, Cal (2016) *Deep Work: Rules for Focused Success in a
    Distracted World*. Piatkus Little, Brown Book Group. Kindle Edition,
    p. 159.

59 In 2010 and 2011.

60 Research by Matthew Killingsworth and Daniel Gilbert: it's fascinating to note the researchers concluded the subjects' mind-wandering was generally the cause, not the consequence, of their unhappiness.

61 https://www.hs-neu-ulm.de/fileadmin/user_upload/Über_uns/Familie_und_Soziales/BIZEPS/Mindfullness_meditation_improves_cognition.pdf

62 Newport, Cal (2016) *Deep Work: Rules for Focused Success in a Distracted World*. Piatkus, Little, Brown Book Group. Kindle Edition, pp. 33–34.

Chapter 6

1 Leslie, Ian (2014) *Curious: The Desire to Know and Why Your Future Depends on It*. Quercus. Kindle Edition, location 243–244.

2 IDEO, 'Unlocking creativity' course.

3 The founder of the Young Entrepreneurs' Organization, Verne Harnish, asserts that Bill Gates learned this technique from his mentor, Warren Buffett.

4 https://www.cnbc.com/2019/07/26/bill-gates-took-solo-think-weeks-in-a-cabin-in-the-woods.html

5 Leslie, Ian (2014) *Curious: The Desire to Know and Why Your Future Depends on It*. Quercus. Kindle Edition, location 1,313.

6 A little curious, I recently had my DNA tested through the genomics and biotechnology company 23andme (www.23andme.com), revealing that I am 67.5 per cent British and Irish, 21.5 per cent French and German and 10.8 per cent broadly North-Western European.

7 https://quatr.us/greeks/pandoras-box-greek-mythology.htm

8 Nesta, Oxford Martin School and Pearson (2017) 'The future of skills employment in 2030'.

9 Gratton, Lynda 'Human resource strategy in transforming companies'.

10 Professor Gratton recounted this incident at the HR Strategy Forum at London Business School in 2018: https://events.streamgo.co.uk/

paving-the-way-for-the-next-decade/events/lifelong-learning-your-competitive-advantage

11 https://www.edutopia.org/blog/why-curiosity-enhances-learning-marianne-stenger

12 https://www.cell.com/neuron/abstract/S0896-6273(14)00804-6

13 Rowson, Jonathan Dr (2012) 'The power of curiosity: How linking inquisitiveness to innovation could help to address our energy challenges', RSA Social Brain Centre, p. 11, referencing the work of psychologist Daniel Berlyne.

14 https://www.cbsnews.com/news/ohio-teen-hospitalized-after-playing-video-games-for-at-least-4-straight-days/

15 https://www.bbc.co.uk/news/world-asia-pacific-12541769

16 https://www.wired.com/2015/12/psychology-of-clickbait/

17 Rowson, Jonathan Dr (2012) 'The power of curiosity: How linking inquisitiveness to innovation could help to address our energy challenges', RSA Social Brain Centre, p. 11, referencing the work of Professor George Lowenstein of the University of Pennsylvania. An economist by training, his work brings psychological considerations to bear on models and problems that are central to economics.

18 Rowson, Jonathan Dr (2012) 'The power of curiosity: How linking inquisitiveness to innovation could help to address our energy challenges', RSA Social Brain Centre, p. 11.

19 Academics call this epistemic curiosity.

20 Rowson, Jonathan Dr (2012) 'The power of curiosity: How linking inquisitiveness to innovation could help to address our energy challenges', RSA Social Brain Centre. This diagram is based on the work by the British and Canadian exploratory psychologist, Daniel Berlyne (1924–1976), reproduced in the RSA report into curiosity. I have altered some of the labelling and invented the Roam, Surf, Sample and Focus labels.

21 Rowson, Jonathan Dr (2012) 'The power of curiosity: How linking inquisitiveness to innovation could help to address our energy challenges', RSA Social Brain Centre, p. 21.

22 https://www.technologyreview.com/s/607886/curiosity-may-be-vital-for-truly-smart-ai/

23　Chamorro-Premuzic, Tomas (2014) 'Managing yourself: Curiosity is as important as intelligence', *Harvard Business Review*.

24　In an interview in *The New York Times*: https://www.inc.com/empact/bill-gates-warren-buffett-and-oprah-all-use-the-5-hour-rule.html

25　http://www.theceugroup.com/9-famous-people-who-embrace-lifelong-learning/

26　https://www.nytimes.com/2017/01/16/books/obamas-secret-to-surviving-the-white-house-years-books.html

27　As far as I know, the five-hour rule was coined by Michael Simmons, founder of Empact, a US company devoted to encouraging entrepreneurs.

28　https://www.entrepreneur.com/article/317602

29　https://science.howstuffworks.com/innovation/famous-inventors/10-ben-franklin-inventions9.htm

30　Isaacson, Walter (2017) *Leonardo Da Vinci*. Simon & Schuster UK. Kindle Edition, location 175.

31　Livio, Mario (2017) *Why? What Makes Us Curious*. Simon & Schuster. Kindle Edition, location 982.

32　https://study.com/academy/lesson/reticular-activating-system-definition-function.html

33　https://www.wired.com/2010/08/the-itch-of-curiosity/

34　https://blog.bufferapp.com/connections-in-the-brain-understanding-creativity-and-intelligenceconnections

35　http://uk.businessinsider.com/robert-palladino-calligraphy-class-inspired-steve-jobs-2016-3?r=US&IR=T

36　https://www.businessinsider.com/the-full-text-of-steve-jobs-stanford-commencement-speech-2011-10?IR=T

37　https://blog.bufferapp.com/connections-in-the-brain-understanding-creativity-and-intelligenceconnections

38　Kleon, Austin (2012) *Steal Like an Artist: 10 Things Nobody Told You About Being Creative*. Workman Publishing Company. Kindle Edition, location 98.

39　Isaacson, Walter (2017) *Leonardo Da Vinci*. Simon & Schuster UK. Kindle Edition, location 196–197.

40　Leslie, Ian (2014) *Curious: The Desire to Know and Why Your Future Depends on It*. Quercus. Kindle Edition, location 537–541.

41 Adapted from Leslie, Ian (2014) *Curious: The Desire to Know and Why Your Future Depends on It*. Quercus. Kindle Edition, location 228–229.

42 Sutherland, Rory (2019). *Alchemy*. Ebury Publishing. Kindle Edition, location 1309.

43 Leslie, Ian (2014) *Curious: The Desire to Know and Why Your Future Depends on It*. Quercus. Kindle Edition, location 591–593.

44 Isaacson, Walter (2017) *Leonardo Da Vinci*. Simon & Schuster UK. Kindle Edition, location 198–201.

45 Stone, Brad (2013) *The Everything Store: Jeff Bezos and the Age of Amazon*. Transworld Digital. Kindle Edition, location 255.

46 https://www.youtube.com/watch?v=MUPHNQkBdVw

47 This quote is taken from an interview Grazer gave: 'Brian Grazer: A Career in Curiosity' – Talks at Google. The ideas are from his book: Grazer, Brian and Fishman, Charles (2015) *A Curious Mind: The Secret to a Bigger Life*. Simon & Schuster.

48 This idea was introduced to me by a South African colleague of mine, Keith Coats, co-founder of the global futurist firm TomorrowToday, who regularly arranges 'curiosity conversations' with people who'll push him out of his comfort zone. Over the last few years he's spoken to a world champion big wave surfer, a PhD fellow exploring the frontiers of virtual reality and a double lung and heart transplant patient, to mention but three.

49 Kasparov, Garry (2017) *Deep Thinking: Where Machine Intelligence Ends and Human Creativity Begins*. John Murray. Kindle Edition, p. 61.

Chapter 7

1 http://news.bbc.co.uk/1/hi/england/bradford/7962212.stm

2 Fry, Hannah (2018) *Hello World: How to be Human in the Age of the Machine*. Transworld Digital. Kindle Edition, location 238.

3 https://www.theguardian.com/technology/2016/jun/25/gps-horror-stories-driving-satnav-greg-milner

4 Livio, Mario (2017) *Why?: What Makes Us Curious*. Simon & Schuster. Kindle Edition, location 181.

5 Sadly, over time this luminosity has dimmed thanks to some unwise subsequent treatments of the painting, which have made it look darker.

6   https://www.telegraph.co.uk/news/2019/08/13/chaos-louvre-visitors-given-just-minute-mona-lisa/

7   Maxwell, John C. (2014) *Good Leaders Ask Great Questions:Your Foundation for Successful Leadership.* Center Street. Kindle Edition, p. 7.

8   Psychologist Michelle Chouinard from 2007, in Leslie, Ian (2014) *Curious: The Desire to Know andWhyYour Future Depends On It.* Quercus. Kindle Edition, location 558.

9   https://www.psychologytoday.com/us/blog/darwin-eternity/201306/human-herding-how-people-are-guppies

10   The term 'filter bubble' was coined by Internet activist Eli Pariser in his 2011 book, *The Filter Bubble:What the Internet Is Hiding fromYou.* Penguin Press.

11   https://www.theatlantic.com/technology/archive/2018/03/largest-study-ever-fake-news-mit-twitter/555104/

12   Fry, Hannah (2018) *Hello World: How to be Human in the Age of the Machine.* Transworld Digital. Kindle Edition, location 254.

13   With thanks to my London Business School colleague Graeme Codrington and TomorrowToday for this excellent phrase.

14   Goddard, Jules and Eccles, Tony (2013) *Uncommon Sense, Common Nonsense.* Profile Books.

15   Taken from various conversations withTammy Erickson, during our leadership programme breaks at London Business School, 2016–2019.

16   Sawyer, Keith (2013) *Zig Zag: The Surprising Path to Greater Creativity.* Jossey-Bass. Kindle Edition, location 530–532.

17   Sawyer, Keith (2013) *Zig Zag: The Surprising Path to Greater Creativity.* Jossey-Bass. Kindle Edition, location 533–535.

18   https://www.london.edu/faculty-and-research/lbsr/innovation-hacks-straight-out-of-silicon-valley#.WryacojwZPZ

19   I would advise, if you choose this well-known technique, to dig a little deeper into the prescribed method. There's a great description of it here: https://www.mindtools.com/pages/article/newTMC_5W.htm

20   Sawyer, Keith (2013) *Zig Zag: The Surprising Path to Greater Creativity.* Jossey-Bass. Kindle Edition, location 472.

21   https://www.inc.com/eric-markowitz/life-and-times-of-instagram-the-complete-original-story.html

22   https://www.statista.com/statistics/253577/number-of-monthly-active-instagram-users/

23 Maxwell, John C. (2014) *Good Leaders Ask Great Questions: Your Foundation for Successful Leadership*. Center Street. Kindle Edition, p. 15.

24 Gregersen, Hal (2018) 'Better Brainstorming', *Harvard Business Review*.

25 https://www.mindtools.com/pages/article/newTMC_88.htm

26 https://www.forbes.com/sites/jeffboss/2016/08/03/the-power-of-questions/#5ac99be462a5

27 https://www.forbes.com/sites/groupthink/2013/10/04/10-disruptive-questions-for-instant-innovation/#532949506dab

28 These questions are taken from the workshops of Lisa Bodell, CEO of FutureThink, a New York City based innovation research and training firm.

29 Questions adapted from: McKinney, Phil (2012) *Beyond the Obvious: Killer Questions That Spark Game-Changing Innovation*. Hachette Books. Kindle Edition.

Chapter 8

1 https://lifehacker.com/5972825/inspiration-is-for-amateurs--the-rest-of-us-just-show-up-and-get-to-work

2 From IDEO's 'Unlocking Creativity' course.

3 Tharp, Twyla (2008) *The Creative Habit: Learn It and Use It for Life*. Simon & Schuster.

4 Csikszentmihalyi, Mihaly (2013, reprint from 1997) *Creativity: The Psychology of Discovery and Invention*. Harper Collins, p. 363.

5 2019 Netflix documentary *The Creative Brain*: https://www.netflix.com/gb/title/81090128

6 2019 Netflix documentary *The Creative Brain*: https://www.netflix.com/gb/title/81090128

7 A lesser-known story of unintended consequences of a particular invention is the discovery of LSD by Albert Hofmann, although that wasn't a mistake.

8 A portmanteau of the French words *velours* (velvet) and *crochet* (hook).

9 Sawyer, Keith (2013) *Zig Zag: The Surprising Path to Greater Creativity*. Jossey-Bass. Kindle Edition, location 1,339–1,341.

10 Louis Pasteur discovered the process, which became known as pasteurisation, that kills germs.

11 https://psychology.fas.harvard.edu/people/ellen-langer

12 http://keithsawyer.com/

13 Sawyer, Keith (2013) *Zig Zag: The Surprising Path to Greater Creativity*. Jossey-Bass. Kindle Edition, location 1,464.

14 Csikszentmihalyi, Mihaly (2013) *Creativity: The Psychology of Discovery and Invention*. Harper Perennial, p. 352.

15 https://www.opencolleges.edu.au/informed/features/the-value-o f-connecting-the-dots-to-create-real-learning/

16 Kelley, David and Kelley, Tom (2013) *Creative Confidence: Unleashing the Creative Potential Within Us All*. William Collins. Kindle Edition, p. 13.

17 Simon Baron-Cohen, the director of the Autism Research Centre at Cambridge University, has shown this: https://www.theguardian.com/science/2013/jan/04/barack-obama-empathy-deficit

18 https://www.youtube.com/watch?v=XuwP5iOB-gs

19 The term 'emotional intelligence' is now part of our everyday language, mostly due to the 1995 best-seller *Emotional Intelligence* by the psychologist Daniel Goleman.

20 According to Marshall Rosenberg, psychologist and founder of Nonviolent Communication: https://www.bbc.co.uk/news/magazine-33287727

21 https://www.theguardian.com/science/2013/jan/04/barack-obama-empathy-deficit

22 https://www.psychologytoday.com/gb/blog/threat-management/201303/i-dont-feel-your-pain-overcoming-roadblocks-empathy

23 Thanks to Judy Rees, my old colleague from journalism, for introducing me to this phrase.

24 2014 study: https://journals.aom.org/doi/abs/10.5465/amj.2012.0575

25 'Creatively successful firms' as rated by critics.

26 https://www.businessinsider.com/adam-grant-living-abroad-makes-you-more-creative-2016-2?r=US&IR=T

27 Grant, Adam (2016) *Originals: How Non-Conformists Change the World*. Virgin Digital. Kindle Edition (audible version).

28 https://www.bbc.co.uk/programmes/articles/1nS2GZDqHjPn5VQBY wfHRXK/seven-simple-ways-to-boost-your-creativity

29 Harvard researcher Jeffrey Ellenbogen found that after sleep, people
    are 33 per cent more creative, taken from Sawyer, Keith (2013) *Zig
    Zag: The Surprising Path to Greater Creativity*. Jossey-Bass. Kindle
    Edition.

30 Yong, Ed (15 May 2018) 'A new theory linking sleep and creativity:
    The two main phases of sleep might work together to boost creative
    problem-solving', *The Atlantic*. https://www.theatlantic.com/science/
    archive/2018/05/sleep-creativity-theory/560399/

31 https://www.psychologytoday.com/us/blog/the-social-thinker/201712/
    sleep-it-boost-your-creativity

32 https://www.youtube.com/watch?v=-P3UpuGnYKA

33 'Hypnopompic' is the state just after waking; the 'hypnagogic' state is
    that just before you fall asleep.

34 https://www.psychologytoday.com/us/blog/the-social-thinker/201712/
    sleep-it-boost-your-creativity

35 From an interview on Saturday Live, Radio 4, 15 December 2018 on
    the publication of Idle's autobiography *Always Look on the Bright Side
    of Life* for the troupe's controversial 1979 film, *Life of Brian*.

36 du Sautoy, Marcus (2019) *The Creativity Code: How AI is Learning
    to Write, Paint and Think*. Fourth Estate. Kindle Edition, location
    607–608.

37 Isaacson, Walter (2011) *Steve Jobs: The Exclusive Biography*. Little,
    Brown Book Group. Kindle Edition, p. 61.

38 https://www.huffingtonpost.co.uk/entry/harry-potter-synopsis-jk-
    rowling_us_59f1e294e4b043885915a95c

39 https://medium.com/@jeffgoins/dont-waste-your-words-how-to-
    write-a-first-draft-that-is-crappy-but-usable-c5dbf977f5a5

40 https://medium.com/@jeffgoins/dont-waste-your-words-how-to-
    write-a-first-draft-that-is-crappy-but-usable-c5dbf977f5a5

41 Sawyer, Keith (2013) *Zig Zag: The Surprising Path to Greater
    Creativity*. Jossey-Bass. Kindle Edition.

42 Fig, Joe (2009) *Inside the Painter's Studio*. Princeton Architectural
    Press, p. 42.

43 This advice from Tom Peters in his 1991 article 'The Pursuit of
    Luck', which listed 50 strategies: https://tompeters.com/columns/
    the-pursuit-of-luck/

Chapter 9

1 https://www.inc.com/annabel-acton/10-pieces-of-killer-advice-from-famous-creative-ge.html

2 http://creativethinking.net/a-simple-way-to-get-ideas/#sthash. NCFYhh33.v9ULOf5m.dpbs

3 https://brailleworks.com/braille-resources/history-of-braille/

4 https://medium.com/the-0mission/forget-about-the-10-000-hour-rule-7b7a39343523

5 https://www.barnesandnoble.com/blog/every-single-stephen-king-book-ranked/

6 Sawyer, Keith (2013) *Zig Zag: The Surprising Path to Greater Creativity*. Jossey-Bass. Kindle Edition.

7 https://www.linkedin.com/pulse/thinking-strategies-used-creative-geniuses-michael-michalko/

8 https://www.businessinsider.com/richard-branson-fails-virgin-companies-that-went-bust-2016-5?r=US&IR=T

9 Sawyer, Keith (2013) *Zig Zag: The Surprising Path to Greater Creativity*. Jossey-Bass. Kindle Edition.

10 https://www.entrepreneur.com/article/295312

11 2019 Netflix documentary *The Creative Brain*: https://www.netflix.com/gb/title/81090128

12 https://editorial.rottentomatoes.com/article/exclusive-the-storyboards-of-walle/

13 http://99u.com/articles/52154/idea-sex-how-new-yorker-cartoonists-generate-500-ideas-a-week

14 Sawyer, Keith (2013) *Zig Zag: The Surprising Path to Greater Creativity*. Jossey-Bass. Kindle Edition, location 2,294.

15 Sawyer, Keith (2013) *Zig Zag: The Surprising Path to Greater Creativity*. Jossey-Bass. Kindle Edition.

16 I'm indebted to Michael Michalko, author of *ThinkerToys: A Handbook of Creative-Thinking Techniques*, for this metaphor: http://creativethinking.net/combine-what-exists-into-something-that-has-never-existed-before/#sthash.jeEBSktP.dpbs

17 2019 Netflix documentary *The Creative Brain*: https://www.netflix.com/gb/title/81090128

18 https://www.theguardian.com/stage/2016/aug/23/masai-graham-organ-donor-funniest-joke-edinburgh-fringe-2016

19 https://www.streetdirectory.com/travel_guide/155647/motivation/a_sense_of_humor_increases_creativity.html

20 https://www.edwddebono.com/lateral-thinking

21 https://www.laughterremedy.com/article_pdfs/Creativity.pdf

22 https://www.inc.com/yoram-solomon/humor-and-sarcasm-can-make-you-creative-science-says.html

23 https://www.psychologytoday.com/us/blog/the-tao-innovation/201406/the-power-humor-in-ideation-and-creativity

24 Here's a good list of comedy warm-ups: https://learnimprov.com/warm-ups/

25 https://www.iflscience.com/technology/ais-attempts-at-oneliner-jokes-are-unintentionally-hilarious/

26 https://www.psychologytoday.com/us/blog/the-tao-innovation/201406/the-power-humor-in-ideation-and-creativity

27 Taken from the 2019 Netflix documentary *The Creative Brain*: https://www.netflix.com/gb/title/81090128

28 https://www.livescience.com/43639-who-invented-the-printing-press.html

29 https://www.cnbc.com/2018/09/04/8-surprising-facts-you-might-not-know-about-googles-early-days.html

30 https://www.brainpickings.org/2011/10/20/i-steve-steve-jobs-in-his-own-words/

31 I'm endebted to the video explanation of this technique, which I've tweaked a bit: https://www.youtube.com/watch?v=kptxOsZitRs

32 Harford, Tim (2016) *Messy: How to be Creative and Resilient in a Tidy-Minded World*. Little, Brown, p. 9.

33 Kleon, Austin (2012) *Steal Like an Artist: 10 Things Nobody Told You About Being Creative*. Workman Publishing Company. Kindle Edition, location 44.

34 Kleon, Austin (2012) *Steal Like an Artist: 10 Things Nobody Told You About Being Creative*. Workman Publishing Company. Kindle Edition, location 49.

35 https://www.pablopicasso.org/picasso-and-dali.jsp

36 Kleon, Austin (2012) *Steal Like an Artist: 10 Things Nobody Told You About Being Creative.* Workman Publishing Company. Kindle Edition, p. 167.

37 https://www.bbc.co.uk/programmes/articles/38rJrt2ZVRlXCzXCZbB GTlH/ten-huge-bands-who-started-out-as-tribute-or-covers-acts

38 https://www.creativethinkinghub.com/creative-thinking-and-stealing-like-an-artist/

39 I'm indebted to entrepreneur and creativity writer Kevin Ashton for this example: Ashton, Kevin (2015) *How To Fly A Horse.* Cornerstone Digital. Kindle Edition, pp. 66–67.

40 https://www.smithsonianmag.com/innovation/theory-of-relativity-then-and-now-180956622/

41 https://brailleworks.com/braille-resources/history-of-braille/

42 Kleon, Austin (2012) *Steal Like an Artist: 10 Things Nobody Told You About Being Creative.* Workman Publishing Company. Kindle Edition, location 87.

Chapter 10

1 https://www.inc.com/annabel-acton/10-pieces-of-killer-advice-from-famous-creative-ge.html

2 https://www.filmsite.org/pixaranimations.html

3 Isaacson, Walter (2017) *Leonardo Da Vinci.* Simon & Schuster.

4 https://medium.com/the-aspen-institute/the-myth-of-the-lone-genius-6a5146c7da10

5 https://www.nchannel.com/blog/amazon-statistics/

6 Harford, Tim (2011) *Adapt: Why Success Always Starts With Failure.* Little Brown, p. 3.

7 Harford, Tim (2011) *Adapt: Why Success Always Starts With Failure.* Little Brown, p. 2.

8 https://www.theguardian.com/science/occams-corner/2017/oct/04/myth-lone-genius-nobel-gravitational-waves-ligo

9 The 50 years in question were 1951–2001.

10 Nobel Prizes awarded to individuals – 33; Nobel Prizes awarded to teams – 36.

11 He became so renowned for what's now known as 'networking' that the scientific community have invented a special unit of measurement for people who jointly wrote papers with him. If your name appeared

alongside Erdős on an article you are said to have an Erdős number of one. If you wrote a paper with one of these collaborators you have a number of two, and so on. There are 40,000 people with a number of three or lower.

12 In 1973 the sociologist Mark Granovetter published a paper entitled 'The Strength of Weak Ties', in which he talks about and explains their value. Granovetter analogises weak ties to being like bridges that allow us to disseminate and get access to information that we might not otherwise have access to.

13 https://theguardian.com/technology/2010/mar/14/my-bright-idea-robin-dunbar

14 This behaviour is in the same category as the 'curious conversations' introduced earlier in this book.

15 https://www.nytimes.com/2012/02/26/opinion/sunday/innovation-and-the-bell-labs-miracle.html

16 Harford, Tim (2016) *Messy: How to be Creative and Resilient in a Tidy-Minded World*. Little Brown, pp. 80–82.

17 Isaacson, Walter (2012) 'The Real Leadership Lessons from Steve Jobs', *Harvard Business Review*.

18 Catmull, Ed (2014) *Creativity, Inc.* Bantam Press, p. 93.

19 Catmull, Ed (2014) *Creativity, Inc.* Bantam Press, p. 131.

20 Catmull, Ed (2014) *Creativity, Inc.* Bantam Press, p. 88.

21 Sawyer, Keith (2007) *Group Genius: The Creative Power of Collaboration*. Basic Books, p. 16.

22 Sawyer, Keith (2013) *Zig Zag: The Surprising Path to Greater Creativity*. Jossey-Bass. Kindle Edition, location 3,136.

23 https://hbr.org/2014/05/leading-with-humor

24 https://www.humorthatworks.com/benefits/30-benefits-of-humor-at-work/

25 https://www.humorthatworks.com/benefits/30-benefits-of-humor-at-work/

26 https://www.psychologytoday.com/us/blog/the-tao-innovation/201406/the-power-humor-in-ideation-and-creativity

27 https://www.fastcompany.com/3009489/why-humor-makes-you-more-creative

28 Rock, David, Siegel, Daniel J., Poelmans, A.Y. and Payne, Jessica (2015) 'The Healthy Mind Platter', *NeuroLeadership Journal*, Vol. 4.

29 https://www.laughterremedy.com/article_pdfs/Creativity.pdf

30 https://www.forbes.com/sites/jacquelynsmith/2013/05/03/10-reasons-why-humor-is-a-key-to-success-at-work/#28ded47e5c90

31 Li Huang of INSEAD Business School, Adam D. Galinsky of Columbia University: https://www.scientificamerican.com/article/sarcasm-spurs-creative-thinking/

32 https://www.forbes.com/sites/jacquelynsmith/2013/05/03/10-reasons-why-humor-is-a-key-to-success-at-work/#28ded47e5c90

33 https://hbr.org/2014/05/leading-with-humor

34 https://www.streetdirectory.com/travel_guide/155647/motivation/a_sense_of_humor_increases_creativity.html

35 Burt, Gabor George and Anderson, Jamie (2019) 'Use Humor to Energize the Global Workplace', Society for Human Resource Management (SHRM): https://www.shrm.org/ResourcesandTools/Legal-and-compliance/employment-law/Pages/global-using-humor-to-energize-the-global-workplace.aspx

36 https://www.fastcompany.com/3024535/yes-and-improv-techniques-to-make-you-a-better-boss

37 Zak, Paul J. (2014) 'Why Your Brain Loves Good Storytelling', *Harvard Business Review*.

38 With thanks to my London Business School colleague Professor Niro Sivanathan (who's a great storyteller!).

Chapter 11

1 https://medium.com/the-0mission/forget-about-the-10-000-hour-rule-7b7a39343523

2 Harford, Tim (2011) *Adapt: Why Success Always Starts With Failure*. Little Brown, p. 7.

3 Thanks to my London Business School colleague and strategy execution expert Andrew MacLennan for this anecdote.

4 https://www.theatlantic.com/international/archive/2011/11/chinas-steve-jobs-debate-and-deng-xiaoping/248080/

5 https://www.prospectmagazine.co.uk/magazine/the-hunt-for-dark-matter-the-missing-ingredient-without-which-our-universe-would-not-exist-physics-astronomy

6   I'm indebted to Tammy Erickson for this wonderful analogy.

7   Thanks to Eric Ries for this excellent analogy.

8   https://www.ted.com/talks/simon_sinek_how_great_leaders_inspire_
action/

9   https://hbr.org/2009/02/how-to-design-smart-business-experiments

10 https://science.howstuffworks.com/innovation/edible-innovations/
fast-food.htm

11 https://www.youtube.com/watch?v=u00S-hCnmFY

12 Davenport, Thomas H. (2009) 'How to Design Smart Business
Experiments', *Harvard Business Review*: https://hbr.org/2009/02/
how-to-design-smart-business-experiments

13 https://hbr.org/2009/02/how-to-design-smart-business-experiments

14 https://www.washingtonpost.com/business/technology/google-
crunches-data-on-munching-in-office/2013/09/01/3902b444-0e83-
11e3-85b6-d27422650fd5_story.html?noredirect=on&utm_term=.
38c2b7f59bd1

15 I first came across this different spin on the M.V.P. (Minimum
Viable Product) and the four 'Ss' from my London Business School
colleague, Andrew MacLennan.

16 https://simplicable.com/new/business-experiments

17 This involves trying one version of the email, font or brand colour
and then comparing it to another to see which one works best.

18 Ironic, as this is the same format that creates the code for computers
and AI. Writing this book has never been anything less than
thought-provoking!

19 (2013) 'HBR's 10 Must Reads on Innovation', *Harvard Business
Review*, p. 99.

Epilogue

1   Tegmark, Max (2017) *Life 3.0: Being Human in the Age of Artificial
Intelligence*. Penguin Books Ltd. Kindle Edition, location 731–732.

2   Kasparov, Garry (2017) *Deep Thinking: Where Machine Intelligence Ends
and Human Creativity Begins*. John Murray. Kindle Edition, p. 249.

3   Kasparov, Garry (2017) *Deep Thinking: Where Machine Intelligence Ends
and Human Creativity Begins*. John Murray. Kindle Edition, p. 249.

4   https://www.imperial.ac.uk/media/imperial-college/administration-and-support-services/enterprise-office/public/Table-of-Disruptive-Technologies.pdf

5   London Business School panel event, 2019.

6   https://www.forbes.com/sites/falonfatemi/2018/08/17/how-ai-will-augment-human-creativity/#7523edbd711b

7   https://www.forbes.com/sites/falonfatemi/2018/08/17/how-ai-will-augment-human-creativity/#20152a1b711b

8   https://www.forbes.com/sites/falonfatemi/2018/08/17/how-ai-will-augment-human-creativity/#1a7c634d711b

9   Mentioned to me by the MIT academic, technologist and entrepreneur Michael Davies.

10 Daugherty, Paul R. and Wilson, H. James (2018) *Human + Machine: Reimagining Work in the Age of AI*. Harvard Business Review Press, p. 7.

11 Cognizant (2018) '21 Jobs of The Future', Center for the Future of Work, p. 3.

12 http://www.bbc.com/future/story/20151201-the-cyborg-chess-players-that-cant-be-beaten

13 du Sautoy, Marcus (2019) *The Creativity Code: How AI is Learning to Write, Paint and Think*. Fourth Estate. Kindle Edition, location 155–157.

14 Boden's 'Transformational' creativity aligns with psychologist Irving A. Taylor's 'Innovative/Emergent' levels we looked at in Chapter 3. His whole scale was: Expressive, Productive, Inventive, Innovative and Emergent.

Index